Economics
of Unemployment

Economics
of Unemployment

An Historical Perspective

MARK CASSON

The MIT Press
Cambridge, Massachusetts

First MIT Press edition, 1984

© Mark Casson, 1983

First published in 1983 by
Martin Robertson & Company Ltd.,
108 Cowley Road, Oxford OX4 1JF.

Library of Congress catalog card number: 83-62502
ISBN 0-262-03106-X

Printed and bound in Great Britain

Contents

List of Tables and Figures   ix

Preface and Acknowledgements   xiii

1 Unemployment in Historical Perspective   1

   1.1 Back to the thirties?   1
   1.2 An historical controversy   2
   1.3 Structural aspects of unemployment   3
   1.4 The aggregation issue   6
   1.5 Pre-Keynesian analysis of unemployment   8
   1.6 Summary and plan of the book   9

2 The Pre-Keynesian Economists: Their Lives and Times   14

   2.1 Introduction   14
   2.2 Arthur Cecil Pigou (1877–1959)   14
   2.3 Henry Clay (1883–1954)   18
   2.4 Edwin Cannan (1861–1935)   19
   2.5 Unemployment theory in inter-war Britain   23
   2.6 The aftermath of World War I   26
   2.7 Britain's poor performance in the 1920s   27
   2.8 Structural change in inter-war Britain   30
   2.9 Unemployment in inter-war Britain   33
  2.10 Summary   36

3 The Pre-Keynesian Theory of Unemployment   37

   3.1 Basic concepts   37
   3.2 Frictional unemployment   41
   3.3 Wage setting   43
   3.4 Monetary disturbance   48
   3.5 Structural problems   53
   3.6 The contribution of Pre-Keynesian theory   60

4   Disequilibrium Theory   62

    4.1 Introduction   62
    4.2 The short-side rule   62
    4.3 The role of profits in disequilibrium   65
    4.4 The determinants of labour supply   68
    4.5 Money and saving   70
    4.6 Bankruptcy and unemployment   76
    4.7 Fiscal policy and crowding out   79
    4.8 Keynes, the Pre-Keynesians, and the origins of
         disequilibrium theory   79
    4.9 Summary and conclusions   82

5   Job Search and Unemployment   84

    5.1 The impact of job rationing on labour supply   84
    5.2 A simple model of queue unemployment   86
    5.3 Effects of a wage cut   89
    5.4 Unemployment benefit   93
    5.5 Money wage bargaining   96
    5.6 Summary   99

6   Structural Disequilibrium   101

    6.1 Introduction   101
    6.2 The basic model   101
    6.3 Alternative regimes   107
    6.4 Structural disequilibrium under real-wage bargaining   113
    6.5 Labour mobility   115
    6.6 Unemployment benefit and structural adjustment   121
    6.7 Structural disequilibrium in an open economy   122
    6.8 Summary   127

7   Policies for Structural Unemployment   128

    7.1 Industrial transference   128
    7.2 Employment subsidies   130
    7.3 Selective protection   133
    7.4 Rationalization   138
    7.5 Selective investment   142
    7.6 Summary: an evaluation of alternative policies   144

8   The Pre-Keynesian Theory and the Keynesian
    Revolution   147

    8.1 Introduction   147
    8.2 The formulation of the theory   147

8.3   Policy implications of the theory   149
8.4   The apparent failure of industrial transference   153
8.5   Changing ideologies   156
8.6   Keynes' attack on the 'classics'   157
8.7   The short run   159
8.8   The unpopularity of structural change   163
8.9   Summary   164

9   The Determinants of Employment and the Real
    Wage in Inter-war Britain   166

9.1   Introduction   166
9.2   A short-run employment function derived from
      Pre-Keynesian theory   167
9.3   Evidence on the demand for labour   173
9.4   A comparison with other studies   177
9.5   The course of real wages in the inter-war period   179
9.6   Causes of downward money wage rigidity   183
9.7   Summary   188

10 Labour Supply, Unemployment and Migration in
    Inter-war Britain   190

10.1 Introduction   190
10.2 The determinants of labour supply   190
10.3 Time-series estimates of the labour supply function   192
10.4 Cross-section estimates of the labour supply function   197
10.5 The intensity of labour supply, and inter-industry variation
      in the rate of unemployment   202
10.6 Unemployment in an open economy   204
10.7 Regional inequality and industrial structure   209
10.8 Labour mobility between industries and regions   214
10.9 Conclusion   219

11 Pre-Keynesian Theory: Its Relevance Today   222

11.1 Introduction   222
11.2 Demand for labour and the real wage   223
11.3 Money wage rigidity and real wage rigidity   225
11.4 The regional problem and industrial structure in post-war
      Britain   229
11.5 Employment growth and labour migration in post-war Britain   234
11.6 The extent of structural unemployment in Britain:
      a critique of previous studies   236
11.7 Enterprise and the process of structural change   240
11.8 Implications for economic theory   245
11.9 Summary   247

12 Summary and Conclusions   248

Appendices   253

A: The Cross-section Study of Employment   253

B: The Time-series Study of Employment   265

C: The Time-series Study of Labour Supply   268

D: The Cross-section Study of Labour Supply   271

Bibliography   274

Index   292

List of Tables and Figures

TABLES

1.1 Suggested reading programmes for readers with special
    interests   12
2.1 Industrial growth in Britain, 1920–38   29
9.1 Determinants of the growth of employment in 38 UK
    industries 1924–30–35   174
9.2 Log-linear regressions of employment on output, time
    and the own-product wage, using annual data for five
    UK industries, 1920–38   176
9.3 Relative wages for different skills in five British indus-
    tries (1913=100)   181
10.1 Log-linear regressions of labour supply on employment,
    wages, benefits and working population, using annual
    data for five UK industries, 1923–38   194
10.2 Estimation of labour supply function from cross-section
    of 27 UK industries, various periods 1920–35   201
10.3 Influence of industry characteristics on unemployment in
    a cross-section of 27 UK industries, 1924–35   205
10.4 Log-linear regressions of employment on output, time
    and the own-product wage, using annual data for UK
    manufacturing industry, 1920–38   206
10.5 Log-linear regressions of labour supply on various
    explanatory variables, using annual data for UK manu-
    facturing industry, 1923–38   207
10.6 Shift-share analysis of percentage unemployment for
    nine divisions of the UK labour market and thirty
    industries, 1929–36   211
11.1 Log-linear regressions of employment on output and the
    own-product real wage using adjusted quarterly data for
    eight industries, 1965(III)–1974(II)   224

11.2   Shift-share analysis of percentage changes in manufactur-   231
        ing employment in eleven UK regions, 1952–79
A.1   Matching of industrial classifications 1924, 1930, 1935   253
A.2   Comparison of univariate distributions for full and
        reduced samples   260
A.3   Comparison of the full and reduced sample estimates of
        the effect of the growth of earnings on the growth of
        employment in the cross-section study of UK industries
        1924–30–35   262
D.1   Industry characteristics data used in cross-section study
        of labour supply   271

FIGURES

4.1   Disequilibrium in the labour market   63
4.2   Derivation of labour supply   68
4.3   Determination of the money price level under real-wage
       bargaining   75
4.4   Implications of bankruptcy for labour demand   78
5.1   Job search equilibrium   88
5.2   Impact of wage cuts on job search   91
5.3   Effects of unemployment benefit   95
5.4   Price and output determination under money-wage
       bargaining   98
6.1   Full employment equilibrium in a closed two-sector
       economy   106
6.2   A classification of regimes in a closed two-sector economy   109
6.3   A Phillips curve generated by expansionary policies
       applied to a structurally unbalanced economy   112
6.4   Structural wage adjustments   114
6.5   Determination of a structural unemployment equilibrium
       with labour mobility   118
6.6   Equilibrium in an export industry   125
6.7   Effects of a decline in export demand   125
7.1   Industrial transference   129
7.2   Effects of an employment subsidy   131
7.3   Effects of protection   136
7.4   Price discrimination under rationalization   139

7.5 Rationalization as a solution to structural unemployment 140
9.1 Derivation of a short-run Pre-Keynesian employment
     function   172
9.2 Time path of real and money wages in Britain, 1920–38   183

Preface and Acknowledgements

The object of this book is to examine the explanation of British unemployment advanced by a small group of economists in the 1920s—the most notable of these economists being Keynes' Cambridge colleague A. C. Pigou. These economists were concerned about low productivity and the high level of real wages in Britain, and also about the apparent inability of the labour force to respond to structural changes in demand.

By focusing upon a small group of economists and emphasizing their preoccupation with structural factors it is possible that a distorted impression of the inter-war unemployment situation could be given. This book should therefore be read in the context of more general studies of the inter-war period. Hancock (1960, 1962) and Winch (1969) provide useful surveys of economic thinking on unemployment, while there are valuable reviews of the economic history of the period by Alford (1981) and Howson (1981), amongst others.

The analytical core of the book involves a reformulation of the unemployment theory of the 1920s in modern terms. Some historians of thought may object to this procedure, but its justification is quite straightforward. By formalizing the theory it is possible to test it econometrically, and to examine its continuing relevance in the post-war period. It is also interesting to notice that, when formalized, the theory anticipates a number of recent analytical developments in labour economics. The author has, at times, used his own judgement in supplementing the earlier ideas with some more modern ones. Where this is done, it is always explicitly noted, so that standards of historical scholarship have not been too seriously infringed.

I am grateful to Dr W. R. Garside of Birmingham University for inviting me to present a conference paper from which this book has developed. I benefited greatly from the discussion of this paper, and also from the discussions at staff seminars at Bath, Brunel and Reading. Several people have been kind enough to comment on the manuscript in its earlier stages, especially Paul Cheshire, John Creedy, Peter Hart, Tim Hatton, Jim Pemberton and Denis O'Brien. I am indebted to Professor Terence Hutchison, both for his comments on the conference paper, and for reading the manuscript in penultimate draft. Valuable comments were also received from the publishers' readers.

I wish to thank the Librarians and staff of the Marshall Library, Cambridge; King's College, Cambridge; Nuffield College, Oxford and the British Library of Political and Economic Science for giving me access to their archives. Sir Norman Chester kindly discussed with me the career of Sir Henry Clay. Huw Rees provided extremely valuable assistance in obtaining statistics on employment in inter-war Britain, and Sue Watts helped with the computing. The manuscript was typed with impeccable precision by Jill Turner. My wife, Janet, read the manuscript and did a great deal to improve its quality. I am very grateful to them all.

I am also grateful to Basil Blackwell for permission to reproduce a table from Bowers, Deaton and Turk (1982) and to Heinemann Educational Books for permission to reproduce a table from Fothergill and Gudgin (1982). Thanks are also due to Tim Hatton for permission to reproduce tables from his recent discussion papers.

1

Unemployment in Historical Perspective

1.1 BACK TO THE THIRTIES?

The economic outlook for the 1980s is most unfavourable. The economies of the Western industrialized world are stagnating; mass unemployment has become an international problem. The situation invites comparison with the slump conditions of the 1930s. The comparison is particularly appropriate if one believes in a 50-year Kondratieff trade cycle. The question naturally arises as to whether a slump of the magnitude of the early 1930s can happen again. From a policy perspective the question is, perhaps, whether the present slump must continue to deepen or whether measures can be taken to reverse the decline.

The analogy with the 1930s is not exact, of course. The international currency system is not yet in total disarray, and protective import duties have not been widely introduced, though the portents are rather ominous in this respect. It must also be recognized that Keynesian techniques of demand management had not been fully developed in the 1930s—where deficit spending was adopted it was usually only on an *ad hoc* basis. It could be argued that with the sophisticated Keynesian policies now available a recurrence of the slump is unnecessary.

But current opinion is divided over whether Keynesian policies are a blessing or a curse (for a modern restatement of the Keynesian stance see Dow and Earl (1982)). Some people argue that Keynesian policies have actually caused the current world recession: more precisely, they argue that the recession results from the need to bring under control an inflationary spiral fuelled by the post-war expansion of government expenditure, and the concomitant increases in public debt and money supply. It is suggested that a major effect of Keynesian policies has been to depress unemployment below its 'natural rate' and/or to validate trade unions' excessive money wage claims. The present recession may be a final opportunity to establish sound currency and salvage the liberal economic order; further application of Keynesian policies would simply revive inflation, and necessitate a subsequent deflation so severe and so socially divisive that it would endanger the established order.

Keynesians, on the other hand, would argue that this anti-Keynesian view overstates the constraint on policy imposed by the inflation–unemployment trade-off. They believe that it is possible to control both inflation and unemployment by augmenting the orthodox Keynesian instruments of demand management with an incomes policy. According to this view, it is failure to find a workable formula for a long-term incomes policy which is at the root of the present problem.

1.2 AN HISTORICAL CONTROVERSY

The current debate over the effects of Keynesian policies is reflected in recent academic controversy over the history of the inter-war period (see e.g. Hatton, 1982b). From the 1950s to the mid-1970s the Keynesian perspective dominated historical writing about the inter-war period. This perspective focuses upon the slump of 1929–33 and on British policy towards unemployment during that period. Its basis is a counter-factual exercise in which the British government is imagined to have increased public spending through deficit finance. Using a Keynesian model it is shown that had such a policy been pursued there would have been beneficial effects on employment and output. The slump is thus attributed to the failure of the government to pursue appropriate fiscal and monetary policies (Middleton, 1981, 1982; Winch, 1969). Keynes is pictured as a 'prophet in the wilderness', arguing for public expenditure against the united opposition of his fellow economists. The economists are alleged to have supported the 'Treasury view' that additional public expenditure would simply crowd out private expenditure and leave output and employment unchanged. Keynes is supposed to have presented cogent arguments—anticipating those of his *General Theory*—for increasing public expenditure, but his opponents could not make the intellectual leap needed to assimilate his new ideas.

Recently the Keynesian orthodoxy has been challenged by adherents of neoclassical macroeconomic theory (Lucas, 1973). Neoclassical theory emphasizes the role of aggregate supply instead of aggregate demand. Neoclassical economists argue that Keynes' analysis depends crucially upon the downward rigidity of the money wage rate and that this assumption is false. They argue instead that, once frictions are allowed for, long-term wage adjustments are inhibited only by the payment of unemployment benefit. Using this approach, Benjamin and Kochin (1979) suggest that the Keynesian interpretation of history is false, and that unemployment in inter-war Britain is explained almost entirely by overgenerous levels of unemployment benefit. This has initiated a very heated debate (see e.g. Hatton, 1980; Metcalf, Nickell and Floros, 1982), with the academic community being asked to choose between two quite polarized interpretations of the evidence (for an analogous debate on the US economy see Lucas and Rapping, 1969, 1972; Rees, 1970; Gordon and Wilcox, 1981).

It is possible, however, that the antithesis between Keynesian and neoclassical explanations of unemployment is a false one. Both theories are essentially macroeconomic: their focus is upon aggregate unemployment rather than upon the structure of unemployment and its incidence on different groups of workers. A central argument of this book is that the clue to the causes of the present high aggregate unemployment is to be found in the structure of unemployment. Once the structural nature of unemployment is properly recognized, it can be seen that controversies between rival schools of macro-economists have merely diverted attention from the underlying problem of structural adjustment.

1.3 STRUCTURAL ASPECTS OF UNEMPLOYMENT

Structural factors are receiving increasing attention in the diagnosis of unemployment. So far, however, it has been historians, geo-graphers and political scientists who laid most stress upon structural unemployment; contemporary economists have had surprisingly little to say on the subject. Economic historians such as Aldcroft (1970), Booth and Glynn (1975), Glynn and Howells (1980), Hatton and Richardson (1962), for example, have all drawn attention to the structural aspects of inter-war British unemployment (see also Buxton and Aldcroft, 1978). Structural factors have also been emphasized by critics of Benjamin and Kochin (see e.g. Collins, 1982). The structural problems of the British economy were much more noticeable in the 1920s than in the 1930s because the overall level of unemployment was lower—so that pockets of unemployment were more conspicuous—and because rearmament had not yet boosted demand in some of the basic industries which were in secular decline.

Geographers such as Coates, Johnston and Knox (1977) and Law (1980) have emphasized the regional inequalities which have prevailed in Britain since 1914. Massey and Meegan (1982) and Fothergill and Gudgin (1982) have drawn attention to the strong regional discrepancies in the rates of employment growth (and job loss) in manufacturing industries in the 1960s and 1970s. Regional inequality has exerted an important influence on the geography of politics in Britain (as it does in all electoral democracies). The political consequences of regional decline are now receiving considerable attention (see e.g. Crick, 1981).

The main reason why economists have had relatively little to say about structural unemployment seems to be a conceptual problem: the lack of a satisfactory definition. Economists such as Cheshire (1973) and Nickell (1982) take a very narrow view of structural unemployment: they identify it with unemployment in one sector which is matched by unfilled vacancies in another sector. Since, however, unemployment in one sector tends to depress demand in other sectors it tends to eliminate any unfilled vacancies there. It is therefore not surprising that this narrow concept of structural unemployment leads these writers to conclude that structural unemployment is of little importance.

There are, however, a few economists who have not been inhibited by conceptual problems from discussing structural aspects of unemployment. The dual labour market theories inspired by Doeringer and Piore (1971) provide an interesting context within which structural factors can be analyzed. So too do theories of technical progress: Freeman, Clark and Soete (1982), for example, have considered the sectoral impact of technical progress on unemployment, adopting an historical perspective somewhat similar to that followed in this book. Finally, some economists have discussed structural unemployment in the context of discussions of sectoral employment growth (see e.g. Lindley, 1980).

One reason for economists' failure to conceptualize structural unemployment properly may be that the concept is most useful in the context of a dynamic rather than a static analysis. Economists who are addicted to static theorizing may be unable to perceive how the identification of a structural component in unemployment adds to their understanding of a situation. On the other hand, the concept of structural unemployment fits naturally into a dynamic theory of economic growth and development.

It is often useful to think in terms of the life-cycle of an economy. In this context, the British economy of the 1920s was certainly mature, and may even have been going senile. It is possible that Western economies which industrialized soon after Britain, are now becoming senile too. Belgium is an example of an economy with problems apparently similar to those of Britain. An important aspect of senility is the inability to cope with change. The quality of entrepreneurship in owner-managed firms declines as industrial power is increasingly acquired through inheritance rather than personal initiative. Corporate managements pursue their vested interests through political lobbying rather than through competition in the market place. What entrepreneurship there is becomes hampered by social convention and by the tax burden imposed by a welfare state.

Failing entrepreneurship is typically reflected in increasing vulnerability to competition; when an entire economy is afflicted then domestic industry as a whole becomes vulnerable to foreign competition. This is what seems to have happened in Britain in the 1920s, and is what seems to be happening to other mature Western economies now. In the 1920s Britain's foreign competition was chiefly from the US and continental Europe; but then, as now, a significant element of the competition was from the Far East, and especially Japan. Japanese competition severely damaged the Lancashire textile industry and would probably have seriously damaged the motor industry had not import duties been in force to protect the infant UK producers. Then, as now, the heavy industries—iron and steel, and shipbuilding, for example—were seriously afflicted with overcapacity. These are industries in which technology has been relatively standardized for some time, and in which developing countries have therefore found it relatively easy to make import-substituting investments which have eroded the mature economies' export trade.

Lack of entrepreneurship cannot be blamed entirely upon employers and industrialists, however. Entrepreneurship is also reflected in the adaptability of labour, and in particular in its willingness to move between jobs in response to relative labour scarcities. A failure of entrepreneurship means that an excessive amount of labour remains attached to declining industries. The most common reason for industrial immobility is probably the inability of labour to adjust to new working methods or to learn new skills. In this respect there may be certain differences between the 1920s and the present day. There is reason to believe that in the 1920s many of the unemployed were craftsmen with obsolete skills who were unwilling to 'trade down' to semi-skilled work. By contrast, it seems that at the moment there are many unskilled or semi-skilled workers who lack the training to take skilled work. This difference is to some extent reflected in the age distribution of the long-term unemployed. In the 1920s the vast majority of long-term unemployed were older male workers—many of them approaching retirement age. There were very few young long-term unemployed; there was still plenty of unskilled work for the young to do. At the moment there are many young people whose only work experience is on government-assisted schemes, and these are by and large the unskilled young workers. There are still many older workers among the long-term unemployed, but they are relatively much less significant than they were.

The world economy is in a constant state of flux. New technologies and methods of work organization are continually being developed and innovated by entrepreneurial nations. As a result, demand for particular products produced in particular locations is always changing. Workers whose jobs are threatened must either accept real wage reductions or transfer to other industries; otherwise they become long-term unemployed. Nations who are continually innovating will produce a range of 'new' products which enjoy a degree of temporary monopoly power. Such nations are likely to be wealthy and to be able to afford high wages. But high wages, by raising workers' aspirations, may encourage them to demand greater economic security—better employment protection, more industrial democracy and so on. Such provisions may create structural rigidities which inhibit the innovation process. New products cease to replace the older ones, the product range becomes increasingly vulnerable to competition, and national income declines. And if workers in the ageing industries refuse to accept real wage cuts as competition intensifies, then structural unemployment will soon become endemic in the economy.

1.4   THE AGGREGATION ISSUE

Keynesian theory cannot provide an adequate account of structural unemployment because the theory is essentially macroeconomic. It explains aggregate unemployment, but not its incidence on different groups of workers.

Keynes' emphasis on macroeconomics is not difficult to explain. In his work he developed the analysis of monetary fluctuations pioneered by Dennis Robertson and Ralph Hawtrey. His major contribution was to provide a simple yet systematic account of the determination of equilibrium output under less than full employment conditions. Keynes was able to keep his model simple because he collapsed the whole of the real side of the economy into a single sector. This allowed him to show that aggregate output was determined by a feedback mechanism based upon a simple multiplier. The theoretical imperative of simplicity combined with Keynes' background in monetary economics led him in this way to develop a purely macroeconomic theory of employment.

Multi-sectoral Keynesian models have subsequently been developed, of course, but despite their apparent sophistication they provide only limited insights into the structure of unemployment. This is because the models are developed almost exclusively with the object of examining how structural interdependencies influence the size of the Keynesian income multiplier. The models assume that all sectors experience Keynesian unemployment to some degree. In addition, the models have little to say about the supply of labour to individual sectors, and in particular about the impact of labour mobility on sectoral labour supplies. These difficulties stem directly from the aggregation across the real sector which is inherent in the Keynesian approach. For this reason the Keynesian approach cannot, without substantial modification, provide a purely structural account of unemployment.

Likewise modern neoclassical theory has followed the macroeconomic approach pioneered by Keynes. One reason is that the theory has been developed partly as a critique of Keynes; the other is that the theory is concerned primarily with the monetary sector, and in particular with the role of aggregates such as the money supply. It is true that neoclassical theory claims to have better microeconomic foundations than Keynes; but these microeconomic foundations do not embody any insights into the structure of the economy. In most cases they merely involve postulates about the rational behaviour of a representative individual, whose actions are grossed up to predict macroeconomic relationships between, say, aggregate unemployment, inflation and money supply.

1.5   PRE-KEYNESIAN ANALYSIS OF UNEMPLOYMENT

To find an adequate theory of structural unemployment it is necessary to go back before Keynes. The outline of a theory of structural unemployment was developed in the 1920s by a small group of British economists who were concerned about the relatively poor performance of the British economy after World War I. These economists distinguished various dimensions of economic structure, and sought to explain their relevance to unemployment. In some cases they distinguished a vertical chain of production linking the primary sector (agriculture and mining) the secondary sector (manufacturing) and the tertiary sector (services). In other cases they distinguished sectors according to their revealed comparative advantage in trade: the export sector, the import-substituting sector and the non-tradeable sector. For some purposes they distinguished industries by age ('old' or 'staple' industries and 'new' industries), by the durability of the product (consumer-good and capital-good industries) or the type of consumer (wage-good and non-wage-good industries), or even by location ('central' and 'peripheral'). All of these characteristics—and many more besides—were held to influence the incidence of unemployment within an industry.

When Keynes introduced his macroeconomic approach to the real sector he went to considerable pains to try and justify his aggregation procedures (Keynes, 1936, ch. 4). His macroeconomic approach was a considerable departure from the Pre-Keynesian approach. In some respects, of course, it represented a theoretical advance, but this advance was achieved only at considerable cost. The enthusiasm with which Keynes' ideas were greeted meant that many of the insights of Pre-Keynesian writers into the structure of unemployment were neglected.

This process of neglect was hastened by serious misrepresentation of Pre-Keynesian writers, begun by Keynes and continued by some of his younger Cambridge colleagues. As a result of these false accounts of their views, it is nowadays widely believed that the Pre-Keynesian economists had no coherent theory of large-scale unemployment. As a corollary to this, it is held that the employment policies they advocated were based upon political prejudice or class ideology rather than upon any analysis of the situation. The promulgation of these views led to an estrangement between Keynes and his senior Cambridge colleagues Pigou and Robertson.

Keynes suggested in the *General Theory* that previous writers on unemployment held 'classical' views which were quite foolish. In fact, nothing could be further from the truth. Keynes' 'classical economist' is very much a straw man. With the possible exception of Lionel Robbins, it is difficult to find any British economist of repute who conforms even roughly to Keynes' 'classical' type. British economists who were contemporary observers of unemployment in the 1920s were not only 'unclassical', they actually anticipated many of the concepts of the *General Theory*. For example, Pigou—often regarded as the archetypal 'classic'—had developed in detail the concepts of money illusion and relative wage rigidities well before Keynes had even started on his *General Theory*. Keynes' predecessors developed a coherent analysis of structural unemployment, and this analysis led them to recommend policies such as rationalization and the industrial transference of labour. They also made some rather pessimistic forecasts of unemployment. Their pessimism appeared to have been falsified by the high post-war employment, but current experience suggests that in the long run their forecasts may well have been correct.

1.6 SUMMARY AND PLAN OF THE BOOK

The main objects of this book are

(1) to summarize Pre-Keynesian economists' views on unemployment, and to show that they anticipated many aspects of the modern theory of unemployment;
(2) to examine the theoretical difficulties they encountered in using equilibrium concepts to analyze disequilibrium phenomena, and in the light of this to reinterpret their analysis using modern disequilibrium theory;
(3) using a model of structural disequilibrium, to appraise some of the selective measures considered—and in some cases advocated—by the Pre-Keynesian economists as a cure for unemployment;
(4) to demonstrate the relevance of the Pre-Keynesian analysis to the inter-war British economy; and
(5) to consider its implications for unemployment today.

The most important Pre-Keynesian writers were A. C. Pigou, Henry Clay and Edwin Cannan (in that order). The lives and times of these economists are described in chapter 2.

Their theory of unemployment is outlined in chapter 3. The theory has two main features:

(1) unemployment is caused by a real wage that is fixed too high in relation to productivity; and
(2) the problem of the real wage is particularly acute in certain sectors of the economy.

The Pre-Keynesian theory anticipated many subsequent developments in unemployment theory. Pigou, for example, described how unemployment can be caused by workers migrating from a non-unionized competitive sector to a unionized sector where they queue for jobs. Pigou also anticipated many of the ideas in Keynes' *General Theory*. Pigou's anticipation of Keynes is not much stressed in the present work, however, because it is already well known that Keynes borrowed most of his ideas from other economists. Indeed, it is suggested in this book that Pigou's economics is of far greater importance than the economics of Keynes; Pigou's claim to fame does not rest merely upon his anticipation of Keynes.

The Pre-Keynesian theory was never systematically expounded. Clay summarized the theory, but in a discursive manner, while Pigou formalized only selected aspects of the theory. The theory can, in fact, be formulated very simply using the concepts of modern disequilibrium theory. This reformulation makes it clear that the logic of the Pre-Keynesian analysis is impeccable. It shows that the Pre-Keynesians were amongst the first to apply disequilibrium reasoning to the unemployment problem; indeed Clower's original statement of disequilibrium theory fits the economics of Pigou much better than it fits the economics of Keynes.

The elements of disequilibrium theory are summarized in chapter 4 and its application to Pre-Keynesian theory is discussed in chapters 5 and 6. This reformulation of the Pre-Keynesian theory sheds new light on two important issues. The first is the relation between disequilibrium theory and job search theory; this is considered in chapter 5. Pre-Keynesian theory suggests that the two theories can be integrated by postulating that workers search, not for wage information, but for rationed jobs. The resulting theory can be used to analyze the migration behaviour of unemployed workers. It was indicated above how Pigou had used this kind of theory to show that the exercise of trade union power could encourage labour to migrate into unionized industries where unemployment was relatively high.

The second issue concerns the concept and measurement of

structural unemployment; this is considered in chapter 6. It is sometimes suggested that unemployment in a declining sector can only be structural if it is balanced by unfilled vacancies elsewhere. This view is entirely false. If wages are rigid only in the downward direction then structural unemployment may persist in the declining sector while the unfilled vacancies in the growing sectors are eliminated by upward wage adjustments. Even if wages are rigid upwards, disequilibrium theory indicates that unemployment in the declining sectors may reduce the excess demand for labour in the growing sectors through the spill-over effects of lower incomes. This shows that the existence of structural unemployment cannot be tested by whether there are labour bottlenecks elsewhere in the economy. Conversely, recognition of a bottleneck problem does not imply that there must be a structural unemployment problem too.

The Pre-Keynesian economists had a coherent set of employment policies which they deduced directly from their analysis. Indeed, their policies can be properly understood only in the context of their theory. A consequence of their fixed real wage postulate is that public expenditure can crowd out private expenditure even at high levels of unemployment. Another consequence is that the impact of the exchange rate on export competitiveness may be neutralized by wage bargaining. On these grounds the Pre-Keynesians ruled out public expenditure and devaluation as long-run employment policies. Because they did not favour wage cuts either, they recommended productivity improvements as the main solution of the real wage problem.

Because their policies were formulated in a medium-run context, they seemed largely irrelevant to the short-run problems of financial instability during 1929–33. Like many other economists, the Pre-Keynesians advocated monetary expansion as a cure for financial instability. They warned, however, that monetary expansion should be only temporary, but their warnings were ignored in the aftermath of the 'Keynesian revolution', with damaging consequences in the long run. Pre-Keynesian policies are discussed in chapter 7, and their relation to Keynesian policies is examined in chapter 8. In discussing the failure of Pre-Keynesian economics to survive the impact of the 'Keynesian revolution', the personalities of the Pre-Keynesians—as described in chapter 2—assume an important role.

The statistical evidence in favour of the Pre-Keynesian theory is quite strong. Chapters 9 and 10 show that data on inter-war Britain are consistent with the view that a disproportionate number of workers were strongly attached to older industries where the real wage was out of line with productivity. An increase in the real wage relative to productivity in certain industries led to a reduction in employment and a less than proportionate reduction in labour supply. Thus unemployment became concentrated in certain declining industries.

The book concludes by considering the social and industrial background to real wage problems, with a view to explaining why they predominate in older industries. It is suggested in chapter 11 that older sectors of the economy which have evolved standardized working practices are prone to growing conflict over the right to manage, and over the appropriation of profits. Innovative sectors avoid these problems because entrepreneurs are more aggressive in creating new jobs and in enforcing managerial prerogatives, and because they attract to their firms the more enterprising workers. In a fairly flexible economy, recurrent waves of innovation readily transfer a mobile labour force from the older sectors to the new ones. This movement of resources to the newer sectors limits the size of the 'aged industry' problem.

It is suggested, very tentatively, that in twentieth-century Britain social attitudes have led to a failure of entrepreneurship and to a relatively low mobility of labour. New industries have failed to develop as they should, and labour has remained attached to older industries where the quality of management is poor. If this conjecture is correct then the real wage problem discussed by the Pre-Keynesian economists may well be one of the major problems facing the British economy today.

Not all readers will want to study every part of this book. The book has been structured so that readers can pick and choose, within

TABLE 1.1
Suggested reading programmes for readers with special interests

Special interest	Chapters										
	1	2	3	4	5	6	7	8	9	10	11
History of thought	√	√	√				√	√			
Macroeconomic theory				√	√	√			√	√	√
Economic history		√	√					√	√	√	√
Structural problems			√			√	√		√	√	√

limits, what chapters they read. Four categories of reader have been distinguished according to their major interests, and these are listed in the left-hand column of table 1.1. The most relevant chapters for each category are indicated by ticks in the appropriate columns. Readers should be able to fill in the bits omitted from their programme using the summary above, and also by referring to the summaries at the end of the omitted chapters.

2

The Pre-Keynesian Economists:
Their Lives and Times

2.1 INTRODUCTION

This book is concerned with the theory of unemployment developed
by a small group of British writers in the late 1920s: Edwin Cannan,
Henry Clay, Arthur Cecil Pigou, and one or two others. These
writers published papers (chiefly in the *Economic Journal*) and
academic monographs (chiefly with Macmillan) in which they
reviewed and criticized one another's work. For the purposes of this
book these writers are dubbed 'Pre-Keynesian', although they are the
writers whom Keynes himself considered 'classical'. They certainly
formed part of the British academic establishment of which Keynes
was so critical. Two of them—Clay and Pigou—served with Keynes
on the Committee of Economists of the Economic Advisory
Council, (Howson and Winch, 1977) and they also testified before
the Macmillan Committee on Finance and Industry, of which
Keynes was a member.

This chapter presents some background material in order to
provide a context for the summary of Pre-Keynesian analysis
presented in chapter 3. The impatient reader may prefer to skip this
chapter, and refer back to it when necessary. Sections 2.2–2.4 present
brief biographies of the three leading Pre-Keynesian economists.
Section 2.5 discusses their relations with their contemporaries.
Sections 2.6–2.9 survey economic conditions in inter-war Britain,
and indicate the kind of problems the Pre-Keynesian economists had
to diagnose.

2.2 ARTHUR CECIL PIGOU (1877–1959)

Pigou read history and moral sciences at Cambridge, was elected a
Fellow of King's College in 1902 and became Girdler's Lecturer in
1904. He was responsible for much of the basic teaching in the

Economics Tripos established in Cambridge in 1903. At the age of 30 he succeeded Alfred Marshall to the Chair of Political Economy, being preferred to the more senior Herbert Somerton Foxwell, and held this chair until his retirement in 1943. The conventional view of Pigou is articulated by Austin Robinson (see also Johnson, 1978):

Pigou was throughout his life a devoted—some would say too devoted and uncritical—pupil of Alfred Marshall. Pigou's course of lectures became the principal channel through which the oral tradition of Marshall's economics was passed down. . . . [It] was he, more than any other, who brought up a generation of Cambridge economists in the conviction that (in his oft-repeated words) 'it's all in Marshall'. . . . Keynes gave those generations of students their enthusiasms, their sense of the importance of discovering solutions to the economic problems of the world. Pigou gave them their training in the disciplines and techniques of economic reasoning. Clarity of analysis and a willingness to follow an argument through to the end were the essence of his own exposition and of what he demanded in others (E.A.G. Robinson, 1971, p. 815).

This view of Pigou as someone of narrow vision is rather belied, however, by the subject-matter of his early work. *Robert Browning as a Religious Teacher* (1901) was his first, unsuccessful, attempt at a fellowship thesis for King's. His earliest economics books were *The Riddle of the Tariff* (1903), *The Principles and Methods of Industrial Peace* (1905), *Protective and Preferential Import Duties* (1906), *Wealth and Welfare* (1912) (later retitled *The Economics of Welfare*), and *Unemployment* (1914). The subjects of these books do not suggest an interest in purely abstract theorizing but rather in applying theory to important social and political issues.

As a young man Pigou was certainly active in politics. In the early days of Joseph Chamberlain's campaign he went on tour, giving Free Trade lectures. 'Public speaking was something he thoroughly enjoyed: he loved the cogent close-knit argument and the finished phrase'. As President of the Cambridge Union his eloquence was legendary, and according to Philip Noel-Baker, he preached a 'warm but practical idealism' (Saltmarsh and Wilkinson, 1960, p. 7). This practical idealism is apparent throughout Pigou's early writings. His *Unemployment* book, for example, begins as follows:

It is thought by many that the attitude of economists in the face of obvious social evils is unduly contemplative; that conditions, which involve the misery of untold thousands and the withering of incalculable human promise, are for them no more than the theme for ingenious disquisitions, and the excuse for a number of scarcely comprehensible formulae. Assuredly this is a mistaken view. The compelling motive that leads men to economic study is seldom a mere academic or scientific interest in the movements of the great wheel of wealth. It is rather the sense that, in the world of business and of labour, justice stands with biassed scales; that men, women and children stagger often into an abyss that *might* be fenced and guarded; that the lives of many are darker than they need be; that the wealth, on which western nations pride themselves, bears but a faded flower of welfare. In these things lies the impulse to economic investigation; and the removal, or at least the mitigation, of the evils they portray is the goal of the economist's search. In the ideal of which he dreams, and, be it hoped, in the ardour and constancy of his vision of it, there is nothing that need divide him from the fiercest orator of the market place (Pigou, 1914, pp. 9–10).

As a conscientious objector during World War I, Pigou spent his vacations driving an ambulance at the front, first in Flanders, and later in Italy. Towards the end of the war he worked in the Board of Trade, and he later served on the Cunliffe Committee on Currency and Foreign Exchanges after the War (1918), the Royal Commission on the Income Tax (1919–20) and the Chamberlain–Bradbury Committee on the Currency and Bank of England Note Issues (1924–5). He supported the recommendation of this last committee that Britain should return to the Gold Standard at the pre-war parity at the earliest opportunity (Moggridge, 1972), although, as he admitted later, he had not personally considered the issue of *whether* Britain should return to gold, but only the more limited question of *when* the return should be made. On the latter issue he believed that Britain may as well return sooner rather than later, as later the British economy might be even weaker than it already was.

Pigou was never very happy serving on committees, however; he complained of too much 'gassing' and 'jaw'. He preferred his own company, and that of a few carefully chosen friends. Mountaineering was his main hobby, while misogyny restricted his social life. In 1927 he was taken seriously ill with heart trouble whilst playing squash, and thereafter he suffered intermittent phases of debility throughout his life. He became increasingly withdrawn, and his friends believed him to have become a hypochondriac. This withdrawal is reflected in his writing, which until the late 1920s was lively and incisive, but degenerated into little more than analytical taxonomy in the 1930s. In 1927, for example, he published two major pieces of work: *Industrial Fluctuations* and a paper on Wage Policy and Unemployment. Thereafter he produced only 'pudding-like tomes'

(Collard, 1981) such as *The Theory of Unemployment* (1933) and *The Economics of Stationary States* (1935). The most useful book from this later period is *Employment and Equilibrium* (1941).

Pigou achieved posthumous notoriety in 1979 when Donald McCormick (alias Richard Deacon) 'exposed' Pigou as a Russian spy (Deacon, 1979). Deacon refers to a coded diary written by Pigou, which is located in the 'Deacon Papers', but despite extensive inquiries this has not come to light. It is certainly true that in the 1930s Pigou was accused of being a socialist sympathizer because of his view, expressed as *Socialism and Capitalism* (1935) that central planning made it easier to stabilize employment through public works. Had he been a spy, however, it is difficult to see why he should have 'blown his cover' in this way. The idea of a coded diary is somewhat absurd, anyway, because Pigou's handwriting was so bad that few people could decipher his ordinary correspondence. Saltmarsh and Wilkinson (1960, p. 15) recall that his handwriting could often only be interpreted by an expert at Miss Pate's typewriting establishment. Once he wrote a telegram 'Expect me 5 o.c. Pigou', and the message arrived 'Export me 500 pigeons'.

Pigou's response to the publication of Keynes' *General Theory* was distinctly hostile. He believed that Keynes had misrepresented his views and the views of some of his fellow economists. In particular, Pigou felt that Keynes had drawn freely upon the ideas of their teacher Alfred Marshall, and their mutual colleague Dennis Robertson, and that, rather than acknowledge his debt, Keynes had decided for reasons of political expediency to criticize those who had inspired him (Robinson, 1977). Pigou also had certain theoretical objections, which he later crystallized as the omission of the wealth effect of price changes on the determination of output (Pigou, 1945, 1949). His hostile review seriously damaged Pigou's reputation with younger economists. At Cambridge Pigou seems to have become an isolated, if not comic, figure so far as the young Keynesians were concerned. They were inclined to reject Pigou's criticisms of Keynes out of hand, on the grounds that his health was affecting his mental faculties, although as Collard (1981, pp. 128–9) points out, there was considerable disagreement among the Keynesians about precisely what Pigou's errors and misunderstandings were.

Pigou continued writing on economics long after his retirement, and in 1950 published a retrospective view of the *General Theory* in which he recanted some—though by no means all—of his earlier criticisms. It is arguable that this book demonstrates a better appreciation of the true significance of the *General Theory* than does the more polemical writing of those who were so quick to ridicule his own work.

2.3   HENRY CLAY (1883–1954)

Clay pursued a varied career as social worker, academic, civil servant and man of affairs. As an academic he was 'a tool-user rather than a tool-designer—and frequently impatient of the tools provided' (Jewkes and Jewkes (1971), p. 227).

Graduating from Oxford with a second-class degree in *literae humaniores,* he took a job as secretary of a charity and afterwards became the warden of a settlement in Sheffield. Between 1909 and 1917 he lectured on economics for the Workers' Educational Association and published in 1916 a widely used textbook which 'by reason of its lucidity and the homeliness of its examples, broadened public interest in economic matters'.

After a spell of work at the Ministry of Labour and an assignment as special industrial correspondent to the New York *Evening Post,* he was elected in 1922 to the Stanley Jevons Chair of Political Economy at Manchester University, and transferred in 1927 to a newly established Chair of Social Economics there. This was a period of intense creative effort, with numerous perceptive commentaries on the industrial situation flowing from his pen. Clay was also much in demand, both at home and abroad, as an arbitrator, and as an adviser on industrial relations.

Clay was very diffident in his role as an academic economist. When in 1926 Cannan suggested that he should stand for the chair in London from which he was retiring, Clay expressed considerable surprise.

The suggestion that I should stand for your chair in London surprised me very much. I have always felt that as a Professor of Economics I was a fraud. I don't distrust my own opinions on economic questions more than other people distrust theirs; but I have not reached them by the methods of the scholar or scientist. My reading of English Economics has been scrappy—so much so, that if I set myself to fill in all the gaps, I should have reached the retiring age before I finished; I know no foreign economic literature; I don't know enough mathematics to follow our Cambridge friends, however suspicious I may be of their results; and I cannot suppress my interest in current political and social questions sufficiently to stick to any one part of the field of economics and so do some serious work on it (Clay, 1926, p. 1).

Clay was a strong advocate of rationalization, and in 1930 he joined the Bank of England as adviser to the newly established Securities Management Trust, whose role was to allocate government funds for the regeneration of private industry. He served on the Royal Commission on Unemployment Insurance and in 1933 was appointed economic adviser to the governor of the Bank, Lord Norman (of whom he later wrote a biography). Though dissimilar in temperament—Norman a 'prima donna', Clay 'gentle, scholarly, sensitive and undogmatic'—they agreed upon the basic tenets of economic policy, and made a formidable team.

Clay was instrumental in the establishment in 1938 of the National Institute of Economic and Social Research. During the war he held a variety of senior posts in Whitehall; he was appointed Warden of Nuffield College, Oxford in 1944 and was knighted in 1946. He was killed in a road accident in 1954.

Clay was not a profound or original theorist, but he showed considerable skill in identifying relevant areas of theory and applying them to the contemporary industrial situation. His eclectic use of theory sometimes led to minor inconsistencies in his arguments, but this is more than compensated for by the breadth of view and judgement apparent in his writings. Two books in particular provide valuable introductions to Pre-Keynesian thought: *The Post-war Unemployment Problem* (1929) and *The Problem of Industrial Relations and Other Essays* (1929). Taken together, these books afford a convincing diagnosis of the structural problems of the British economy in the 1920s.

2.4   EDWIN CANNAN (1861–1935)

Cannan entered Balliol College, Oxford, to read History, but owing to illness he switched to the pass school, where he read political economy as one of his subjects. Writing in 1912, he recalled that

At Oxford I underwent in regard to my social philosophy the kind of change which in regard to religion is described as 'conversion'. As I listened to Mr A. L. Smith, the Historical Spirit entered into me, and I became a new man. I . . . took to heart the truth that all important change is gradual, and that social institutions are not created by the sudden efforts of inspired geniuses but grow 'of themselves', usually slower than oak-trees (Cannan, 1912, pp. 10–11).

The historical spirit seemed to me to be urgently required in dealing with economic doctrine. I had been strongly influenced by Adolf Held's *Zwei Bucher zur Socialen Geschichte Englands,* in which Adam Smith, Malthus and Ricardo are treated as mortal men affected by their environment instead of strange, inexplicable phenomena suddenly created by some unknown force in the midst of a world of nothingness (Cannan, 1912, p. 17).

The seed sown by the Historical Spirit blossomed into Cannan's best known work, *A History of the Theories of Production and Distribution in English Political Economy from 1776 to 1848* (1893), which attracted considerable attention for its trenchant criticisms of the classical economists. His mastery of classical economics established Cannan as an authority on the theory of population and the law of diminishing returns (cf Robbins, 1927). Cannan's reputation for independent thought and forceful expression secured for him an invitation to lecture on economics at the newly established London School of Economics (Robbins, 1949, p. 142). He was appointed Professor of Economics in the University of London in 1907, and retired in 1926. His two-year lecture course on economic principles was published as *A Review of Economic Theory* (1927).

In 1895 Cannan discovered a set of student's notes of Adam Smith's Glasgow lectures, which he published in a learned edition as *Lectures on Justice, Police, Revenue and Arms* (1896). Then in 1904 he published an edition of *The Wealth of Nations* which remained standard until the Glasgow edition of 1976. His wide-ranging interests and his literary style are indeed reminiscent of Adam Smith. He wrote papers and short polemical articles for the press on a wide variety of subjects, many of which were republished in two volumes of essays, *The Economic Outlook* (1912) and *An Economist's Protest* (1927).

Robbins (1971) recalls Cannan in his 60s as

A short thickset figure in not very well-cut clothes, his doctor's cap perched at a somewhat aggressive angle over a grey-bearded face. . . . Despite superb command in his written work of a wholesome English prose, he was a poor lecturer, apt to mumble into his beard or, when he spoke up, not necessarily in full control of the tonality of his voice. . . . There was therefore little in outward appearances or pedagogic practice which might be expected to establish outstanding influence on the students who sat under him. Nevertheless, such influence existed. . . . Once one had tuned in to

Cannan, so to speak, everything he said seemed to matter—the
keen ones would turn up early to get seats in the front rows so as not to miss
any sentences which were more than usually enveloped in the beard. We
discussed his every *obiter dictum*. We relished and put into wider circulation
his pawky humour. . . . Cannan was not incapable of misinterpreting his
sources, great scholar though he was. But what came through in the large
. . . was a weight of erudition, a broad feeling for history and institutions,
an invincible common sense, a combination whose impressiveness it is
difficult to exaggerate (Robbins, 1971, pp. 83–5).

Cannan's historical outlook and his broad concern with issues of
social policy were typical of the Oxford-trained economists of the
day. In this respect, his work resembles that of W. J. Ashley, A. J.
Toynbee and L. L. Price (Kadish, 1982).

As a young man Cannan had flirted with the Fabians, but he was
no political radical. He was fond of debunking generalizations—
whatever their political complexion—which claimed to be true for all
times and in all places. He rebutted allegations of capitalist profiteering, and at the same time condemned employers for managing
according to medieval traditions.

Cannan's staunch independence is illustrated by an episode in
which he was called to testify before the Coal Industry Commission
(Cannan, 1919b). The chairman, Lord Sankey, was somewhat taken
aback when the distinguished professorial witness not only criticized
the employers but recommended the gradual introduction of syndicalism into the industry. Neither did his views please the radical
intellectuals on the commission, who wanted to 'plan' the industry
bureaucratically rather than surrender control to the workers.
Among the commissioners he displeased was Sidney Webb, founder
of the London School of Economics, who had been instrumental in
appointing Cannan to his chair. The commissioners suppressed part
of Cannan's evidence, and Cannan was obliged to publish it
separately. Afterwards, Cannan gave this advice to his Assistant,
Hugh Dalton (later Chancellor of the Exchequer in the post-war
Labour government). When giving evidence to a Royal
Commission:

You must make up your mind whether you're going to talk for the public,
or for the Bluebook. If the latter, you must be prepared to make an
apparently poor show, e.g. Pigou, who made things worse by smiling at
the commissioners all the time. If the former, you should aim at saying
smart things, and making cheap scores. When in a hole, and asked a
question you can't immediately think of a good answer to, begin talking at

the same time as your questioner. Then the shorthand reporter will get confused and take it down wrong, and you'll be able to correct the proofs and think out the best answer at leisure (Dalton, 1953, pp. 113–14).

Cannan was a staunch supporter of sound currency. He argued that it was governments, and not the banks, that regulated the supply of credit and thereby influenced the money price level. He recalls an episode in Oxford where 'in the stress of the examination it occurred to me to write that the ideal of credit would be attained when coin was so superseded that there remained but "a single sovereign at the Bank of England, which no-one would want because anyone could have"' (Cannan, 1912, p. 11). This mental aberration did not last long, however. He refers elsewhere, with evident approval, to the 'oft-recurring refrain' (Cannan, 1927, p. xi) of his book on *Money* (1918) that 'to maintain the value of a currency due limitation of issue is necessary'. In fact, to support his argument against war-time currency expansion, he edited a special reprint of the Bullion Report of 1810, entitled *The Paper Pound of 1797 to 1821* (1919).

Cannan was highly critical of Cambridge monetary theory, which suggested that banks' deposit creation and discount policy could influence prices. Cannan's criticisms are obviously over-stated, and Keynes (1924, p. 68) complained with considerable justification that 'Professor Cannan is unsympathetic with nearly everything worth reading—as it seems to me—which has been written on monetary theory in the last ten years' (quoted in Gregory, 1927, pp. 59–60).

Cannan enjoyed independent means; he chose to live in Oxford and commute to London. He was a town councillor, and made a special study of roads. One of his more unusual pastimes was detecting minor errors in the successive editions of Marshall's *Principles* (Fay, 1935). Marshall, apparently, took the rather unorthodox view that errors in his work were his wife's responsibility, and passed on Cannan's criticisms for her to deal with. Cannan was an energetic cyclist, a hobby he pursued in the company of A. L. Bowley and F. Y. Edgeworth. Although they were good friends, he preferred that they did not talk mathematical economics to him (Bowley, 1934). During the General Strike, in his 65th year, he cycled up to London to give his lectures (Dalton, 1927, p. 27) though soon afterwards he acquired a 'baby Austin', and explored the countryside in a more relaxed fashion instead. He continued to write during his retirement, but his style became increasingly outdated as rigour supplanted vigour as the criterion of professional excellence.

He became preoccupied with the dangers of monetary expansion during the slump (Cannan, 1931, 1933). He had always deplored extravagance in public spending—as early as 1893 he had denounced the government for wasting paper by using too wide a margin in its printed reports. He was unable to join Pigou in his qualified support for his public works, and his increasingly inflexible stance diminished his influence in academic circles. By the time of his death—just a year before the publication of the *General Theory*—his reputation was, as Robbins (1949) notes, under something of a cloud.

2.5 UNEMPLOYMENT THEORY IN INTER-WAR BRITAIN

The Pre-Keynesian economists mentioned above were not, of course, the only British economists studying unemployment in the years before the publication of the *General Theory*. They were, however, the most important of the economists who addressed themselves specifically to the question of the relatively high level of unemployment which had been discerned in the 1920s.

Until recently, when scholars looked back upon the economic thought of the inter-war period, their interest centred upon aggregative theories of unemployment and upon the precursors of Keynes (see e.g. Eshag, 1963; Patinkin, 1982). These precursors include the theories of the trade cycle developed by Dennis Robertson (1915, 1926); Ralph Hawtrey (1919) and Frederick Lavington (1922), and the theory of the multiplier developed by Richard Kahn (1931). By and large, these theories are concerned with short-run disturbances to employment and output, and emphasize the role of expectation formation and of lags in the circular flow of money income (Macfie, 1934). Pigou was also interested in the trade cycle, and his work on *Industrial Fluctuations* (1927) repays detailed study. However, most of these theories have already been examined in detail by other scholars (see e.g. Presley, 1979; Davis, 1981) and no attempt is made to summarize them here. They will only be considered in this book in so far as they have a bearing upon the determination of unemployment in the medium run.

Underconsumptionist theories also flourished in the inter-war period (Bleaney, 1976). Although they are interesting for their emphasis on the importance of aggregate demand, most of the theories were flawed in one way or another, as contemporary critics such as Durbin (1933) and Nash (1935) were quick to point out.

Nevertheless the popularity of writers such as Major Douglas indicates the difficulties experienced by the professional economists of the day in winning public support for their analysis of unemployment.

At the opposite end of the spectrum from the underconsumptionist theories are the Austrian theories of the trade cycle, inspired by the work of Friedrich Hayek (1931, 1933). The popularity of Austrian ideas at the London School of Economics seems to have been partly responsible for the eclipse of academic interest in the Pre-Keynesian theory (see chapter 8). A particular strength of the Austrian theory is that, like the Pre-Keynesian theory, it emphasizes the structural aspects of the economy, and in particular the interaction between the capital goods and consumption goods industries. The theory of 'roundaboutness' in production provides a dynamical link between monetary factors (the money rate of interest) and the structural balance of the real sector of the economy (the ratio of capital goods production to consumption goods production).

The weakness of the Austrian theory as expounded by Hayek (1933), Lachmann (1940) and others, was that it was a theory of wages and prices rather than a theory of output and employment. Unlike the Pre-Keynesian theory, the distinction between price adjustments and quantity adjustments was not properly made. An interesting blend of Pre-Keynesian and Austrian Theory is provided by J. R. Hicks' *Theory of Wages* (1932). Although chiefly remembered for its analysis of bilateral monopoly in wage bargaining, this book provides a convenient summary of Pre-Keynesian thinking on unemployment, and attempts in the later chapters to integrate the Pre-Keynesian analysis with the Austrian theory of the trade cycle. A much more dogmatic, and less successful, Austrian analysis of unemployment was given by Lionel Robbins in *The Great Depression* (1934).

It is sometimes suggested that it was from an Austrian standpoint that W. H. Hutt developed his critique of the *General Theory*. His book, *The Theory of Idle Resources* (1939), though now well known, was sadly neglected at the time. Without denying Hutt's attachment to Austrian methodology, it appears that this early critique relies heavily upon the Pre-Keynesian literature. The 'orthodox economics' described by Hutt is essentially the Pre-Keynesian theory; thus while Hutt refers to Cannan and to Pigou, he does not refer by name to Hayek or to Mises. Hutt's arguments may thus be viewed, not as an alternative to the Pre-Keynesian theory, but as a restatement and elaboration of them.

Finally, it should be recognized that the Pre-Keynesian economists drew upon a large body of statistical evidence compiled by the social investigators of the period. The social statistics movement had acquired considerable momentum in late Victorian and Edwardian Britain. The survey work of Charles Booth in London and B. Seebohm Rowntree in York, together with the historical work of Sidney and Beatrice Webb, provided valuable evidence on the relation between unemployment and poverty. Much of the evidence is summarized in the Majority and Minority Reports of the Royal Commission on the Poor Laws, 1909 (for further information see Garraty (1978) and Williams (1936)).

Statistical inquiries were continued in the inter-war period (Kent, 1981). Bowley and Hogg (1925) examined whether poverty had diminished since before the war and concluded that, owing to various factors such as higher real wages of unskilled workers, it had. Hilton (1924, 1928) examined Ministry of Labour statistics to analyse the dynamics of spells of unemployment. A number of investigators concerned themselves specifically with the problems of juvenile unemployment (Jewkes and Jewkes, 1938), which was particularly troublesome in the textile industries and the distributive trades (Casson, 1979, ch. 2; Sims, 1978). The New Survey of London Life and Labour was organized by H. Llewellyn Smith (Smith, 1930–5) to re-examine the problems studied by Booth over 30 years earlier. The Merseyside Survey was conducted by D. Caradog Jones (1934), a survey of Southampton was carried out by P. Ford (1934), and so on. A more general study was conducted by the Pilgrim Trust (1938) with a view to ascertaining the problems of the unemployed in declining urban areas (see also Singer, 1939a,b, 1940). Mention should also be made of the somewhat unorthodox sociological investigations of E. Wight Bakke (1933). Although these later surveys came too late to influence Pre-Keynesian thought, they provide invaluable information upon the incidence of unemployment and upon the attitudes of the unemployed.

Statistical evidence on unemployment was collated by William Beveridge (Beveridge, 1909, 1930, 1931). Although this work attracted considerable attention, Beveridge's own thinking on unemployment was not particularly original, and underwent considerable change during the inter-war period as he came under the influence of different scholars (Harris, 1977). Beveridge was first and foremost an administrator with a particular interest in social policy. In the 1920s his outlook was broadly Pre-Keynesian; in the early

1930s he came under the influence of Hayek and Robbins while he was Director of the London School of Economics; and in the late 1930s he changed, along with many others, to a Keynesian stance.

2.6   THE AFTERMATH OF WORLD WAR I

At the beginning of the inter-war period Henry Clay was in his mid-30s, Pigou in his early 40s and Edwin Cannan in his late 50s. The loss of life during World War I had been on an unprecedented scale. It seemed to many people that a new and better social order should be rebuilt from the ruins of the old one. Prior to the war there had been a great deal of agitation for industrial reform (Phelps Brown, 1959). Clay believed, like many others, that now was the time, at the end of hostilities, to introduce a new order built around industrial democracy.

The restoration of the *status quo* in industry is as difficult as it would be in the political organisation of Europe. Is it not as undesirable? With all its suffering the war has been an opportunity. . . . [On] the thought that industry is plastic and can be given new shape rests the hope that makes of reconstruction an ideal and not merely a toilsome restoration of an unsatisfactory past (Clay, 1918, p. 145).

But the political and business establishment did not perceive the necessity for any change in the social order. Disregard for the welfare of the troops was superseded by the maxim of 'business as usual' now that hostilities had ceased. There was a speculative boom on the stock market and a good deal of profit-taking as businesses were refinanced with fixed-interest debt. 'Reform' was no part of the vocabulary of the government or the press. But the establishment could not contain the situation.

Throughout Europe the established order of things seemed to be breaking up. The Russian Revolution had added to the restlessness of workers weary of war and disillusioned by the coming of peace. Central Europe was in turmoil. In Britain, even before the end of the war in November 1918, the Labour Party had adopted a socialist constitution. And the confidence of the authorities was shaken by a police strike which forced Lloyd George to intervene personally to concede pay increases. Mutinies provoked by the demobilisation arrangements took place at Folkestone and Calais and several thousand angry soldiers demonstrated on the Horse Guards Parade. . . . The return of a Parliament of 'hard-faced men who look as if they have done well out of the war' reinforced the trade union belief of the pre-war years, intensified by syndicalist and guild socialist propaganda and the shop stewards' wartime challenge, that only by industrial action could they hope to achieve their ideals. The cost of living was shooting up, profiteering was rife and workers could see little evidence of the arrival of the 'land fit for heroes' which Lloyd George had promised them.

Trade union membership more than doubled between 1914 and 1920, when it reached 8,348,000. Ten days after the signing of the armistice, the Wages (Temporary Regulation) Act ended the prohibition on lock-outs and strikes. . . . Within a month, while the election was taking place, the first major official strike for more than four years, in the cotton industry, was already under way (Wigham, 1976, p. 47).

The government was forced to appease the agitators. The Coal Industry Commission was set up, to which workers' leaders were invited to testify (though their testimony was subsequently ridiculed by the press). As already noted, Cannan was summoned as a witness to this commission. Tax reform was mooted; Pigou was appointed to serve on a Royal Commission, which recommended measures that Pigou felt would effect a substantial improvement in the distribution of the 'national dividend'.

The agitation for reform did not, however, survive the collapse of the post-war boom in 1920. Its chief legacies were not changes in legislation, but changes in working practices negotiated privately between employers and trade unions. There was a widespread reduction in the standard working week from 54 to 48 hours, and official recognition of shop stewards in many industries. This reduction in standard hours was one of the greatest ever in the history of British labour (Bienefeld, 1972). The main legislative changes were the extension of the national insurance scheme and the establishment of wage boards and arbitration machinery (Sells, 1923; Chang, 1936). The rules, customs and procedures instituted in 1919–20 provide the framework of industrial relations in many industries to this day.

2.7   BRITAIN'S POOR PERFORMANCE IN THE 1920s

The collapse of the post-war boom in 1920 was perceived at the time as part of an inevitable cyclical fluctuation in trade. But a recovery of the kind anticipated was very slow in coming. By 1924 there was growing realization that there had been a permanent rather than transitory change in the level of economic activity. The idealism which had inspired Pigou, Clay and Cannan to support the reforms of 1919–20 gave way, to some extent, to greater 'realism'.

It became apparent that, because of the interruption to production caused by war, many British export markets had been lost for good. The standardized nature of the technologies in the staple export trades—textiles, shipbuilding and steel, for example—made it easy for overseas customers to establish import-substituting local production. It is doubtful if many of these overseas markets could have been retained for long in any case; the decline of some of the export industries had begun well before the outbreak of the war. The acquisition of industrial disciplines and skills by workers in Europe and the Far East upset the old balance of comparative advantage; it was no longer economic to transport raw materials to Britain for processing and fabrication before shipping them onwards to the final market.

British labour was becoming less competitive. The reduction in the standard working week, though it undoubtedly enhanced productivity per hour by reducing the incidence of fatigue, on balance probably reduced productivity per man per working week. New working practices may also have impaired productivity (e.g. the abolition of split shifts on the railways). The increased power of shop stewards facilitated organized resistance to the introduction of Taylorist scientific management and Fordist work organization in the traditional craft industries. Whether organized resistance was in fact necessary is questionable, however, since British management was also slow to adopt new professional practices based upon cost accountancy, line and staff organization and the like. For these and other reasons productivity growth in British staple industries lagged behind the growth of productivity in many other countries.

Labour costs in the staple industries showed little tendency to fall. There was no reduction in the weekly wage to compensate for the reduction in the working week. Union membership, though adversely affected by the depression, remained higher than pre-war and an increased number of industries was covered by minimum wages set by Trades Boards. The improved unemployment insurance system introduced in 1920 was partly financed by an increase in the compulsory contribution from employers, which amounted to a tax upon the employment of labour (see section 3.3 below). By contrast the newly industrializing countries had almost unlimited supplies of labour available at a reservation wage set by very low incomes in the agricultural sector.

TABLE 2.1
Industrial growth in Britain 1920–38

Industry	Annual rate of growth of			
	Output	Employment	Capital	Output per man
High-growth industries				
Vehicles	6.6	3.0	5.4	3.6
Building and contracting	5.4	1.8	1.8	3.6
Timber and furniture	5.2	0.2	—	5.0
Electricity, gas, and water	5.0	2.5	3.3	2.5
Non-ferrous metals	4.8	1.2	1.4	3.6
Electrical engineering	4.7	3.6	2.3	1.1
Building materials	3.7	2.1	−0.5	1.6
Food	3.6	1.5	0.6	2.1
Clothing	2.7	−0.2	2.3	2.9
Precision instruments	2.7	−0.3	—	3.0
Medium-growth industries				
Paper and printing	2.6	1.3	2.0	1.3
Metal goods not elsewhere specified	2.5	0.4	—	2.1
Tobacco	2.2	0.5	2.4	1.7
Leather	2.1	−0.2	2.2	2.3
Chemicals	1.9	0.4	1.4	1.5
Mechanical engineering	1.7	−2.0	0.3	3.7
Low-growth industries				
Iron and steel	1.1	−2.4	0.7	3.5
Textiles	0.2	−1.4	−0.9	1.6
Mining and quarrying	0.2	−2.3	0.7	2.5
Drink	−0.2	0.8	0.4	−1.0
Shipbuilding	−2.7	−4.6	−0.8	1.9
Manufacturing	2.6	−0.1	0.7	2.7

Source: Adapted from Aldcroft (1970), p. 121.
Notes: High-growth industries are industries having an annual growth rate higher than the average for manufacturing as a whole. Medium-growth industries are industries growing at less than the average rate, but more than half the average rate. Low-growth industries are industries growing at less than half the average rate.

The major factor reducing the cost of British labour was the falling relative price of wage-goods—notably food. The opening up of new continents by railways, coupled with the increasing mechanization of agriculture, led to a rapid expansion of world food output and a dramatic fall in its price. Much of the overseas agricultural expansion, in the Empire and in Latin America, was financed by the export of debenture capital from London in the late nineteenth century and the first decade of the twentieth century. The fall in the price of wage-goods benefited industrial labour all over the world, however, and did nothing to improve the comparative performance of British labour.

The position of British labour was further worsened by a relative increase in the cost of complementary productive inputs such as energy. The best coal seams were becoming exhausted and Britain did not have cheap indigenous supplies of alternatives such as oil or hydroelectric power; moreover the distribution systems for electricity and gas left a great deal to be desired.

Productivity was by no means stagnant in the staple industries, but the productivity gap between Britain and the rest of the world narrowed considerably, with the result that output in the British staple industries grew only slowly and in most of them employment actually fell. Table 2.1 shows how the staple industries predominate in the low-growth category.

2.8   STRUCTURAL CHANGE IN INTER-WAR BRITAIN

Output growth in inter-war Britain was largely the result of structural change. The high-growth industries were mainly the new industries, in particular those based upon the technologies of internal combustion and electricity. Without question the leading sector was the motor industry, and this industry's demand for components in turn stimulated the electrical and mechanical engineering industries, the rubber industry and so on. The innovation of the mass-produced motor vehicle indicates a degree of entrepreneurial vision which parallels that of the early industrial revolution. Ford, Austin, Morris and others recognized that standardization, quality control and long production runs were crucial in achieving low unit costs, and were willing to commit resources to back their judgement that there was a very large market for low-price vehicles. They invested heavily in assembly lines and scientific work measurement. To ensure the quality of his inputs Ford went so far as to integrate backwards into steel production at his Dagenham works; Austin produced in the Midlands where there was a tradition of precision engineering, while Morris produced in Oxford using migrant workers (many from the depressed Welsh coal-fields) and displaced agricultural workers whom he trained himself.

The new industries were different from the old ones in a number of important respects. Whereas in the old industries Britain had traditionally enjoyed a technological lead—albeit one that had been eroded as the pace of technical advance slowed and foreigners had learnt from British experience—in the new industries it was the United States (in vehicles and electrical engineering) and Germany (in chemicals and pharmaceuticals) which held the lead. In the pre-war period Britain had lent abroad to finance foreign purchases of British capital goods embodying British technology; in the inter-war period foreign firms began to invest in Britain or to license production by British firms. Investments by US firms were particularly notable because they were direct investments of which the essence was foreign control of British production. This reflected the fact that the technology was no longer embodied in the capital equipment, but was 'disembodied'—or, more strictly, it was embodied in management practices and in labour skills. Scientific supervision of the mode of production was the essence of the US technologies, and necessitated continuing control by the parent firm overseas.

The labour skills required by the new industries were rather different from those of the old. They were not the 'craft' skills of the pattern-maker, the boiler-maker or the railway engineer. Rather they were disciplines such as punctuality, precision, a steady rather than erratic work rate, and so on. The work was 'semi-skilled' and the craft unions chose to denigrate it rather than to absorb the semi-skilled within their ranks. Craft workers became a dwindling 'aristocracy of labour', and the semi-skilled workers' interests were represented by the general unions, who became a growing force in the new industries.

The new industries were very much geared to consumer goods rather than capital goods and to the domestic market rather than the export market. British production in the new industries was import-substituting, and was stimulated by trade barriers which prevented foreign high-technology firms from sourcing the British market by imports. The logic of the situation dictated that within Britain, production should be located as close as possible to the centre of the market. In the consumer durable industries, for example, where production costs were kept low by long production runs, the reduction of the transport costs of components and the distribution costs of the finished product was a dominant factor. It was important to locate close to the major source of component supply—the Midlands—and to the major centre of demand—the high-income residential South-east (Political and Economic Planning, 1939; Barlow Commission, 1940).

The new industries therefore avoided the industrial centres based upon the old industries, in spite of the ready availability of the surplus labour they had shed. The few new plants that did locate in the old areas had rather mixed fortunes. It seems that redundant skilled workers from the old industries were either unable or unwilling to 'trade down' successfully to semi-skilled work. The new industries preferred to locate on green-field sites and rely upon migrants from the old areas to meet their labour requirements. It is possible that the migration process may have been a self-selection mechanism which meant that only the most enterprising and ambitious workers presented themselves for employment on the green-field sites. In spite of a quite substantial volume of migration, however, very many unemployed workers remained attached to the depressed areas.

At the end of the war the demobilized troops had generally returned to the industries from which they had been conscripted. The restructuring of industry for which the Pre-Keynesian economists had hoped at the end of the war had not been accomplished. The apparent failure of workers to transfer from declining industries was strongly censured by the Pre-Keynesians. They began to feel it an abuse of the unemployment insurance system that workers should remain indefinitely on the dole in industries where the chances of re-employment seemed very low. This was totally against the actuarial principles which underlay the financing of the insurance scheme. The 'realism' regarding Britain's poor productivity gave way, in some cases, to cynicism about the exploitation of the insurance scheme for personal self-interest (this is especially true of Cannan and Clay). This cynicism also affected the Pre-Keynesians' attitudes towards the claims of pressure groups for subsidies or protection. As a result, the economic literature of 1929 and after shows little of the idealism that was so apparent 10 years before.

2.9   UNEMPLOYMENT IN INTER-WAR BRITAIN

Unemployment generally was high in inter-war Britain, both relative to other countries at the time and to the post-war situation. Following the end of the speculative boom in 1920 unemployment rose sharply in 1921 and then there was gradual recovery, with intermittent setbacks—notably in 1926—until 1929, when Britain became engulfed in the world-wide depression which followed the Wall Street Crash. International trade contracted sharply as the world payments system disintegrated under speculative pressure, and as tariff levels were increased by countries seeking to defend their industrial base. Between 1930 and 1933 aggregate unemployment in Britain averaged about 15 per cent, though the incidence of unemployment in some areas of the North-east and South Wales exceeded 50 per cent.

The slump of 1929–33 did not create widespread social and industrial unrest of the kind seen in 1919—the Jarrow march of 1931, for example, was quite a peaceful affair. It seems that many workers believed the slump to be largely unavoidable: their attitude was one of resignation rather than of protest. Their demands were chiefly for the alleviation of the symptoms rather than for a cure; and alleviation was to some extent available through the unemployment benefit and supplementary benefit schemes.

It was chiefly the intellectuals who protested. The insensitivity to unemployment amongst the business elite encouraged the view that industrial capital was concentrated in the hands of a 'traitor class'. Since moderation in the pursuit of a new social order had failed, it seemed that more extreme measures were called for. Many intellectuals believed that the command economy of Stalinist Russia had solved the unemployment problem. They deluded themselves that in a Stalinist Britain they would assume important roles in a bureaucratic elite. In this 'climate of treason', subversive views were quite common among academics and artists (Boyle, 1979). However, except in one or two cases (notably the Webbs), admiration for the Stalinist system did not survive an examination of it at first hand.

Although the slump was serious in Britain, it was not so catastrophic as in other countries which had grown accustomed to higher levels of growth in the 1920s and, having enjoyed lower levels of unemployment, did not have the same social provision for the unemployed. In Germany and Japan export-led growth was seriously interrupted and economic advancement was increasingly sought through military influence rather than through trade. Rearmament in Western Europe had its beneficial effects, however, for it reduced the idle capacity in the heavy engineering industries, and boosted employment generally through a multiplier effect. From 1933 there was steady recovery in Britain towards a situation of relative prosperity at the outbreak of war in 1939.

There was also a steady if unspectacular growth in service employment, particularly in banking, insurance, distribution and professional services. Productivity in the service industries is notoriously difficult to measure; available statistics suggest that it was stagnant, if not declining. In the case of financial and professional services it seems likely that the measurement of productivity growth is biased downwards because it fails to take proper account of improvements in the quality of the services. In retailing, on the other hand, it is possible that productivity did indeed diminish because although quality improvements were effected through the growth of high-street chain stores and department stores, surprisingly few of the smaller retailers closed down as a result. It is quite possible that the low productivity in retailing is a reflection of 'disguised unemployment' arising from the fact that the owners of small shops remained in business simply because they could not find other work.

The increasing responsibilities of central and local government in the field of education, health and social welfare led to expansion in the civil service and in local government administration. At the same time the growth of new science-based industries using sophisticated marketing methods created a new type of professional manager. As a result there grew up a new middle class of salaried administrators earning secure, though not exceptionally high, incomes.

A notable feature of the inter-war period was the significant growth in building and related trades. Much of this building involved residential construction of family homes in the suburbs and retirement bungalows along the south coast. The boom in building had much to do with the aspirations of the new middle class. Unlike their Victorian and Edwardian predecessors, whose life was built around the small businesses they owned, the new middle class sought to detach themselves as much as possible from the 'polluted' industrial environment. They sought the gentrified exclusivity of the country and the wholesomeness of the sea air.

Economic events conspired to fulfil their dreams. Falling food prices wiped out agricultural land values and provided abundant supplies of cheap building land in the countryside. Workers thrown off the land were available as building labourers or to provide local services for the new village residents. The cheapness of mass-produced motor cars made commuting from the country a feasible proposition even where the railway system was inadequate.

Increased household ownership of vacuum cleaners, sewing machines and other labour-saving consumer goods produced by the new industries reduced the burden of housework. This encouraged women to switch from housework (whether as housewives or as domestic servants) to work in factories and offices. Increased female labour force participation was also stimulated by the experience of war-time employment in munitions factories and elsewhere, which had given women a taste of the social benefits of going out to work. Another effect of the war was that military casualties left many women as heads of households—either as widows, young spinsters, or wives supporting disabled husbands. Finally, as employment prospects for men in the old industries declined, their wives sought work in order to maintain the family income. Although employment opportunities for female operatives declined in some industries (e.g. textiles), many women found suitable work in the new industries or in the expanding service sectors, which offered clerical and administrative work.

At the outbreak of World War II the British economy was in very different shape from what it had been at the end of World War I. It is estimated that net national income grew at an average of 2.1 per cent per annum over the period 1920–38, and industrial productivity by 2.8 per cent. Massive residential development had occurred—particularly in the South-east—and many of the new suburban homes were equipped with labour-saving durables. In contrast, Wales, Merseyside, the North-east and elsewhere had become very depressed, having experienced unprecedented levels of unemployment during the slump. On average material welfare had increased substantially, but new inequalities in the distribution of well-being had arisen. The stylized inequality of the pre-war period between the capitalist and worker had been eclipsed by a new stylized inequality between the affluent semi-skilled or professional worker in the Midlands and South-east and the unemployed craftsmen in one of the depressed areas.

2.10 SUMMARY

The Pre-Keynesian economists lived through turbulent times. The inter-war British economy was under the constant stress of structural change. Superimposed upon its underlying structural problems were the usual short-term fluctuations in employment, and also the very serious shock of the world slump 1929–33. During the 1920s the attitudes of the Pre-Keynesians changed from practical idealism to realism, and even cynicism, as they became increasingly aware of the magnitude of Britain's economic problems, and the lack of the social and political will to solve them. The Pre-Keynesians' attitudes are very important in understanding both their analysis of unemployment and their response to the major policy issues of the time. Their analysis of unemployment is examined in the following chapter. Their policy response is considered in chapter 8.

3

The Pre-Keynesian Theory of Unemployment

3.1 BASIC CONCEPTS

This chapter summarizes the main aspects of the Pre-Keynesian theory of unemployment. Although individual writers differed both in the factors which they chose to emphasize, and upon certain points of analytical detail, it is reasonable to talk of 'the' Pre-Keynesian theory, because all the writers used a common framework. When they differed they were at least agreed upon what their differences were about. In this respect the situation was very different from the late 1930s when there was a breakdown in communication between the Pre-Keynesian economists on the one hand and the Keynesians on the other.

The chapter contains several lengthy quotations. The object of quoting at length is to demonstrate that the Pre-Keynesian writers did not merely make passing reference to the various aspects of unemployment, but gave a full analysis of them. Allowing the Pre-Keynesians to speak in their own words reduces the possibility that their views are misrepresented. Short quotations can, of course, be taken out of context, but with long quotations the context of the discussion is usually quite explicit.

The analytical apparatus of the Pre-Keynesian economists is Marshallian, though the respect they had for Marshall seems to have varied considerably. Pigou revered Marshall, while Cannan was as critical of Marshall as he was of other great economists, and referred to him, rather contemptuously, as 'old Marshall' (Robbins, 1971). In the case of Pigou, Marshallian analysis is combined with the utilitarian ethics of Henry Sidgwick and with ideas drawn from Edwardian writings on unemployment by William Beveridge, Sidney and Beatrice Webb, and others. While Cannan used Marshallian analysis too, he also drew inspiration from classical economists such as Adam Smith and John Stuart Mill.

It was not until the turn of the century that unemployment began to be perceived as a problem in its own right. The popular view in the nineteenth century was that unemployment was just one of several factors connected with family poverty, along with intemperance, bad housing, lack of education, and so on. By and large unemployment was regarded as a manifestation of personal inadequacy, which in turn was caused by unsatisfactory social conditions. But as social conditions improved unemployment did not disappear. It became apparent that it was concentrated in trades which used casual methods of labour recruitment. Cyclical fluctuations in unemployment could also be discerned. Although economists were already familiar with cycles—Pigou was particularly impressed by the statistical investigations of William Stanley Jevons—they had hitherto been associated mainly with prices (including wage rates and interest rates) rather than with quantities such as employment. Samuel Jones Loyd (Lord Overstone) and H. S. Foxwell (1886) were among the few economists who gave serious attention to the issue prior to Marshall (Eshag, 1963). The evidence of systematic variations in unemployment persuaded economists that unemployment was not so much a problem of personal inadequacy—i.e. of unemployability—but a problem of the industrial system itself.

By the time that Pigou had succeeded to Marshall's chair at Cambridge, the fiscal controversy which had hitherto absorbed much of his attention had abated, and he turned his attention to the emerging issue of unemployment. Pigou's pocket-book on the subject, *Unemployment* (1914), may be considered the first major work of Pre-Keynesian theory. Pigou discusses at the outset the key distinctions between voluntary and involuntary unemployment, short-term and long-term unemployment, and full-time unemployment and short-time working. In doing so he elucidates the value judgements which underlie Pre-Keynesian theory, and illustrates its sophistication in relation to its Keynesian counterpart. According to Pigou

. . . unemployment clearly does not include all the idleness of wage earners, but only *that part of it which is, from their point of view and in their existing condition at the time, involuntary*. There is, therefore, excluded the idleness of those who are definitely incapacitated from wage-earning work by extreme old age, infirmity or temporary sickness. There is also excluded the idleness of those who are idle, not from necessity, but from choice. . . . Yet again, there is excluded the idleness of the great mass of the vagrant class, whose ambition is, in large part, just to avoid work. And, finally, there is excluded the 'playing' of those workpeople who are idle on account of a strike or lock-out. . . . The amount of unemployment, let us therefore say, which exists in any industry, is measured by the number of hours' work . . . by which the employment of the persons 'attached to' or 'occupied in' that industry falls short of the number of hours' work that these persons would have been willing to provide at the current rate of wages under current conditions of employment. The precise definition of this rate . . . has been accomplished with reasonable success by the draftsmen of the British National Insurance Act. Unemployment prevails, from the point of view of that Act when a man cannot obtain the work he desires

(1) otherwise than in a situation vacant on account of a stoppage of work due to an industrial dispute.

(2) in the district where he was last ordinarily employed, otherwise than at a rate lower, or on conditions less favourable, than those which he habitually obtained in his usual employment in that district, or would have obtained had he continued to be so employed.

(3) in any other district, otherwise than at a rate of wage lower, or on conditions less favourable, than those generally obtained in such district by agreement between associations of employers and of workmen, or, failing any such agreement, than those generally recognised in such district by good employers (Pigou, 1914, pp. 14–17).

Although the terminology is the same, it is clear that Pigou's concept of involuntary unemployment differs substantially from that of Keynes. Keynes defined involuntary unemployment to be unemployment that could be alleviated by a mild inflation of product prices. Pigou's concept accords much more with the ordinary sense of the word 'involuntary': it describes unemployment for which the individual worker cannot reasonably be held responsible. Pigou does not shirk from the moral judgement implicit in his concept of involuntary unemployment. He seems to recognize that what it is reasonable to expect of a worker seeking a job is culturally determined. Cultural values are in turn likely to be reflected in the law governing the provision of benefits to the unemployed.

Pigou's involuntary unemployment is thus unemployment which may reasonably be attributed to a failure of the economic system. As such, it may include frictional unemployment as well as cyclical unemployment, in so far as frictions are caused by shortcomings in labour market practices and institutions (see section 3.2 below). It should not be inferred that Pigou excluded the strictly Keynesian type of unemployment from his discussion. It will be shown in section 3.4 that Pigou anticipated many of Keynes' ideas on this subject.

Pigou, following Beveridge (1909) and others, was particularly concerned about the adverse consequences of long-term unemployment.

. . . when unemployment comes about in such a way that certain individuals are rendered definitely 'unemployed' for several weeks, or even months, at a time there emerges a further very important element. This form of unemployment threatens to inflict permanent injury on the industrial character of those on whom it falls. It is not merely that technical skill is injured through lack of practice, though this, in some instances, may be a matter of real significance. The main point is that the habit of regular work may be lost, and self-respect and self-confidence destroyed, so that, when opportunity for work does come, the man, once merely unemployed, may be found to have become unemployable (Pigou, 1914, pp. 32–3).

Pigou also recognizes that

. . . the volume of unemployment prevailing at any one time may be either concentrated upon a small number of workpeople or scattered fairly evenly over a large number. . . . [We] may lay it down broadly that, in industries where bad times are predominantly met by the dismissal of hands, unemployment will be concentrated fairly closely upon a limited number of men, the same least efficient persons being selected for dismissal on nearly every occasion; while in industries such as coal-mining and the cotton industry, where bad times are predominantly met by the practice of short-time (or a short working week) unemployment will be spread widely among many men. Thus . . . the practice of meeting bad times by dismissals is roughly equivalent to the concentration of unemployment, and the practice of meeting them by short-time to the spreading of unemployment (Pigou, 1914, pp. 192–3).

Pigou's utilitarian calculus, based upon a diminishing cardinal utility of income, leads him to prefer (subject to certain qualifications) an equal incidence of unemployment achieved by short-time working.

The aggregate suffering involved when one man has two pounds and a second man has nothing is obviously greater than it would be if one pound belonged to each of them. . . . [Thus] the social evil resulting from a given volume of unemployment would be least when that volume was spread evenly over the working classes, and . . . it would be made greater by every advance in the direction of greater concentration (Pigou, 1914, p. 202).

His main qualification is that the relief of poverty may be easier to administer when unemployment is concentrated upon a few.

Suppose, for example, that, in some industries, the conditions are such that, when unemployment is spread evenly among all the persons attached to an industry, none of these persons can earn sufficient for independent self-support, and all, therefore, need to have their incomes eked out by public or private benevolence; and suppose, further, that, by the concentration of all the work on one group of these persons and of all the unemployment on another group, the former group would be raised to the stage of adequate self-support, while the latter were thrown more completely on the hands of charity. In that case it will hardly be disputed that social evil would, on the whole, be made less by a concentration of unemployment in the way described. We seem, therefore, to be led to the general conclusion that, as regards grades of workpeople so well situated that all their members can attain to adequate earnings when unemployment is spread among them evenly, the spreading of unemployment is better than its concentration; while, as regards grades so badly situated that the spreading of unemployment forces the earnings of all below a reasonable subsistence minimum, concentration is better than spreading. In the former case the evil results of a given volume of unemployment would be diminished if the manufacturers in any industry were persuaded to adopt a policy of organised short-time in periods of depression. In the latter case the results of such a policy would be, not beneficial, but injurious (Pigou, 1914, pp. 202–3).

3.2   FRICTIONAL UNEMPLOYMENT

Pre-Keynesian analysis of the causes of unemployment may be examined under four heads: frictions, wage setting, monetary disturbance and structural problems.

The Pre-Keynesians recognized that frictions were an important cause of short-term unemployment. The problem was seen as one of synchronizing the demand and supply of labour: e.g. filling vacancies as quickly as possible in order to reduce the lags in the re-employment of labour. The problem did not receive much analytical attention, however, because the remedies were believed to be quite straightforward: improved information flow through employment exchanges and a more efficient system of short-term production planning. As was often the case, the Pre-Keynesian view was stated most succinctly by Clay:

In certain employments the volume of work varies from day to day. Work at docks, which depends ultimately on the volume of goods to be moved, but is constantly dislocated by wind and tide, affords the chief example of daily fluctuation. The effect on employment depends on the method of engagement. The work offers an opening for a regular staff, capable of handling the minimum of work to which the docks are ever reduced, with a mobile reserve to deal with fluctuations above that minimum. If each taking-on station, as was formerly the practice, acts independently, each will require a reserve of its own, and the industry as a whole will have a reserve in excess of its needs. Moreover, the chance of a job under the system of casual engagements will attract to the industry more than can be employed even at its busiest, with a necessary consequence in chronic under-employment. Some occupations, again, fluctuate with the seasons, either because their materials come in at certain seasons only, or because the demand for their products is seasonal. Variations in employment due to these fluctuations, like the time lag in the fitting of available workers into available jobs, are the less difficult elements in the problem to distinguish. Moreover, to distinguish them is to indicate appropriate remedies; a system of employment exchanges to bring together vacancies and workers and to eliminate unnecessary movement in search of work, some system of vocational guidance for new entrants to industry, the concentration of casual jobs by a system of preference upon the minimum number of workers wanted, and the dovetailing of seasonal jobs. If these elements are not dealt with, it is not for want of knowing how to deal with them, but due to lack of will (Clay, 1929a, pp. 4–5).

In the latter part of the 1920s economists were naturally pre-occupied with explaining the extraordinary length and depth of the depression which followed the collapse of prices in 1920. Most of them recognized the necessity of finding separate explanations of short-term unemployment and long-term unemployment. Casting around for an explanation for rising short-term unemployment they identified an association with the institution of unemployment insurance in 1911 and its extension in 1920. During the 1920s the worker's entitlement to unemployment insurance was fairly quickly exhausted, and so it was quite reasonable to suppose that its incentive would affect mainly the short-term unemployed; the long-term unemployed remained dependent upon relief.

Cannan anticipated recent neoclassical literature by arguing that the main effect of unemployment benefit was upon the duration of job search. He suggested that when the replacement ratio (the ratio of benefits to wages) is high, workers will take longer in searching for a job:

. . . especially in the occupations in which the superiority of employment over unemployment is least the insurance scheme has reduced the economic pressure which used to make persons grab at every chance of employment, take what they could get regardless of every inconvenience, and stick to what they had got regardless of every disagreeableness—which made them, like the old British army 'ready to go anywhere and do anything'. And it is commonly recognised that no individual thinks of the alternatives open to him being 'Take what you can get now, or go on the dole till this Government or the next lets your time run out, and then become a pauper (or 'publicly assisted person') for the remainder of your life.' He takes the alternatives to be 'Take what you can get now, or hold out another week, when something better may turn up.' 'Sooner or later', says Professor Clay, the unemployed workman is obliged 'to accept work outside his own district or trade if it is available.' There is much virtue in the 'later'; the magnitude of the turnover of labour (the number of new engagements) is so great that a very little average delay will make a very large addition to the unemployment (Cannan, 1930, pp. 46–7).

Clay provides a more sophisticated argument which related unemployment insurance to employers' hiring practices. The gist of his argument is that employers take advantage of the insurance scheme to extend the system of casual labour. An employer faced with fluctuating product demand can accommodate peaks either by building up and then running down inventories, or by taking on and laying off more labour. To take on and lay off labour easily it is necessary to have workers standing by ready for occasional employment. Unemployment insurance subsidizes the employer by maintaining, at someone else's expense, a stand-by army of unemployed.

The system of organised short-time makes it possible to dove-tail periods of wage-earning with periods of unemployment relief. Employers have adapted their engagement of labour to these conditions, and thus spread the available employment over a larger number of workers than the industry could employ full-time, at the same time throwing on the unemployment fund the burden of maintaining the surplus labour when it is not in employment. Instituted as a device for tiding over a temporary depression, this system has been prolonged, as year succeeded year of unemployment, and has had the effect of substituting intermittent and irregular employment for regular work in industries in which such conditions were formerly rare (Clay, 1929b, p. 336).

3.3   WAGE SETTING

The Pre-Keynesian economists' main explanation of the rising long-term unemployment in the 1920s was that real wage rates were set at too high a level.

In the post-war period . . . there is strong reason to believe, that, partly through direct State action, and partly through the added strength given to work people's organisations engaged in wage bargaining by the development of unemployment insurance, wage-rates have, over a wide area, been set at a level which is too high . . . and that the very large percentage of unemployment which has prevailed during the whole of the last six years is due in considerable measure to this new factor in our economic life (Pigou, 1927a, p. 355).

Clay (1929b, p. 323) noted that trade union membership had grown from 2½ million in 1910 to 8 million in 1920 and had remained at just over 5 million even after the onset of the depression and the General Strike (see also Clay, 1929c). This, he argued, strengthened the hand of trade union negotiators:

Trade union control of wages, and the analogous control of public wage-fixing authorities, may be most simply regarded as an application of monopoly price policy to labour. The monopoly is seldom, if ever, complete; but what monopoly is? It gives the seller of labour no control over the demand for his services; it merely enables him, so far as it is effective, to select the point on the demand curve at which he will hold the price, until a general rise in demand absorbs at that price all the union members, instead of allowing competition for employment always to force wages down to the point at which the whole supply of labour is absorbed (Clay, 1929b, p. 329).

While Clay regarded the spread of trade unionism as a general phenomenon, Pigou had recognized as early as 1914 that the degree of unionization differed significantly between sectors of the economy. He considered the consequences for unemployment of a situation in which one sector of the economy is unionized while in the other sector wages are set competitively. His analysis is of particular interest as it anticipates recent theories of labour migration and of wage inflation.

It sometimes happens that . . . the wage rate over the main part of the industrial field is freely adjusted by competitive forces so as to absorb all the workpeople assembled there, but that, at one or more selected points, it has been somehow raised above the level proper to free competition. An abnormally high rate of the kind contemplated may be established from time to time, or even for long periods together, if, in any industry or place, the workpeople happen to possess a particularly strong Trade Union. No doubt, even when a Union has power to enforce an abnormally high rate, it will not always find it to its interest to exercise that power. . . . In some cases, however, a group of workpeople—coal miners, for example, or doctors—render a service for which no adequate substitute can be found. . . .

[L]et us suppose . . . that the actual wage has been raised artificially to 10 per cent above this [the competitive] level. Then, as a first approximation, it would appear that new men will be drawn into the occupation affected until the *expectation of earnings* in it (this expectation being interpreted to mean the wage rate multiplied by the chance of employment) is reduced to the level of the earnings that prevail outside; and this evidently implies the creation of 10 per cent unemployment. Furthermore . . . in estimating the relative advantages of different occupations, workpeople are apt to pay more attention to the money wage, which is obvious and readily known than to the probability of unemployment, which is a much more obscure matter. This means that a 10 per cent rise in the wage rate above the general level is likely to cause so many men to attach themselves to the industry that their average earnings are actually lower than those obtainable for similar work elsewhere. In other words, *more than 10 per cent* of the men assembled there will, on the average, be unemployed. There is, indeed, no reason to suppose that, of these men, any individual will be unemployed permanently; but the aggregate volume of unemployment will be permanent, and it will be made up of separate items of unemployment, experienced now by some individuals and now by others (Pigou, 1914, pp. 52-5).

This argument needs to be qualified, however, to take account of the different methods of hiring that prevail:

[It] has been tacitly assumed that, in the occupation affected, workpeople are engaged in such a way that an outsider, who contemplates attaching himself to the occupation, may reckon on a prospect of employment approximately as good as that of the men who are attached to it already. . . . Things work out quite differently, however, if the work available in the industry is concentrated rigorously upon a defined group of persons who constitute, in effect if not in name, a permanent staff. . . . In that case the fact that the wage rate is artificially high will not have the effect of assembling as camp-followers of the industry any persons other than those for whom full employment can be found. . . . We may conclude, therefore, that the establishment of an artificially high wage rate in any part of the industrial field involves unemployment only when the method of engagement prevailing there is of what may be called the casual type, and that it does not involve unemployment when, so to speak, the concentrated type of engagement prevails (Pigou, 1914, pp. 56–7).

To deter unemployment in high-wage industries, Pigou recommends the practice of recruitment from preference lists. It does not matter whether the names on a list are 'set out in alphabetical order or order of merit or any other order, provided only that workpeople, as they are wanted, are engaged in strict accordance with the position of their names on the list' (p. 58). Lists could be administered by trade unions or, better still, by a labour exchange 'focussing the demand for a whole industry or district'. Once the worker had put his name on the list there would be nothing further he could do to improve his chances of employment in the high-wage industry, and he could therefore afford to take temporary work elsewhere until his name came up.

According to Clay, trade union bargaining strength after World War I had been greatly increased by the institution of unemployment insurance. This had left trade unions free to negotiate over wage rates by shifting the responsibility for the employment consequences of wage bargains on to the government. Clay laid far greater stress on this aspect of unemployment insurance than he did upon its impact on frictional unemployment.

Before the war the consequence [of refusing a wage reduction] would have been unemployment, and unemployment would have involved, for the small minority of wage-earners covered by trade union unemployment insurance, a drain on the union funds; for the great mass of wage earners, who had no such resource, early and extreme hardship. It was impossible for the representatives of the wage-earners in wage negotiations to ignore unemployment.

Today things are different. Successful resistance to a reduction may still involve unemployment, but unemployment does not involve the same certainty or degree of distress. Before the war the provision for unemployment relief was partial and inadequate. Today there is a system of unemployment relief that covers all the industries that are liable to serious unemployment. Then the spokesmen of the wage-earners had to consider the employment situation, because their clients would be the chief sufferers, if their wage-policy restricted employment; now, in such a case, they may nevertheless persist in their policy, since they are conscious that their clients are not without resources, if all cannot be employed at the level of wages exacted (Clay, 1929b, p. 335).

Another implication of the extension of unemployment insurance concerns the impact of the employer's contribution on the demand for labour.

An important increase in costs associated with labour is the greatly increased extent and scale of insurance contributions. . . . This *increase* in the tax on employment—for that is what incidentally it is—amounts to £20,000,000 in respect of insured industry as a whole. . . . This considerable addition to wages, represented by the employer's compulsory contributions under the State insurance schemes, has never, so far as I have been able to ascertain, been taken into account in fixing wage-rates. It is nevertheless an addition both to the real income of the wage-earners and to the labour costs of the employers (Clay, 1929a, p. 97).

According to Clay, therefore, the shifting of part of the employer's contribution on to the workers through real wage adjustment has been resisted using the monopoly power of the trade unions. There is, however, some inconsistency here. A monopoly model suggests that union labour will receive a fairly stable mark up on the monopoly wage—reflecting the elasticity of demand for unionized labour—and this in turn implies that the monopoly wage will vary in accordance with labour market conditions. It would not be inflexible and it would, to some extent, endogenize changes such as the introduction of the employer's contribution.

It is just possible, of course, that the growing strength of the trade union monopoly will exactly offset the deteriorating competitive position of labour, but this coincidence seems unlikely. In fact Clay, having expounded the monopoly argument, goes on elsewhere in the same paper to advocate an alternative to the pure monopoly model. In discussing the sluggishness of wage adjustment he considers two hypotheses. The first, which he rejects, is that the administrative procedures of collective bargaining cause undue delay in renegotiating wages. The second, which he supports, is that collective bargaining provides a forum in which non-economic factors can come into play.

[Collective bargaining] opens the door to the influence of non-economic factors. The mere fact of publicity, or organised discussion, invites appeal to social and ethical standards of 'fair' and 'living' wages, to pseudo-principles such as the sanctity of pre-war *real* wages, to the unpopularity of reducing rates of wages of the lower-paid workers, none of which have any bearing on the capacity of industry to pay wages and provide employment. Economists in the seclusion of a private circular may state baldly that 'the fundamental hindrance to recovery . . . lies in the abnormal relationship between the movement of the cost of materials and that of the cost of labour', but directors of large companies, who may be candidates for Parliament, will not commit themselves publicly to such unpopular opinions (Clay, 1929b, pp. 334–5).

In effect, therefore, what Clay is left with is not a monopolistic mark-up of the competitive wage but a wage that is established by social and political criteria rather than strictly economic ones. The monopoly model explains the nature of the threat which gives labour a strong bargaining position—namely the power to disrupt production which is conferred by control of the labour supply. But the model does not adequately describe the objectives which govern the monopolist's stipulation of the wage.

It seems rather narrow-minded of Clay to regard social and ethical standards as 'non-economic', since if such standards influence economic behaviour they are surely economic in the broadest sense. The standards may be subjective—that is, people may differ in their perceptions of them—but that is no excuse for failing to analyze them, and is certainly no excuse for condemning them. Clay's attitude is, unfortunately, typical of many economists, and little has been learnt by economists, since Clay wrote, about the way that social and political motives influence wage bargaining.

On the whole, it can be said that the Pre-Keynesian analysis of frictional unemployment and of wage-setting anticipates many recent developments in the theory. The analysis of the effects of unemployment insurance is in some respects more sophisticated than that of present-day economists. The Pre-Keynesian arguments about wage setting anticipate some of the recent work on real wage resistance, though the Pre-Keynesian economists came no nearer than do contemporary writers to finding a strictly economic rationale for real wage resistance in the face of the declining competitive position of labour.

3.4 MONETARY DISTURBANCE

It is widely held that Pre-Keynesian economists failed to appreciate the significance of the fact that wages are negotiated in money terms. Failure to recognize this, it is said, led them to assert a false dichotomy between the real and money sectors of the economy. This is a gross distortion of the truth. Some of the Pre-Keynesians— notably Pigou—were much more sophisticated than this. They recognized that money wages were sticky in the short run. They recognized the role of money illusion in labour supply. They recognized that trade union concern over wages relativities might be a major cause of money wage stickiness. They recognized that when money illusion is present, a mild inflation will reduce the real wage and thereby stimulate employment and output. All this was clearly stated in the Pre-Keynesian literature up to 1930. What the Pre-Keynesians denied was that money illusion could be exploited in the long run to reduce the real wage. They believed that if there were persistent inflation, trade unions would seek to link money wage settlements to the price level, and so would effectively stipulate for a real wage.

Given this view, the logic of the Pre-Keynesian position is impeccable. Because the real wage is fixed, the supply of real output is fixed also, and because the supply of output is fixed, public expenditure will crowd out private expenditure in the product market. It is a modern fallacy that unemployment is incompatible with pure crowding out. Keynesians are correct to assert that pure crowding out will not occur with unemployment caused by a too high money wage, but likewise the Pre-Keynesians were correct to assert that pure crowding out would occur with unemployment caused by a too high real wage.

Money wage stickiness was regarded by Clay as a major cause of normal cyclical unemployment:

If a fall in prices is brought about by a policy of deflation [i.e. monetary restriction] . . . it will almost certainly cause unemployment. This result would not follow if all prices, including the prices of labour, capital and credit, were affected at the same time in the same degree; but this never happens. Deflation causes unemployment by bringing about a divergence between costs and selling prices, and so discouraging and depressing industry. . . . There is, in the upward and downward movement of trade, an inevitable *time lag* between the movement of expenses and the movement of selling prices. The chief elements in expenses that lag in this way are wage-rates and fixed interest charges. If wage-rates are maintained while prices fall by a third, the real cost of labour, other things remaining equal is increased by half; the burden of debentures or other loans raised when the price index is 200 is doubled if the price index falls to 100. The collapse of the post-war boom is only the most striking instance of this dislocation (Clay, 1929a, pp. 65–6).

A possible explanation of money wage stickiness is money illusion in labour supply. Pigou recognized the importance of money illusion in labour supply as early as 1914. He considers a situation in which a scarcity in the supply of gold has caused the price index of wage goods to fall from 30s to 28s.

If the workpeople affected fully understood what had happened, they would know that a wage of 28s, now that prices are reduced, is exactly equivalent to a wage of 30s before they were reduced, and, consequently, unless some ground could be shown for claiming an increase in real wages, there would be no resistance to the proposed reduction in the nominal rate. But the workpeople do not understand what has happened. Thinking—as most other people also think—in terms of money, they do not look through the nominal wage to the real wage which it symbolizes . . . Consequently, they resist the reduction, and their resistance causes the wage rate to fail from time to time properly to adjust itself to the demand for labour. In other words, variability in the purchasing power of the standard is, in view of the universal tendency to think in terms of money, a potent influence hampering the plasticity of wage rates (Pigou, 1914, pp. 80–1).

In his testimony to the Macmillan Committee on Finance and Industry, Pigou elaborated his views on money wage stickiness. This testimony has a very modern ring to it. Amongst other things, Pigou notes that money wage bargaining has the characteristics of a Prisoner's Dilemma, and emphasizes that wage negotiators face the problem of filtering out from aggregate data the real and monetary disturbances that are relevant to labour market conditions.

It does not happen in fact, if you contract the money income stream 10 per cent, that the money wages are contracted 10 per cent. In fact what happens is that real wages go up when the money income stream is contracted.

These resistances are strong for several reasons. First, a reduction in money wage rates would only be innocuous to the real wages rates of the workers in any group, provided that all other groups allowed similar reductions to take place. Suppose that one group of people alone allowed their money wage rates to fall and other people did not, the stuff they bought would not have fallen proportionately, and so they would actually lose. Though it would be true, if everybody all round agreed to a 10 per cent reduction of money wages, when the income stream had fallen 10 per cent, that nobody would lose, yet if one began and the others did not follow, he would lose. Since there is no organized system for treating wages all round, somebody has to start; and naturally nobody wants to start. It is the same principle as the principle of Sunday closing. It would be to the general advantage if everybody would Sunday close; but it is by no means to the advantage of an individual that he should Sunday close, if his competitors do not. That is the sort of principle. That is the first thing.

Secondly, it would be very difficult to distinguish in practice between conditions in which prices are coming down because the money income stream has been contracted, and conditions in which they are coming down because there is increased efficiency. If they are coming down because there is increased efficiency, then you can employ the same number of men as before at a higher real wage, and so the higher real wage will not push people out of employment. In that case, when prices are falling for that reason, there is no ground for reduction in money wages. But it is almost impossible to distinguish in practice between the occasions on which prices are falling for what I may call currency reasons and the occasions in which they are falling for the other sort of reasons. Naturally the wage-earners will think that they are falling for the other sort of reasons, and that will be another cause for resisting reductions of money wages.

Thirdly, many groups of wage-earners hold that their real wage rates are too low to start with. Consequently, even if you prove to them that they would not lose anything by reducing their money wages in proportion to the general price fall, they nevertheless will say: 'No, we ought to have higher real wages, and we must take this chance of getting higher real wages by keeping our money wages up when prices are falling.' That would be a third reason which would cause resistance.

A fourth, and an important reason in practice, is that the wage-earners would be very much afraid that, if they let their money wages drop when prices are falling, they would not be able to get them up again when prices are rising, so they very likely would prefer unemployment for a time rather than run the risk of accepting a wage reduction which they will not be able to win back later on. That will be another reason which would prevent them accepting a reduction.

All these are reasons for what you may call stickiness in money rates of wages. Further, these resistances are strengthened and made more effective by the unemployment insurance system. If that was not there, the pressure to accept a reduction of money wages when there was a lot of unemployment would be much stronger than it is now. Then the resistances are very much strengthened by the general public sense since the war that you do not want to cut down people's wages. There is a general feeling that it is the last thing you would like to do if you can help it (Pigou, 1931, p. 84).

It is interesting that Keynes was a member of the committee to which Pigou was testifying, and was in fact the first to question Pigou after these particular remarks. It is also worth noting that, before concluding, Pigou added the following rider:

Then I come to a more difficult matter. It seems at first sight that when you have got an equilibrium with real wages too high and a certain amount of unemployment, that this equilibrium is a stable one. But the danger of the thing, as I see it, is that this new position is not really a stable position, but it is a position that carries in itself the seeds of its own worsening. For this reason: first, owing to the unduly high wages, the rates of profit become abnormally low. That reacts in two ways. First, it stimulates people to hoard money, so to speak to sit on their deposits instead of investing, which tends to push down the money income stream still further and start a cumulative downward movement, which again, since money wages do not adjust themselves to the money stream, causes a still further increase of real wages and so still further unemployment, and so on. Secondly, you get the same sort of reaction through foreign lending, because, the rates of profit here having been reduced through this process I have been trying to describe, it becomes relatively more profitable to lend abroad as against investing at home. In so far as you do that, there is a tendency for gold to be drawn abroad, and so for the stock of money (deposits) indirectly to be lessened; and so for the money income stream to be lessened on that side too. So there you get a cumulative process, once you get the thing out of adjustment, by which it tends to get more and more out of adjustment. If money wage rates were allowed to fall this would not happen; but, as it is, once you have got the thing wrong, it tends to get more and more wrong. Maintaining money wages in face of a contracted income stream means more real wages. That sets up causes which make the income stream contract more and more. That reacts to get the money wages more and more out of adjustment, and so the thing goes on. That is the danger (Pigou, 1931, p. 84).

Given his emphasis on money wage stickiness, it seems, at first, surprising that Pigou was unwilling to recommend monetary expansion as a long-run cure for unemployment (though he recognized its value in the short run). He had two main reservations about such a policy. First, he was strongly committed to the international Gold Standard as a mechanism not only for promoting international trade but as an integral element in world political unity. Monetary expansion under the Gold Standard would almost certainly cause a balance of payments deficit and precipitate a sterling crisis. Secondly, he did not believe that money illusion was sufficiently strong to be exploited for purposes of demand management:

all these devices such as devaluation, and inflation, and so on, act only in so far as the wage earners are, so to speak, bamboozled. If a workman realises that the raising of prices through inflation is going to hit him he will normally ask for an increase in money wages corresponding to the rise in prices, and you only get your decrease in real wages if, when you bring about those price rises by inflation and all the rest of it, you somehow prevent the workman from asking for a corresponding rise in his money wages (Pigou, 1931, p. 58).

It is not only wages that are denominated in money terms: much business debt is too. Notice that in the earlier quote, Clay refers not only to the effect of deflation on real wages but also its effect on the real value of debenture debt. The increase in real wages affects employers' marginal costs, while the increase in the real value of debenture debt affects their overhead costs. If marginal costs and overhead costs both rise the firm may be threatened with bankruptcy: the increase in marginal costs causes output and employment to contract and this means that there are fewer units of output to spread the overheads over—just at the time when the real cost of overheads is increasing. Bankruptcy is a direct threat to employment—it affects not only the firm's marginal workers—those who would be laid off as a result of increased real wages—but intra-marginal workers too. All the jobs will be lost until financial reorganization is effected. If bankruptcies are widespread then financial institutions themselves may become insolvent, and the process of financial reorganization may be interrupted for some time.

The relation between bankruptcy and unemployment is a point often overlooked in modern theories of monetary policy. It must have seemed an obvious point to Clay, who was able to observe at first hand the fate of the textile firms in Manchester during the financial collapse of 1929. These firms, like many others, had expanded using fixed interest debt in the post-war boom of 1919–20 and found it increasingly difficult to meet their financial obligations as prices fell. Their increasing reliance on short-term borrowing to finance long-term interest repayments created an unstable situation and led eventually to catastrophe.

3.5 STRUCTURAL PROBLEMS

Structural problems arise when both industry and labour are immobile. The immobility of industry means that certain groups of workers are not substitutable in performing certain jobs. Thus if industry is unable to relocate, then workers residing at one location cannot be substituted for workers at another location. The immobility of labour means that different kinds of jobs are not substitutable opportunities for any given worker. Thus if workers cannot migrate, then employment opportunities at some other location cannot be substituted for existing employment.

The two main dimensions of economic structure are location and skill. These dimensions are associated with the barriers of distance and training respectively. In applied work the structure of the labour force is also analyzed by age, sex, race, religion, etc. These are important because they affect where people live and what kind of skills they have; perhaps more significantly, they are often used as indicators of skill by employers who are uncertain of the quality of the labour they are hiring.

Structural problems reflect the industrial composition of the

economy. It was implicitly assumed by the Pre-Keynesian economists that industry was immobile. It could not relocate because of
the need to minimize transport costs to raw material sources and to
final product markets, and it could not easily substitute skills because
of the absolute superiority—over a range of factor prices—of a
particular technology and mode of production (system of work
organization). The assumption of immobility probably reflected the
Pre-Keynesian's concern with the older basic industries; as Dennison
(1939) and Wensley and Sargent Florence (1940) noted, the newer
industries were much more footloose. Since by assumption industry
was immobile, the structural problem was perceived as one of the
immobility of labour.

. . . labour is only imperfectly mobile. Where industrial development is not
dislocated by war or other catastrophe, the adjustment to changing
demands can usually be made by directing the new generation to new work
without disturbing the old generation in the old work; but it is not possible
to re-direct and re-distribute the industrial population with every change in
the demand for labour. The mere distance of new work from the old
involves a time-lag in the adjustment of labour-supply to the demand, if the
labour is able to move. But labour is not always able to move; there may be
no housing accommodation where the new work is developing; the
unemployed worker may be a member of a household the other members
of which are in work, as is so often the case in textile districts. Or the
worker may not be able to adapt himself to the needs of the new work.
Quite apart, therefore, from fluctuations in the aggregate volume of
employment, there must always be some loss of work, due to the
impossibility of fitting workers, whose mobility and range of capacity are
limited, to the kinds of work available (Clay, 1929a, pp. 3–4).

In this quotation Clay clearly recognizes the importance of immobility
caused by workers' commitments to their family and to their
traditional trade. Clay was not entirely consistent in this, however, for
elsewhere he invoked theoretical principles which implicitly assume
that workers are basically indifferent (within limits) to where they live
and the kind of work they do. The Pre-Keynesian economists were
inclined to identify maximum social welfare with a state in which a
uniform wage prevailed in all locations for all occupations 'of equal
difficulty and disagreeableness, which require equally rare natural
abilities and an equally expensive training'. The fact that people living
in certain areas and working in certain industries might prefer lower
wages in their present work to higher wages for 'similar' work
elsewhere, was largely ignored. Implicit in such theorizing is the view

that immobility is simply the consequence of obstacles which are largely avoidable, and that if these obstacles were removed uniform wages and maximum social efficiency would, in principle, prevail.

Pre-Keynesian economists analyzed structural factors in considerable detail. Even Pigou, who is perhaps best known for his view that the real wage was 'on average' 5 per cent too high in the mid-1920s, conceded that the real wage was not too high in all industries. In an important paper, written in 1927, he accepted that

. . . a part of this extra unemployment [in the post-war as compared to the pre-war period] is due to the abnormal growth of the metal industries during the war, and to the fact that the distribution of work people between different occupations has not yet been adjusted to peacetime conditions (Pigou, 1927a, p. 356).

Indeed, the analytical core of Pigou's 1927 paper is a two-sector model of the UK economy in which one sector is at full employment while the other sector experiences unemployment due to a too high real wage. It is unfortunate, though, that in the introduction to this paper Pigou appears to reject a structural explanation of unemployment. He argues that

Had this been the dominant factor, however, we should have expected to find a marked shortage of labour in important groups of industries to balance the excess in engineering, ship-building, and so on; and of such marked shortage there is no sign (Pigou, 1927a, p. 356).

This argument is entirely fallacious—and Pigou himself appears to have recanted later. The alleged lack of evidence for a shortage of labour appears to refer to lack of unfilled vacancies in the prosperous industries. The number of vacancies that remain unfilled, however, depends very much upon employers' wage policy. If vacancies need to be filled urgently then employers will bid up money wages until all but the least essential vacancies have been eliminated. If this is the case—as it almost certainly was—then the only evidence of a shortage of labour will be the high money wage at which the market equilibrium is achieved.

Nevertheless, while Pigou's argument was strongly challenged, the precise nature of the fallacy was never properly exposed. Pigou had started a hare, and it proved very difficult to catch. Clay was the first to attack Pigou, and he challenged him on two main grounds: first, that he understated the maldistribution of labour, and secondly that he failed to take account of the maldistribution of labour when assessing whether on average the real wage was too high.

A high average real wage may be causally connected with a high percentage of unemployment in industry in three ways.

(1) All or most of the wage rates may be 'too high', having moved up together, or stayed up together when prices fell, thus causing generally diffused unemployment in industry.

(2) Some wage rates may be 'too high' thus causing in the industries in which they have to be paid the bulk of the unemployment in the country.

(3) Some wage rates may be 'too high', not in the sense that they cause unemployment in the industries in which they have to be paid, but in the sense that they involve a level of charges to other industries, that depend on them for services or products, so high that unemployment is caused in these other industries (Clay, 1928, p. 5).

Clay showed that in a cross-section of industries in 1927 unemployment rates varied considerably, and that unemployment tended to be highest in industries where wages had risen *least* between 1914 and 1927. These low-wage industries included many of the producers of intermediate products supplied to other industries: coal, iron and steel, and engineering among them. On these grounds Clay rejected the first and third of his possible explanations and concluded that it must be the second which is correct. He maintained that, in spite of the wage adjustments that had occurred in the declining industries, the adjustments had not been enough. It was the low wages of the depressed industries that were too high, and not the higher wages of the prosperous industries.

For his second line of attack Clay pointed out that

. . . since the distribution of labour has an important influence on the productivity of industry, and therefore helps to determine the wage economically possible, it is not easy to separate the two and to treat the wage level and the maldistribution of labour as independent factors in the causation of unemployment; if labour is ill-distributed, production per head will be low and the average wage compatible with full employment will be low; if labour is ideally distributed, production per head will be high, and the average wage compatible with full employment will be high (Clay, 1928, p. 2).

The argument is valid, however, only if the maldistribution of labour is avoidable. It is possible that labour does not wish to move even when it is able to do so. It is likely that this is because the social cost of moving exceeds labour's share of the real rewards of doing so. In this case labour's desire to avoid the cost of moving will be reflected in the lower equilibrium real wage—the equilibrium real wage identified by Pigou.

Although Clay opposed Pigou's general view of the problem, he does not directly meet Pigou's point about the lack of vacancies in prosperous industries. Cannan accuses both Clay and Pigou of failing to understand the dynamics of the growth of employment in prosperous industries.

What sort of evidence ever exists of an unsatisfied demand for labour beyond the fact that additional labour has, in fact, found employment? Within four miles of my proverbial armchair I have seen in a very few years half a dozen big fields on which two or three agricultural workers were employed gradually covered by factory buildings in which several thousand factory workers are now employed, but I do not remember ever seeing or hearing of the smallest evidence of an unsatisfied demand for labour there. I have seen in a few years all the high roads dotted with garages and petrol stations, each served by at least one and generally more persons who seem to make a fair living, and therefore to satisfy a demand, but I cannot imagine how evidence could ever have been produced at any time of an unsatisfied demand for the labour which they perform. I wonder whether Professor Clay would refuse food to a growing boy because no evidence of an unsatisfied demand for additional weight in bone and muscle could be produced. Since the time of Noah the regular rule has been for industries to expand and employ more and more persons without ever exhibiting signs of an unsatisfied demand. The supply and the demand advance together (Cannan, 1930, p. 52).

Cannan's argument, though correct in principle, is expounded with much rhetoric (for Clay's response see Clay, 1930). A more detached view of the issue was taken by Pool (1938). He argued that potential vacancies in the prosperous industries had been eliminated by the aggressive pricing of labour by the trade unions. The resulting lack of vacancies discouraged workers from moving from the depressed industries; thus Pool's explanation of unemployment in the depressed industries lay with trade union wage-push in the prosperous industries.

The speed of [labour] transfer must depend on the number of vacancies that can be created in the occupations with increased demands which in turn obviously depends on the wage levels maintained therein. If wage rates are rigidly maintained at their increased level in these prosperous trades, the rate of expansion of employment therein must be comparatively slow. And this, of course, is precisely what is likely to happen as a result of adherence to the principle of basing wages on 'what the trade can bear'. As long as the prosperous trades continue to enjoy an enlarged demand for their product, they will be considered capable of paying correspondingly high wages. The fact that workers in depressed trades are willing to transfer and accept jobs in the more prosperous trades at wages lower than those prevailing in the latter is not likely to be allowed to have the effect of bringing down these comparatively high wage rates. No trade union is likely to accept as reasonable the contention that wages ought to be steadily reduced in flourishing trades, in order to enable them to expand more rapidly and so absorb the unemployed and lower-paid workers attached to the depressed trades. Yet this is what is required if the adjustments of the competitive labour market are to be deliberately reproduced under conditions of collective negotiation.

Hence there may arise a deadlock in which workers fail to transfer to better-paid occupations because there are no vacancies for them; there are no vacancies because wages are kept at too high a level in these occupations; and wages are kept at this high level because the existence of unemployment and low wages in depressed trades is not accepted as a valid argument for wage reductions in profitable trades. If the occupational redistribution of workers is impeded in this way, one of two effects must follow: either (i) wages in the trades where labour demand has declined must fall and remain permanently at a level which will permit of the absorption into employment of all the workers attached to those trades, or (ii) if it proves impossible to reduce wages to this level owing to trade union resistance, or because in some trades with inelastic demands wages would have to be reduced below a bare subsistence level, some degree of abnormal unemployment will arise among the workers in these depressed trades. In practice we find, during the post-war years, both relatively low wages and heavy unemployment in the depressed and contracting industries, as compared with those which are prosperous and expanding (Pool, 1938, pp. 38–40).

It can be seen that Pool effectively stands Clay's argument on its head: it is not wages in the depressed trades that are too high, but wages in the the prosperous trades instead. In doing so, however, he overstates his case. In the Pre-Keynesian type of model there cannot be unemployment in any industry—prosperous or depressed—unless the wage there is in some sense too high. Thus Clay must be correct, in some degree, in saying that wages are too high in the depressed industries. On the other hand, Pool's emphasis on wages policy in the prosperous industry is correct, in so far as migrants to that industry can be immediately absorbed into employment only if they can bid down the money wage. If the money wage is maintained by trade union pressure then migrants are prevented from obtaining work in this way. They must wait for vacancies to occur. These vacancies will arise sooner or later either from the general expansion of the industry, or from the natural turnover of jobs due to retirements, etc. but in so far as jobs are obtained later rather than sooner, the incentive to migrate is correspondingly reduced.

Quite apart from his logic, Pool's emphasis upon unionization in the prosperous industries seems a little exaggerated. As noted in chapter 2, many of the expanding industries relied increasingly upon women workers who seem, by and large, to have remained aloof from the trade union movement. Part of the reason may be the hostility of the trade unions: for example, some unions made a point of excluding women from skilled work. In manufacturing industries union power was almost certainly much greater among the skilled maintenance workers—a male-dominated group—than among the semi-skilled process workers. Thus it could be argued that if union power was a problem in the growing manufacturing industries then, in the early days at least, it was chiefly a problem in just one segment of the labour force.

Pigou believed that underlying the specific problem of mobility posed by the need for industrial change in inter-war Britain was a more fundamental structural problem connected with the relative remuneration of skilled and unskilled workers. Writing in 1914, he drew attention to social attitudes which, he believed, tended to concentrate unemployment amongst unskilled workers.

In all ordinary industries the workpeople employed are not exactly alike, but vary considerably in industrial capacity. It is, of course, theoretically possible that the wages of different individuals should be accurately adjusted to their powers, so that the same rate per unit of efficiency is paid to each of them. As a matter of fact, however, various forms of friction exist in the economic world, which hinder the full action of normal economic forces, and thus maintain the wage rates of inferior workmen somewhat nearer to those of good workmen than their comparative efficiency warrants. Consequently, if, as we may suppose, the wages of good workmen in any given industry stand at the level indicated by free competition, the wages of inferior workmen are apt to stand somewhat above that level, and are thus artificially enhanced (Pigou, 1914, pp. 60–1).

This enhancement of the wage leads to a contraction of the demand for labour and so to unemployment among the 'inferior' workmen. A similar argument applies for the economy as a whole:

It happens sometimes that, in respect of some low-grade workpeople, the wage rate is raised throughout all the industries of the country, whether by custom or by law or in some other way, above the level at which, in the prevailing conditions of demand, all the men and women in that grade are able to obtain employment. People have ideas of a rough kind as to the amount of income that is necessary to provide a decent subsistence, and public opinion resents the payment to any class of normal workers of a wage that fails to yield them, when fully employed, an income at least as large as this. . . .

[T]he wage upon which public opinion is likely to fix is not something absolute, but will be higher or lower, according as the country affected is rich or poor. . . . If, in any community, wealth—and therefore the demand for labour—were to increase, while the accepted humanitarian minimum wages remained the same, unemployment would necessarily diminish; and, if the humanitarian minimum rose while the community's wealth remained the same, unemployment would necessarily increase. . . . In real life the two movements, if they occur at all, are likely to be associated together in such a way that the effect[s] they tend to produce upon the average volume of unemployment more or less cancel one another. Hence, neither the level of the humanitarian minimum nor the level of material wealth can be regarded without reserve as a determinant upon which the average amount of unemployment depends. Such a determinant may be found, however—and this is the point of my argument—in the number of workpeople of the lowest grade, so ill-endowed by nature and education as to be incapable of really efficient work, that exist in any country, *as compared with its general wealth*. If two countries are about equally rich and have about equal populations, but in one of them population is distributed among the different grades in such a way that a relatively large number are to be found in the lowest and least efficient grade, that country is likely to have the larger mass of unemployment (Pigou, 1914, pp. 64–7).

3.6   THE CONTRIBUTION OF PRE-KEYNESIAN THEORY

The Pre-Keynesian economists did not, as is sometimes suggested, suppose that all unemployment is frictional, and neither did they believe that unemployment was due simply to a too high *average* real wage. They regarded unemployment very much as a structural problem and, as shown in chapter 7, they sought to reduce it through specifically structural measures.

Their analysis of the labour market was, in many respects, quite sophisticated, and anticipates some recent theoretical developments. These developments are discussed in chapter 4–6 below. Although their views on monetary policy differed sharply from Keynes, this reflects a difference in the underlying assumptions about wage bargaining rather than any logical flaw in their analysis. The Pre-Keynesians believed that in the long run trade unions had the power to neutralize the effect of expansionary monetary policy, so that long-run monetary expansion would be purely inflationary. The discussion and elaboration of the ideas presented in this chapter constitutes the theme for the remaining chapters of this book.

4

Disequilibrium Theory

4.1 INTRODUCTION

The next three chapters attempt to formulate the Pre-Keynesian theory in modern terms. The presentation of older theories in modern terms can encounter many pitfalls. It is very easy to read into early writers whatever aspects of the modern theory one wants to find in them. It is also possible for self-appointed 'interpreters' to make subtle alterations and to insinuate their own ideas, as happened with some of the interpretations of Keynes. The use of lengthy quotations in the previous chapter has, it is hoped, demonstrated that there is a very explicit body of theory waiting to be formalized. Although various extensions of the Pre-Keynesian theory are suggested in this book, a deliberate effort has been made to indicate the stage at which the translation of Pre-Keynesian ideas ends and the improvisation begins.

The reformulation of Pre-Keynesian theory in modern terms demonstrates the underlying continuity which links Pre-Keynesian theory to the modern theory of the labour market. This is useful in setting straight the historical record; it places modern labour market theory firmly in the tradition of Pre-Keynesian thought. It illustrates the extent to which the 'Keynesian revolution' has led to a digression from some of the central issues of labour market theory.

4.2 THE SHORT-SIDE RULE

The present chapter reviews those aspects of disequilibrium theory which are relevant to the interpretation of Pre-Keynesian theory. It is generally accepted that the term 'disequilibrium theory' is a misnomer. The theory in fact generalizes the orthodox concept of equilibrium instead of rejecting it. It extends the concept of equilibrium from an economy where price always adjusts to clear a market to an economy where prices do not adjust and the quantities traded adjust instead.

The basic principle of the theory is that when the market price is inflexible the quantity traded is set at the short end of the market, i.e. at the minimum of demand and supply. This is called the 'short-side' rule. It is a consequence of two postulates: first, that trading is voluntary—so that neither buyers nor sellers can be forced to trade more than they want to—and second, that mutually beneficial trades are never forgone. The first postulate implies that the quantity traded cannot be greater than the minimum of demand and supply, and the second that it cannot be less; hence the two must be equal.

Disequilibrium in the labour market is illustrated in figure 4.1. It is assumed that the economy consists of a fixed number of identical competitive profit-maximizing firms, each employing one variable factor of production, labour, to produce a single homogenous product. There are continuously diminishing marginal returns to labour, so that each firm has a downward-sloping labour demand schedule DD'. There is no free production. The income from production accrues to households, either as wage income or profit (all profits are distributed). There are the same number of households

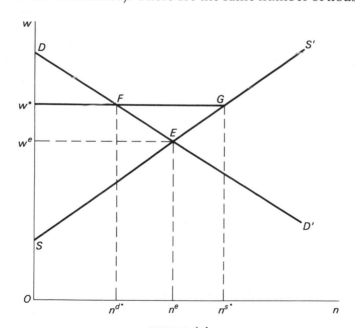

FIGURE 4.1
Disequilibrium in the labour market

as firms, and all households are identical. It is assumed that the representative household has an upward-sloping labour supply schedule SS'. Because there are equal numbers of identical firms and identical households, it is possible to analyze the behaviour of the economy in terms of the relationship between a representative firm and a representative household. Aggregate relationships are obtained simply by scaling up the relationships between individual representative agents.

If the real wage is flexible and the labour and product markets are perfectly competitive then the economy will adjust to the unique full employment equilibrium E, with real wage w^e and employment n^e. Because E lies at the intersection of DD' and SS', everyone who wants work can find it and all firms who have vacancies can recruit sufficient labour to fill them. If, on the other hand, the real wage is too high, at say

$$w^* > w^e \qquad (4.1)$$

then the result is unemployment. The demand for labour is only $n^{d*} < n^e$ because the high real wage increases the cost of labour to the firm and acts as a deterrent to employment. The supply of labour increases to $n^{s*} > n^e$ because the prospect of high wages encourages increased labour force participation (in the present model this involves an increase in the representative household's desired hours of work). Since employment, n^*, is set at the short end of the labour market, it is set in this case by the level of demand F rather than by the level of supply G:

$$n^* = n^{d*} < n^e < n^{s*} \qquad (4.2)$$

Unemployment can be measured in one of two ways, depending upon the norm with which actual employment is compared. The first measure is the shortfall of employment with respect to its full employment level:

$$u_1^* = n^e - n^* \qquad (4.3)$$

while the second is its shortfall with respect to labour supply:

$$u_2^* = n^{s*} - n^* \qquad (4.4)$$

Statistics of registered unemployment are generally based upon the second measure rather than first, and so it is this measure that will be used throughout the rest of the book. It is worth noting, however, that when people talk of the 'waste' of unemployment they are implicitly using the first concept in which the norm is full employment. They are inclined to forget that actual statistics of unemployment reflect not only the deficiency of labour demand with respect to its full employment level, but also the behaviour of labour supply. It will be shown later, for example, that the way that household labour supply responds to employment prospects can strongly influence both the aggregate volume and the industrial distribution of the registered unemployed.

4.3 THE ROLE OF PROFITS IN DISEQUILIBRIUM

The short-side rule described above is really just common sense. The most substantive part of disequilibrium theory is concerned with spill-over effects between markets. When a market is in disequilibrium, some transactors on the long side of the market find their trading plans frustrated. They face a quantity constraint which influences their trading plans in other markets: the breakdown of one planned transaction induces them—and in certain cases forces them—to modify their plans for other transactions.

The modification may operate through either a 'substitution effect' or an 'income effect'. The substitution effect is exemplified by a worker who finds that consumer goods are in short supply. Each individual has a choice of working to earn an income—which he uses to purchase consumer goods—or spending his time in leisure instead. If producers cannot meet all the demand for goods then the frustration of consumption plans will encourage workers to reduce their supply of effort and enjoy more leisure. Workers substitute the consumption of leisure for the consumption of the goods which are in short supply. In this way an excess demand for goods spills over to cause a reduction in labour supply.

The income effect is exemplified by a worker who finds that his labour is in excess supply. If firms do not demand his labour then he becomes unemployed. Lack of employment reduces his wage income and so affects his purchasing power: as a result he is forced to reduce his demand for consumer goods. In this way an excess supply of labour spills over to cause a fall in the demand for goods.

There is, however, a serious ambiguity in the literature concerning the spill-over effect of unemployment upon consumer demand. This ambiguity concerns the role of profits in the transmission of the income effect of unemployment. The ambiguity is inherent in the otherwise masterly analysis of Barro and Grossman (1976). Consider an economy which, for one reason or another, is suffering unemployment. The analysis of the labour market in section 4.2 suggests that the unemployment could be cured by a reduction in the real wage. Sometimes, however, a contrary recommendation is made. It is suggested that an increase in the real wage will increase household wage income and thereby stimulate product demand and encourage firms to expand employment. On these grounds an increase in the real wage is recommended instead.

This argument in favour of higher wages cannot be sustained, however, unless a very strong assumption is made about the determinants of profit. An increase in wage rates will certainly increase household wage income provided that the wage elasticity of firms' demand for labour is less than unity; in this case the proportionate reduction in labour demand will be less than the proportionate increase in the real wage, so that wage income will indeed increase. Firms' profits, however, will fall, and they will fall by more than household wage income increases. This is because firms' profits are squeezed between their higher wage payments on the one hand and their lower real output on the other. Since by assumption profits are always fully distributed to households, household total income will fall, and it will fall by exactly the amount of reduction in firms' real output.

The only case in which an increase in real wages can stimulate employment is when household profit income is exogenous, i.e. independent of firms' employment and output. Malinvaud (1977) makes just such an assumption, and so is able to sustain an argument for high wages analogous to the one above. It is difficult to see, however, precisely how profits can be exogenous. Casson (1981) has suggested that household budgeting decisions may be based upon expectations of profit rather than actual profits, and that because households do not have up-to-date information on firms' production decisions, their expectations of profit may be slow to adjust to actual profits. This leads to behaviour similar to that which would occur were profits exogenous. It can be shown that if household profit expectations are pessimistic then household expenditure will be reduced in line with expected household income and a deficiency of product demand can occur at the prevailing real wage. This causes unemployment, and this in turn reduces firms' actual profits. In this way households' pessimistic profit expectations become self-validating. When unemployment is caused by pessimistic profit expectations an increase in real wages will stimulate product demand and will indeed reduce unemployment.

Once the ambiguity in the treatment of profit is resolved, it becomes clear that the role of real wage policy in alleviating unemployment depends upon the determinants of profit expectations. If household profit expectations stay in line with the profit implications of firms' current production plans then unemployment will occur only if the real wage is too high. The appropriate policy to stimulate employment in this case is to reduce the real wage. If, on the other hand, household profit expectations get out of line and become unduly pessimistic then unemployment may occur through a failure of product demand. Although the best policy is to modify profit expectations, if possible, an increase in real wages may provide a simpler and more reliable alternative.

A number of economists considered the profits issue during the inter-war period. In many cases they assumed for simplicity that all profits are saved and all wages are spent. This assumption has the unfortunate effect of confusing the profits issue with the logically separate issue of whether savings are invested or not. In some cases it led people to argue, rather crudely, that profits are a leakage from the circular flow of income. In England the profits issue was discussed by John A. Hobson and P. W. Martin, and by amateur economists such as Major C. H. Douglas; in the United States William Trufant Foster, Waddill Catchings, and Alvin H. Hansen, amongst others, addressed the issue.

The Pre-Keynesian economists paid little attention to this discussion. They cold-shouldered Hobson, and were openly dismissive of the amateur economists. They were content with an implicit assumption that household budgeting decisions were always based upon correct expectations of profit. Keynes made a similar assumption about household behaviour, and so this particular issue was never a point of controversy between Keynes and the Pre-Keynesians (although some commentators have suggested that this was so). It must be recognized, however, that in the *General Theory* Keynes gave a leading role to profit expectations. When analyzing the impact of entrepreneurial expectations on the investment decision, Keynes emphasized that profit expectations are subjective and highly volatile. It was a major contribution of the *General Theory* to show that through the investment multiplier volatile profit expectations can influence aggregate product demand.

Throughout the remainder of this book, the Pre-Keynesian assumption that households correctly anticipate their profit income will be used. This assumption rules out effective demand failures caused by unduly pessimistic profit expectations. It is not denied that pessimistic profit expectations can have a major influence on unemployment; it is simply that the issue is logically distinct from the issues emphasized by Pre-Keynesian theory.

4.4 THE DETERMINANTS OF LABOUR SUPPLY

In section 4.2 a simple model of the labour market was presented in which both the demand and supply of labour depend only upon the real wage. The form of the labour demand function derives from the assumptions made about the technology of production, but the derivation of the labour supply function was not discussed. It was assumed for the sake of simplicity that labour supply depends only upon the real wage and is an increasing function of it. This assumption is, however, quite *ad hoc*: neither of these properties follows from the conventional assumptions that households regard consumption as a good, labour as a bad, and that there is a diminishing marginal rate of substitution between the consumption of goods and the enjoyment of leisure. For unless the income effect of a change in household profit receipts is zero, labour supply will depend upon profits as well as upon the real wage. Furthermore, unless the income effect of a change in the wage rate is small, labour supply may become a backward-bending function of the real wage.

The first problem can be suppressed by recognizing that profits are themselves a function of the real wage, because the real wage influences output and employment, and hence the profitability of firms. The labour supply curve SS' in figure 4.1 can therefore be reinterpreted as a 'reduced form' supply curve which takes account both of the direct effect of the wage rate on labour supply and its indirect effect on labour supply operating through household profit income. This reinterpretation preserves the simplicity of the diagrammatic treatment—it avoids the need to shift the supply curve every time the wage rate, and therefore profits, change—but it does not avoid the basic analytical complexity associated with the profit-dependence of labour supply. While the supply curve remains unique and well-defined, its derivation under disequilibrium conditions becomes quite difficult.

To avoid such difficulties it is necessary to impose further restrictions on household preferences. A sufficient condition for labour supply to be an increasing function of the real wage alone is that each household has a utility function of the form

$$u = c^d - \varphi(n^s) \tag{4.5}$$

where u is household utility, defined up to a monotone-increasing transformation, c^d is real consumer demand, n^s is labour supply, and φ is an increasing, and indeed accelerating, function of labour supply: φ', $\varphi'' > 0$. Assuming no saving, the household budget constraint is

$$c^d = wn^s + \pi \tag{4.6}$$

where w is the real wage and π is real profit. The first-order conditions for a maximum of (4.5) subject to (4.6) determine the labour supply function

$$n^s = n^s(w) \tag{4.7}$$
$$(+)$$

where the positive sign in parentheses indicates that n^s is always an increasing function of w.

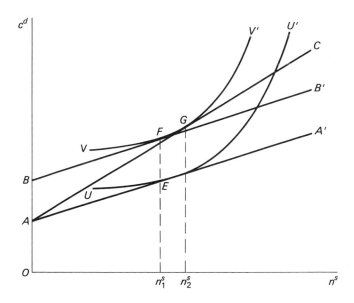

FIGURE 4.2
Derivation of labour supply

The derivation of labour supply is illustrated in figure 4.2. Household preferences are exemplified by the sample indifference curves UU' and VV'. The restriction (4.5) means that any two indifference curves have the same slope at a given level of labour supply. Initially the household receives profit income OA and faces a wage rate measured by the slope of the budget line AA'. Equilibrium is at E where the budget line AA' is tangent to the indifference curve UU', giving labour supply n_1^s. If profit income increases to OB then the budget line shifts up to BB', parallel to AA', and the equilibrium moves to F directly above E. Labour supply is unchanged at n_1^s and so the whole of the additional profit income is spent on additional consumption of goods and none on additional enjoyment of leisure. If, on the other hand, profit remains unchanged but the wage rate increases then the budget line rotates about A to AC, giving a new equilibrium at G, to the right of E and F. Labour supply has increased to $n_2^s > n_1^s$ as a result of the higher real wage.

This establishes that when household preferences conform to the utility function (4.5) labour supply is independent of profits and is an increasing function of the real wage; consequently labour market behaviour can be analyzed using the simple supply curve SS' shown in figure 4.1.

4.5   MONEY AND SAVING

Money and saving have little role in the Pre-Keynesian theory of unemployment. It seems natural to regard this as a serious shortcoming, on the grounds that the introduction of money and saving will fundamentally alter the character of the theory. Such an inference is incorrect, however. The consequences of introducing money and saving depend very much upon the nature of the theory into which they are introduced. Keynesian theory is a theory of money wage bargaining, and the role of money and saving is therefore crucial. The Pre-Keynesian theory, on the other hand, is essentially a theory of real wage bargaining. Although Pigou and others recognized the importance of money illusion, they did not believe that it could persist in the long run—certainly not long enough to be exploited for policy purposes by the government. Because in the long run money wage bargaining is not involved, the introduction of money into Pre-Keynesian theory merely augments the theory of unemployment with a separate theory of the money price level.

Although adherents of the Quantity Theory, the Pre-Keynesian economists did not think entirely in terms of the mechanical analogies of money circulation favoured by Irving Fisher. They analyzed money chiefly in terms of the supply and demand for money balances. The main influence on the money supply is the government's fiscal stance. Assuming a closed economy with no bonds, it is the government's budget deficit that regulates changes in the money supply. Consider the change in the money supply over a unit period: let M be the initial nominal money stock, G government expenditure (fixed exogenously in nominal terms) T tax receipts (generated by a lump sum tax on income and fixed in nominal terms) and M^s the money supply at the end of the period. To standardize the notation with that introduced earlier, all these variables are interpreted in *per capita* terms. The government budget constraint then implies that

$$M^s = M + G - T \qquad (4.8)$$

Money is demanded chiefly for transactions purposes: real money balances generate services by enabling their holder to avoid the difficulties of barter. The Pre-Keynesians also recognized the precautionary motive, and even discussed something very like a speculative motive, but these refinements had little role in their theory of unemployment. In formal terms, the gist of Pre-Keynesian theory is that real money balances enter into the household utility function in the same way as do consumption and leisure. Utility is higher the lower the velocity with which the household's money balances circulate. Assuming that money balances are used chiefly in connection with consumption expenditure, the inverse of the velocity of circulation is

$$k = M^d / P c^d \qquad (4.9)$$

where M^d is the household's nominal demand for money balances and P is the money price level.

It is convenient to restrict the utility function so that the introduction of money balances does not complicate the determinants of labour supply. This can be done by generalizing the utility function (4.5) to

$$u = c^d k^a - \varphi(n^s) \qquad (4.10)$$

where $0 < a < 1$ is a parameter governing the intensity of money demand. Given that there are no bonds, money is the only financial

Disequilibrium Theory

asset, and so the household budget constraint becomes

$$Pc^d + (M^d - M) + T = Wn^s + \Pi \tag{4.11}$$

The three expenditure terms on the left are nominal consumption, nominal saving and nominal tax payments, while the terms on the right represent nominal wage and profit income.

The first-order conditions for a maximum of (4.10) subject to (4.9) and (4.11) determine the labour supply, consumer demand and money demand functions

$$\begin{aligned} n^s = n^s(w) \\ (+) \end{aligned} \tag{4.12}$$

$$c^d = (1 - \alpha)x \tag{4.13}$$

$$m^d = \alpha x \tag{4.14}$$

where $m^d = M/P$ is household demand for real money balances and x is post-tax real wealth:

$$x = (Wn^s + \Pi + M - T)/P \tag{4.15}$$

Equation (4.12) shows that labour supply is determined in exactly the same way as before. Equation (4.13) is reminiscent of the Friedman long-run variant of the Keynesian consumption function (Friedman, 1957). This equation is important because it demonstrates that a linear homogeneous relation between consumption and wealth may be derived by a simple restriction (4.10) upon the household utility function. This result refutes the common belief that Keynesian-type consumption behaviour can only be derived when there is employment rationing in the labour market. It supports Keynes' own view, that the consumption function is a 'psychological law' (Keynes, 1936, p. 114) rather than Clower's view (Clower, 1965) that it is a relation prefaced upon disequilibrium. This matter is discussed further in section 4.8 below. Equation (4.14) is an immediate consequence of (4.13): it shows that the demand for real money balances is also directly proportional to real wealth.

Given the earlier assumption about household profit expectations, it is only when the real wage is above its equilibrium level that the household will be employment-constrained. In this case the household moves off its supply curve (4.12). Supply is now effectively determined by the amount of employment on offer, and the earlier concept of supply becomes a purely notional one. If n denotes the constraining level of employment then when the household is employment-constrained equation (4.12) is replaced by

$$n^s=n \qquad (4.12')$$

and equation (4.15) becomes

$$x=(Wn+\Pi-T+M)/P \qquad (4.15')$$

To complete the model of a monetary economy it is sufficient to formalize the theory of the firm which underlies the earlier derivation of labour demand, n^d. The representative firm maximizes nominal profit

$$\Pi=Py^s-Wn^d \qquad (4.16)$$

where y^s is product supply, subject to the production function

$$y^s=\gamma(n^d) \qquad (4.17)$$

where $\gamma'>0$, $\gamma''<0$. The first-order condition for a maximum of (4.16) subject to (4.17) determines the labour demand, product supply and real profit functions

$$n^d=n^d(w) \atop (-) \qquad (4.18)$$

$$y^s=y^s(w) \atop (-) \qquad (4.19)$$

$$\pi=\pi(w) \atop (-) \qquad (4.20)$$

where $\pi=\Pi/P$

An important property of the economy may be deduced by summing the budget constraints of government (equation (4.8)), households (4.11) and firms (4.16). When combined with the equation of aggregate product demand

$$y^d=c^d+G/P \qquad (4.21)$$

these equations give Walras' Law:

$$P(y^d-y^s)+W(n^d-n^s)+(M^d-M^s)=0 \qquad (4.22)$$

Equation (4.22) states that the total value of all excess demands in the economy is zero. Amongst other things, it implies that if the labour and product markets are in equilibrium then the money market must be in equlibrium too. This result indicates that the analysis of equilibrium can be confined to just two of the three markets: it is the money market that is excluded below.

When the real wage is flexible the economy will adjust to a full-employment equilibrium E analogous to that depicted in figure 4.1. Formally, the full employment equilibrium is determined by the solution w^e of the equation.

$$n^d(w)=n^s(w) \tag{4.23}$$
$$(-) \quad (+)$$

Back substitution into equations (4.18) and (4.19) determines the equilibrium employment n^e and equilibrium output y^e.

If on the other hand the real wage is fixed above the equilibrium level at

$$w=\bar{w}>w^e \tag{4.24}$$

then employment is set at the short end of the labour market:

$$n=n^d(\bar{w})<n^s(\bar{w}) \tag{4.25}$$

The corresponding level of output is

$$y=y^s(\bar{w}) \tag{4.26}$$

This unemployment equilibrium corresponds to the point F in figure 4.1.

Note that employment and output are determined entirely on the real side of the economy: monetary variables have no influence. This is because money illusion is absent. The product market equilibrium

$$y^d=y^s \tag{4.27}$$

determines the money price level through a real balance effect. If equation (4.15) is combined with equations (4.16) and (4.23), or equation (4.15′) is combined with equations (4.12′), (4.16) and (4.25), it can be shown that

$$x=y^s+(M-T)/P \tag{4.28}$$

Substituting (4.28) into (4.13), (4.13) into (4.21) and (4.21) into (4.27) gives, after some rearrangement,

$$P=[G+(\frac{1}{\alpha}-1)M^s]/y \tag{4.29}$$

Since by assumption $0<\alpha<1$, equation (4.29) implies that the money price level varies directly with government expenditure and with the money supply, and inversely with real output. Price adjustments ensure that when there is excess demand for the product, prices are bid up, reducing the real value of nominal government expenditure and encouraging households to save in order to maintain the real value of their money balances. This means that both public and private expenditures are reduced in real terms, and so the excess demand is eventually eliminated. Product supply is unaffected because it is determined exclusively on the real side of the economy.

The determination of the price level is illustrated in figure 4.3. The lower quadrants illustrate the determination of output on the real side of the economy. The upper quadrant illustrates the money side of the economy and shows how the output level determines price. In the bottom left-hand quadrant the labour market is shown experiencing unemployment caused by a too-high real wage. At the wage $\bar{w}_1$ labour supply exceeds demand and employment n_1 is set at F on the demand curve. In the bottom right-hand corner the production function translates employment n_1 into output y_1. In the top right-hand corner price and output are related by the hyperbola XX'. The output y_1 can be disposed of on the product market at an equilibrium price P_1.

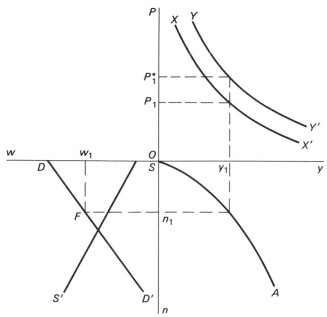

FIGURE 4.3
Determination of the money price level under real-wage bargaining

The slope of the hyperbola XX' depends upon nominal government expenditure, money supply, and the intensity of household money demand, as measured by the parameter α. Equation (4.29) indicates that if government expenditure is set to zero then a pure Quantity Theory relationship is obtained in which the price level is directly proportional to the money supply. The constant of proportionality is the velocity of circulation, and in this instance it is governed by the parameter α. If the money supply were to increase, or households' intensity of demand for real money balances were to diminish (α were to fall) then the price level would rise. The hyperbola would shift out, for example to YY', and the price level would increase to P^*_1. Aggregate output would be unaffected by such a monetary change.

4.6   BANKRUPTCY AND UNEMPLOYMENT

One of the objects of this book is to show that the Pre-Keynesian economists anticipated many of the recent developments in the analysis of unemployment. In some respects, however, Pre-Keynesian thinking even now remains ahead of contemporary developments. This is certainly true of their theory of structural disequilibrium which is formalized in chapter 6. It is also true of their discussion of bankruptcy and its effect on unemployment. This section gives a very simple account of the subject which is broadly in line with the Pre-Keynesian view. It is presented in terms of a modification of the theory of labour demand.

Bankruptcy arises when a firm cannot meet its contractual commitments, and escape is impossible (e.g. no option clause or moratorium on payments is available). It is analysed below in terms of default on debenture repayments. It is assumed for simplicity that debentures are issued at the beginning of each period and repaid at the end (i.e. the contract period is unity). Profit recipients have limited personal liability, and so the firm becomes bankrupt when the full repayment of debentures would imply negative profits. When a firm goes bankrupt it is forced to shut down production and lay off its workers; trading under receivership is assumed to be impossible.

Let the nominal value of the debenture obligations of the representative firm be D and let actual payments be L. The firm maximizes nominal net profit

$$\Pi' = Py^s - Wn^d - L \tag{4.30}$$

subject to the production function (4.17) and a bankruptcy condition which allows the firm to break even by shutting down production and defaulting on its debenture obligations:

$$L=D \qquad \text{if } y^s>0$$
$$0 \leq L \leq D \qquad \text{if } y^s=0 \tag{4.31}$$

The introduction of the constraint (4.31) creates a discontinuity in the firm's labour demand and product supply at the critical real wage at which the firm just breaks even. Below this critical wage labour demand and product supply are 'normal', i.e. they are positive, and vary inversely with the real wage. Above the critical wage labour demand and product supply are zero independently of the real wage. Household real gross profit income, $\pi=(\Pi'+L)/P$, also becomes a discontinuous function of the real wage:

$$n^d= \begin{cases} \underset{(-)}{n^d(w)} & \text{if } w \leq w^* \\ 0 & \text{otherwise} \end{cases} \tag{4.32}$$

$$y^s= \begin{cases} \underset{(-)}{y^s(w)} & \text{if } w \leq w^* \\ 0 & \text{otherwise} \end{cases} \tag{4.33}$$

$$\pi= \begin{cases} \underset{(-)}{\pi(w)} & \text{if } w \leq w^* \\ 0 & \text{otherwise} \end{cases} \tag{4.34}$$

The critical real wage w^* is determined by substituting the functions $n^d(\ .\ )$ and $y^s(\ .\ )$ which appear in equations (4.32) and (4.33) into the profit equation (4.34) and setting the left-hand side to zero; this determines the critical real wage as an increasing function of the real value of the firm's debenture obligations:

$$w^*= \underset{(+)}{w^*(D/P)} \tag{4.35}$$

The implications of bankruptcy are illustrated in figure 4.4. The demand for labour becomes infinitely elastic at the critical wage OD,

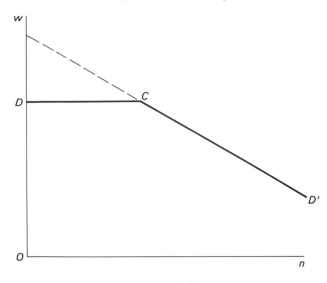

FIGURE 4.4
Implications of bankruptcy for labour demand

generating a kink at *C*. Bankruptcy can occur either if workers
stipulate a very high real wage, in excess of *OD*, or if the real value of
debenture payments is increased, so that *OD* falls below the
prevailing wage. If the nominal value of debentures was indexed to
the price level then the real value of debenture payments could not
increase within the contract period. Indexation of debentures is fairly
unusual, however, so that the real value of debenture payments will
increase if the price level falls. According to the Pre-Keynesian
economists, a falling price level was a major cause of bankruptcies in
the inter-war period.

   This derivation of a kinked labour demand curve is analogous to
the derivation of the shut-down point in the microeconomic theory
of the firm. The debenture obligations correspond to avoidable fixed
costs, and the avoidance of fixed costs generates kinks both in the
labour demand curve and the product supply curve. The present
formulation has the virtue of stressing the macroeconomic implications of the analysis. It shows, for example, that trade union real
wage push may destroy employment by bankrupting heavily capital-
ized firms. In particular, trade union resistance to money wage cuts
during a period of falling prices serves to increase the real wage at the
same time that the real value of debenture obligations is increasing,
and so is very likely to threaten bankruptcy.

4.7   FISCAL POLICY AND CROWDING OUT

Real wage bargaining has important implications for the effectiveness of fiscal policy. Consider, for example, the consequences of an increase in government expenditure financed by an increase in the money supply. The additional government expenditure increases nominal product demand, and this causes money prices to be bid up. If the money wage were fixed then the rise in money prices would reduce the real wage. Assuming there was unemployment initially, this would stimulate additional product supply. Labour demand would increase and unemployment would be reduced. With real wage bargaining, however, the rise in product prices will induce a compensating rise in money wages as trade union leaders seek to protect their members against the increase in the cost of living. The real wage will remain the same and hence product supply will not increase. The rise in money prices will reduce the real value of government demand. It will also encourage households to save more in order to increase their money balances, and so household demand will contract. Thus with product supply fixed because of the fixed real wage, money prices rise until the higher level of nominal demand corresponds to the original level of real demand. Thus the effect of higher government expenditure is simply to 'crowd out' private expenditure through higher product prices. The multiplier effect of the expenditure is zero.

A similar result is obtained when the government expenditure is financed by increased taxation. In this case, crowding out operates not only through the price level but also through the reduction in household incomes caused by the higher level of taxation.

It can be seen that real wage bargaining is a major constraint on the government's ability to 'manage' the economy through fiscal policy. Only if product prices are fixed will additional government expenditure reduce unemployment. This may be the case in the short run, but not in the medium run. In the medium run, prices will rise, wages will rise to maintain the worker's standard of living, and output and employment will remain exactly the same as before.

4.8   KEYNES, THE PRE-KEYNESIANS, AND THE ORIGINS OF DISEQUILIBRIUM THEORY

If Pre-Keynesian theory can indeed be cast in disequilibrium terms, then it is natural to inquire to what extent the Pre-Keynesians can be said to be pioneers of disequilibrium theory. This leads to the supplementary question 'Did the use of disequilibrium theory originate with the Pre-Keynesians rather than with Keynes?'

In discussing issues of this kind, it must be recognized that there are limits to the extent to which the historian of thought can see into the minds of his subjects. There is a strong subjective element in the inquiry which cannot be avoided. It is, however, possible to ask whether what the Pre-Keynesians said about unemployment is consistent with a disequilibrium interpretation. This claim would be refuted if the writers clearly contradict one or more of the postulates of the theory, or violate its logic in a serious way. (On the other hand, minor flaws in the argument may be admitted on grounds of ordinary human fallibility.) It is claimed that the Pre-Keynesian theory summarized in chapter 3 is, by and large, consistent with the disequilibrium theory presented in this book.

A more subjective issue is whether the Pre-Keynesians recognized the generality of the disequilibrium principles which underpin their arguments. On the whole, it seems that they did not. It is certainly difficult to find any conclusive evidence that they did. They appear to have improvised their theory to deal with the specific circumstances with which they were confronted—a situation by no means unusual in the progress of economic thought.

Turning to Keynes, his analysis is broadly consistent with a particular version of disequilibrium theory, namely the fixed money wage—flexible money price version of the Barro and Grossman model (Barro and Grossman, 1971, 1976; Casson, 1981, ch. 6). On the question of Keynes' own grasp of disequilibrium principles, however, matters are much less clear. In the *General Theory*, Keynes is very obscure on fundamental issues, such as the process of labour market adjustment, the microeconomic foundations of the consumption function, and the relevance of Say's Law of Markets.

Wage rigidity is crucial to the disequilibrium theory of the labour market, yet Keynes is ambivalent on the issue. As Leijonhufvud (1968) points out, Keynes is apt to regard wage rigidity more as a policy recommendation than as a behavioural assumption. The Pre-Keynesians were much clearer on this point than was Keynes: as shown earlier, they recognized both short-run money wage rigidity and long-run real wage rigidity.

Clower (1965) has suggested that Keynes' specification of the consumption function implies a recognition of an employment constraint on household earning power. This view depends upon the postulate that in the absence of an employment constraint, a consumer demand function contains only 'price' variables, and no quantity or value variables such as income. This postulate is not so self-evident as it seems, for under certain conditions the representation of a consumer demand function may not be unique.

It has been shown above (section 4.5) that when household preferences satisfy certain conditions, household consumption expenditure is related in a determinate way to household income, independently of prices. Thus in the model above, real consumption is a linear function of real income whether or not there are employment constraints. Thus the Keynesian consumption function may be a conventional consumer demand function expressed in an unconventional way. The consumption function may be no more than what it appears to be at a superficial level: a simplifying assumption about household behaviour. It follows that the form of the Keynesian consumption function does not necessarily imply recognition of employment constraints by Keynes.

Clower links Keynes' specification of the consumption function to his attack on Say's Law of Markets. Clower forges this link through his 'dual decision hypothesis', which he claims underlies Keynes' views of household behaviour. The 'dual decision hypothesis' is a dynamic postulate which captures the flavour of Keynes' verbal reasoning very well. Unfortunately it is neither necessary nor sufficient for Clower's purposes. A violation of Say's Law occurs when there is an excess demand for money balances. This leads to a deficiency of product demand, and can occur quite independently of dual-decision behaviour. An excess demand for money balances is most likely to occur when investors are afraid to commit themselves to real investment and prefer to hold liquid assets such as money instead. This case of strong liquidity preference is emphasized throughout the *General Theory,* and represents one of Keynes' most original contributions.

The main link between liquidity preference and disequilibrium theory is that the excess demand for money balances will only persist if money wages are rigid downwards. Despite Keynes' ambivalence on the subject, there will be a multiplier impact on output and employment only if the money wage fails to adjust. Thus while disequilibrium reasoning underpins Keynes' analysis, contrary to Clower's claims, it does not constitute anything like a unifying theme in Keynes' formal model.

One of the ironies of Clower's interpretation is that his formal model of disequilibrium (Clower, 1965, section 7) actually fits Pre-Keynesian analysis much better than it fits Keynes. Clower's model illustrates the case of a too high real wage rather than a too high money wage. He shows that a too high real wage induces firms to contract output, which reduces household incomes and so in turn induces a contraction in demand. This is precisely the case discussed by the Pre-Keynesians, and is certainly not the case discussed by Keynes. As the preceding section has shown, in the Pre-Keynesian case discussed by Clower, the multiplier effect of government expenditure is always zero. Since there is no multiplier, it is difficult to see how Clower's model can correspond to the case considered by Keynes. Equally though, it is easy to see why the Pre-Keynesians did not discover the multiplier. When real wage bargaining prevails, it is always zero.

4.9   SUMMARY AND CONCLUSIONS

This chapter has presented a simple model in which unemployment is caused by a too high real wage. The model illustrates the application of the short-side rule to the labour market; this rule implies that when there is an excess supply of labour, employment is set by the level of labour demand and not by the level of labour supply. The model also analyzes the spill-over effects of unemployment caused by a too high real wage. A high real wage is associated with a lower level of employment, and hence with lower levels of both household income and product supply. It is shown that the spill-over effect on product demand caused by the lower level of household income reduces product demand to a level compatible with the reduced level of product supply. So far as financial markets are concerned, the only spill-over is that lower real incomes reduce the transactions demand for money and thereby tend to raise the money price level.

It is widely believed that disequilibrium theory has a Keynesian pedigree, or, conversely, that Keynes' major contribution to economics was to think in disequilibrium terms. This is false. It has been shown, on the one hand, that a key Keynesian concept—the consumption function—is not necessarily prefaced upon the existence of a disequilibrium. The consumption function may be simply what Keynes asserted it to be—a psychological law which can be derived by imposing simple restrictions on a household utility function.

On the other hand, it has been shown that Pre-Keynesians thought in disequilibrium terms. The crucial difference between Keynes and the Pre-Keynesians does not lie here, but in their views of wage bargaining. The Pre-Keynesians believed in real wage bargaining while Keynes emphasized money wage bargaining. This is, indeed, the difference that Keynes himself pointed to at the beginning of the *General Theory*. The conflict between these two views can be resolved quite easily if the Keynesian view is regarded as a short-run view of wage bargaining, and the Pre-Keynesian view as a medium-run or long-run view.

The analysis of real wage bargaining in a monetary economy shows that the dichotomy between real and money sectors does not rest upon the existence of full employment. Neither does it rest upon the view that all unemployment is voluntary. It is a general property of real wage bargaining—at least it is when analyzed using simple models of the kind above. A further consequence of real wage bargaining is that pure 'crowding out' between public and private expenditure prevails. Crowding out applies irrespective of the level of unemployment. This is because when there is real wage bargaining the supply of output is totally inelastic with respect to prices—it is governed entirely by the stipulated real wage. Thus if government demand for output increases the money price of output will be bid up, but no additional output will be forthcoming. It is inevitable, therefore, that to the extent that real government demand increases, real private demand will contract.

5

Job Search and Unemployment

5.1 THE IMPACT OF JOB RATIONING ON LABOUR SUPPLY

This chapter presents some original material which has been inspired by a reading of Pre-Keynesian theory. The chapter is largely self-contained and can, if desired, be omitted on a first reading. It is concerned with the integration of disequilibrium theory and job search theory. The conceptual framework is suggested by Pigou's analysis of the influence of trade union wage setting on labour supply, as described in section 3.3. The analysis in this chapter demonstrates that the Pre-Keynesian theory is not a mere historical curiosity. The theory provides a research agenda which offers promising prospects for future theoretical development.

The disequilibrium theory outlined in chapter 4 is quite satisfactory as a theory of the determinants of employment, but is less satisfactory as a theory of labour supply. Consider, for example, the effects on employment and labour supply of an increase in the real wage. If the real wage increases then firms will shed labour, and they have no reason to re-employ people so long as the real wage remains high. On the other hand, workers who have been made redundant may be discouraged from offering to supply as much labour as they were accustomed to supplying before. Recognizing that so long as the real wage remains high their prospects of re-employment are low, they may withdraw from the labour force altogether.

Implicit in this 'discouraged worker hypothesis' is the assumption that searching for work is costly, and that the worker can avoid these costs by withdrawing from the labour force. This is certainly a view in which the Pre-Keynesian economists seem to have concurred. It has the important implication that the level of labour supply cannot be considered independently of the level of labour demand. Buoyant labour demand encourages labour supply, and conversely, depressed labour demand discourages labour supply. Unemployment is the difference between actual employment and labour supply. Although superficially it seems that an increase in labour demand will raise employment and reduce unemployment by about the same amount, this is not necessarily so. Because an increase in labour demand also stimulates labour supply, the supply could increase by the same amount as the demand so that unemployment would remain unchanged. Employment could increase without unemployment having fallen. Likewise a fall in labour demand may discourage labour supply to such an extent that, although employment falls, unemployment may not increase.

To formalize these ideas it is necessary to develop a theory of job search. Neoclassical economists have developed a theory in which unemployed workers search across vacancies currently on offer from employers in order to find the most attractive wage. Search takes time and effort. If a worker refuses a job offer in order to carry on searching full-time for a better job then search involves a loss of current earnings. Each worker remains unemployed just so long as he believes that the improvement in his wage he can achieve by continuing search outweighs the costs involved (Alchian, 1971). This theory affords an important insight into unemployment, but for present purposes it needs to be substantially modified. The theory asserts that there are always suitable vacancies on offer because if business conditions are depressed, employers can cut the real wage. Workers who remain unemployed do so not because they cannot find a job, but because they do not like the wages on offer. The neoclassical theory therefore implies that all idle workers are 'voluntarily' unemployed. Pre-Keynesian economists were quite clear, however, that in inter-war Britain real wages could not be cut in this way. National basic wages, set by collective bargaining or statutory wages boards, set a floor to wage offers throughout most of manufacturing industry. Employers adjusted to changing conditions not by altering the stipulated wage but by altering the number of jobs on offer. Vacancies were not, therefore, freely available, but were rationed. This seems, on balance, to be a reasonable view of the inter-war labour market, certainly for the period 1922–35, when demand for labour was relatively depressed.

The rationing of vacancies alters fundamentally the character of the job search process. When vacancies are rationed, workers undertake search as a competitive strategy in which each worker hopes to locate any given vacancy before the others do. Jobs which in the neoclassical theory are 'rationed' by wage rates are now rationed by search effort instead. Workers 'prospect' for vacancies and it is the outcome of this prospecting process which decides who finds employment and who does not.

The Pre-Keynesian view of the labour market was essentially that of a casual labour market in which a minimum wage is enforced. Labour turnover is high, with workers being regularly hired and fired. Each worker typically has several spells of employment throughout his life, with unemployment intervening between them. During spells of unemployment the worker prospects for vacancies in competition with others who are unemployed.

The prospecting process is well described by the Todaro migration model, (Harris and Todaro, 1970; Todaro, 1969, 1976) from which the model below is adapted. The Todaro model is itself a special case of a general class of models in which there is non-price rationing by personal frustration. Typical of the genre are models of congestion in the access to unpriced public goods, where an equilibrium is achieved at the margin where the disutility of the congestion just offsets the utility of the user services derived from the good. A closer analogy is a queueing system in which an underpriced service is rationed by the frustration of waiting to be served. The analogy is not exact, of course, because the queue accords a single set of priorities based upon sequence of arrival. To obtain the model described below it is necessary either to multiply the number of servers so that each server corresponds to a separate employer who opens for business at random (creates a vacancy) and serves only the first person in the queue (the first applicant for the job); alternatively the single-server assumption could be maintained so that people are served by random selection from a waiting crowd.

5.2   A SIMPLE MODEL OF QUEUE UNEMPLOYMENT

It is assumed that labour is hired on one-period contracts, and that hiring begins from scratch each period. There is a uniform basic wage which sets a floor to the actual wage. If there is an excess demand for labour then employers bid up the wage until it has been eliminated. If there is an excess supply of labour then the wage is bid down only as far as the basic wage. If excess supply persists then at this stage active job search confers priority in obtaining a job. A person actively seeks a job when he spends the same amount of time per day looking for it as he intends to spend at work when he has found it. It is assumed that where there is an excess supply of labour each individual believes that it is necessary to actively seek work in order to obtain a job. Under the assumed conditions this belief is self-validating for no vacancies will remain unfilled for non-searchers to take. It is assumed that the disutility of seeking work is exactly the same as the disutility of working. Thus disutility is related, not to employment *per se,* but to the sum of the time spent in employment and job search. This sum is known as active labour supply, n_a^s; it is on active labour supply, and not the supply of employment, that individuals' preferences depend. Finally, it is assumed that active labour supply enters into the household utility function in exactly the same way as does the supply of employment in equation (4.10).

Workers plan ahead over a large fixed number of periods. A worker plans the same level of consumption, saving and active labour supply throughout the time span that is within his planning horizon. He does not vary his consumption or active labour supply depending upon whether or not he is employed. It is assumed that his desired holding of money balances is sufficient to tide his consumption over interruptions to wage income associated with periods of job search. Thus, over the planning period as a whole, consumption is related to employment, but within the planning period variations in employment above the average are accommodated by changes in money balances. This is a strong assumption, and is crucial for the analysis that follows.

Everyone actively seeking work has the same probability of finding it. Everyone correctly estimates this probability. When there is an excess supply of labour the probability of finding a job is equal to the ratio of labour demand to active labour supply. When there is no excess supply of labour the probability of finding a job is unity.

Under these conditions the introduction of job search creates just one crucial change in the model of section 4.5: the original relationship between labour supply and the real wage is transformed into a relationship between active labour supply and the expected wage:

$$n_a^s = n_a^s(\hat{w})$$
$$(+) \tag{5.1}$$

The expected wage is given by

$$\hat{w} = (n^d/n^s)w \tag{5.2}$$

where, in the light of earlier assumptions, $n^d/n^s \leq 1$. The expected

wage is the average wage income received per unit of active labour
supply; it is the worker's wage income averaged over the total hours
spent either in work or in finding a job. The reason why this is the
only change in the model is that firms' behaviour continues to be
governed by the real wage alone. Given a competitive product
market, and the elimination of excess demands in the labour market
through wage competition, firms always produce on their labour
demand and product supply curves. Thus household wage and profit
incomes are exactly the same as before. This means that although the
expected wage governs the representative household's active labour
supply, it does not influence its actual wage income, and therefore
has no spill-over effects elsewhere in the economy.

   Job search unemployment equilibrium is illustrated in figure 5.1.
Both the actual wage and the expected wage are measured along the
vertical axis. The demand curve DD' is drawn with respect to the
actual wage, w, while the active labour supply curve SS' is drawn
with respect to the expected wage. Full employment equilibrium is

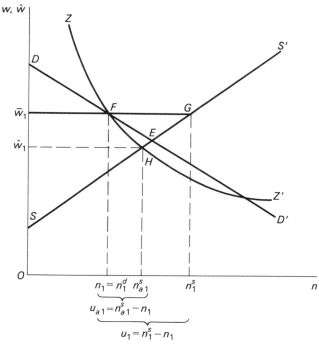

FIGURE 5.1
Job search equilibrium

at E, exactly as in figure 4.1. Suppose, however, that the real wage is fixed above its full employment equilibrium level at, say, $\bar{w}_1$. Firms decide to produce at F. If workers believed that they could obtain employment with certainty at the wage $\bar{w}_1$ then their labour supply would be fixed at G—the level predicted by orthodox disequilibrium theory. It is assumed, however, that they base their decisions instead upon the expected wage, using equation (5.2). Since w is fixed at $\bar{w}_1$ and n^d is therefore fixed also, this equation determines an implicit relation between $\hat{w}$ and n_a^s, whose locus is indicated in the figure by ZZ'. The hyperbola ZZ' passes through the equilibrium of the firm at F. The intersection H of ZZ' with the active labour supply schedule SS' determines the equilibrium expected wage $\hat{w}_1$ and labour supply n_{a1}^s. At H the intensity of job search is such that the expected wage is just sufficient to compensate the searchers for the marginal effort involved.

The expected wage $\hat{w}$ can never exceed the actual wage w and so, since the active labour supply curve is upward-sloping, the labour supply induced by the expected wage cannot exceed the supply that would be induced by the certain payment of the actual wage. Thus the unemployment $u_{a1} = n_{a1}^s - n_1$ predicted by the job search theory can never exceed the unemployment $u_1 = n_1^s - n$ predicted by orthodox disequilibrium theory. When the full employment wage prevails both theories, quite naturally, predict zero unemployment. When the wage is fixed above the full employment level, the job search theory predicts lower unemployment than the orthodox theory. The difference between these two predictions measures the strength of the 'discouraged worker' effect.

5.3   EFFECTS OF A WAGE CUT

It was noted at the outset that the discouraged worker effect can generate some unusual behaviour in the statistics of the registered unemployed. This can be analyzed by considering the effect on unemployment of a cut in the actual real wage. Intuitively a cut in the real wage should reduce unemployment, but in practice the reduction in unemployment may be significantly less than the number of new jobs created. Under certain extreme conditions a cut in the real wage may stimulate employment but increase the amount of unemployment also!

Combining equations (5.1) and (5.2) gives

$$wn^d(w) = \hat{w}n_a^s(\hat{w}) \tag{5.3}$$

and total differentiation of (5.3) yields the following key result:

$$\eta^s = (1 - \eta^d)\hat{\eta}^s / (1 + \hat{\eta}^s) \tag{5.4}$$

where

$$\eta^s = (dn_a^s/dw)w/n_a^s \tag{5.5}$$

$$\eta^d = -(dn^d/dw)w/n^d \tag{5.6}$$

$$\hat{\eta}^s = (dn_a^s/d\hat{w})\ \hat{w}/n_a^s \tag{5.7}$$

Equation (5.4) expresses the elasticity of active labour supply with respect to the actual wage as a function of the wage-elasticity of labour demand and the expected wage-elasticity of labour supply. Since it has earlier been assumed that $\hat{\eta}^s > 0$, it is an immediate consequence of (5.4) that $\eta^s \gtrless 0$ as $\eta^d \gtrless 1$. This means that a cut in the actual real wage will reduce active labour supply if the elasticity of labour demand is less than unity, but will increase labour supply if the elasticity of labour demand exceeds unity. This result indicates that the elasticity of labour demand is crucial in determining whether a cut in real wages increases or decreases labour supply.

If the elasticity of labour demand exceeds unity then the question arises as to how large the increase in labour supply will be relative to the increase in labour demand. If the increase in labour supply is nearly as large as the increase in labour demand then the effect of the wage cut on unemployment may be very small. Totally differentiating unemployment with respect to the real wage and applying equation (5.4) shows that the reduction in proportional unemployment induced by a unit proportional wage cut is

$$du_a'/(dw/w) = (n^d/n_a^s)\ (\eta^d + \hat{\eta}^s)/(1 + \hat{\eta}^s) \tag{5.8}$$

where

$$u_a' = (n_a^s - n^d)/n_a^s \tag{5.9}$$

Similarly it can be shown that the absolute reduction in unemployment induced by a unit proportional wage cut is

$$du_a/(dw/w) = n^d\eta^d + n_a^s(1 - \eta^d)\hat{\eta}^s/(1 + \hat{\eta}^s) \tag{5.10}$$

It follows from equation (5.8) that percentage unemployment is

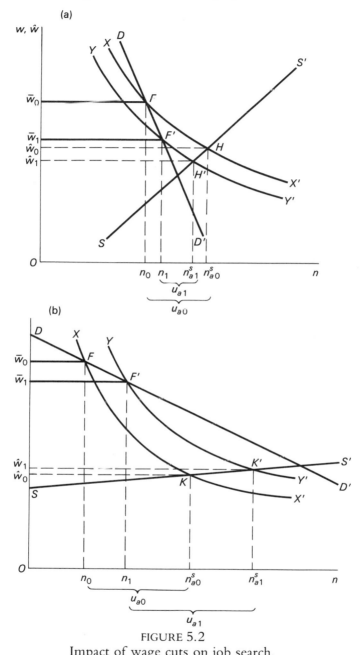

FIGURE 5.2
Impact of wage cuts on job search.
(a) Effect of a wage cut with an inelastic demand for labour.
(b) Effect of a wage cut with an elastic demand and elastic active supply

always reduced by a wage cut. Equation (5.10), on the other hand, shows that *absolute* unemployment is not necessarily reduced. Absolute unemployment may be increased by a wage cut if

$$\eta^d > 1 \text{ and } \hat{\eta}^s > (n^d/n_a^s)\eta^d/(\eta^d - 1) \tag{5.11}$$

i.e. if the elasticity of labour demand exceeds unity and labour supply is highly elastic with respect to the expected wage.

These results are illustrated in figure 5.2. The top part of the figure illustrates an inelastic demand for labour. A wage cut from $\bar{w}_0$ to $\bar{w}_1$ produces very little increase in employment: the proportional increase from n_0 to n_1 is much smaller than the proportional reduction in the wage from $\bar{w}_0$ to $\bar{w}_1$. The effect of the wage cut is to reduce total wage income. This is reflected in the fact that the new expected wage locus YY' passing through the new equilibrium F' lies below the original locus XX' through the initial equilibrium F. Since the new locus is lower, it intersects the upward–sloping supply curve SS' at H' below H. The expected wage falls from $\hat{w}_0$ to $\hat{w}_1$ and the active labour supply responds by contracting to $n_{a1}^s < n_{a0}^s$. Employment has increased only marginally, but since labour supply has fallen, the fall in unemployment from u_{a0} to u_{a1} is a quite significant one.

The bottom part of the figure illustrates the case where labour demand is elastic, and labour supply is elastic also. It shows that if the wage is cut, then despite the fact that employment will rise substantially, unemployment may actually also rise. A small proportional cut in the wage from $\bar{w}_0$ to $\bar{w}_1$ generates a large proportional increase in labour demand from n_0 to n_1. Employment and wage income both rise, and the increase in wage income tends to push up the expected wage. The new expected wage locus YY' lies above the original locus XX'. Labour supply is determined, as before, by the intersection of the expected wage locus with the labour supply curve. With a highly elastic labour supply curve SS', the intersection K' with YY' may lie far to the right of the intersection K with XX'. Labour supply increases substantially as a result, from n_{a0}^s to n_{a1}^s. As shown, the increase in supply $n_{a1}^s - n_{a0}^s$ exceeds the increase in demand, $n_1 - n_0$, so that despite the fact that employment has risen, unemployment is higher than before: $u_{a1} > u_{a0}$. Admittedly this case is somewhat extreme, but it is a striking illustration of the difficulties of interpreting statistics of job search unemployment. The significance of this effect during the inter-war period is examined in chapter 10.

5.4 UNEMPLOYMENT BENEFIT

This section applies the theory of queue unemployment, developed above, to analyze the impact of unemployment benefit on the level of unemployment. It is assumed to begin with that unemployment benefit is set in real terms (this assumption is relaxed in section 5.5). This implies that government indexes the nominal benefits paid. The assumption of indexation is not unreasonable because the level of unemployment benefit is usually fixed with reference to the needs of subsistence living, which is a real and not a monetary concept. The period that elapses between the revision of nominal benefits is analogous to the contract period referred to above. The analysis below assumes a period of time exceeding the contract period. It is therefore a medium-run rather than a short-run analysis.

If unemployment benefit is fixed in real terms then with real wage bargaining the dichotomy between the real and money sectors, described in section 4.5, is preserved. Unemployment benefit influences unemployment through the labour market alone. The monetary implications of unemployment benefit are reflected purely in the price level. The increase in the government budget deficit leads to an increase in the money supply. In the context of the product market, unemployment benefit receipts stimulate households' nominal consumption demand, but because the real wage is fixed, product supply remains unchanged. Excess demand is eliminated by a rise in price which reduces the real value of both government and households' nominal demands.

It is assumed that unemployment benefit is paid only to those genuinely seeking work. Much of the political controversy surrounding unemployment benefit concerns the effectiveness with which claimants are screened; for present purposes this is regarded as a problem of social administration rather than economics, and so is excluded from the analysis.

The main effect of unemployment benefit is to alter the relation between the actual wage and the expected wage. Let the real level of unemployment benefit be fixed at $b < w$, so that total unemployment benefit payments are

$$a = b(n_a^s - n) \tag{5.12}$$

where, in the light of earlier assumptions,

$$n_a^s \geqslant n = n^d \tag{5.13}$$

Averaging over periods of employment and unemployment gives

$$wn^d + a = \hat{w}n_a^s \qquad (5.14)$$

Substituting (5.12) and (5.13) into (5.14) gives an implicit equation for the expected wage:

$$(w-b)n^d(w) = (\hat{w}-b)n_a^s(\hat{w}) \qquad (5.15)$$

Differentiating equation (5.15) with respect to b gives

$$du_a/db = (u_a/\hat{w})\hat{\eta}^s/(1+\hat{\eta}^s - \psi) \qquad (5.16)$$

where

$$\psi = b/\hat{w} \qquad (5.17)$$

is the replacement ratio for the expected wage. Since by assumption $b<w$, and $\hat{w}$ is a weighted average of b and w, $\psi \leqslant 1$.

Equation (5.16) has several important implications.

(1) Since $du_a/db=0$ if $u_a=0$, the introduction of unemployment benefit has no effect on the full employment equilibrium. This may seem at first sight to be a trivial result. It reflects the assumptions that all leisure-seeking 'scroungers' are disqualified from benefit, and that there is no frictional unemployment, i.e. job search only occurs when vacancies are rationed. The result is interesting, nevertheless, because it emphasizes that when benefits are carefully administered, and job matching is easy to achieve, then a change in the level of unemployment benefit may have no effect on unemployment. If real wage adjustments maintain the economy in equilibrium then that equilibrium will be independent of benefit levels.

(2) Since $\hat{\eta}^s>0$ and $\psi \leqslant 1$, it follows that $du_a/db>0$ if $u_a>0$. This means that when there is unemployment to begin with the introduction of unemployment benefit will always increase it by stimulating active labour supply. More generally, the benefit-sensitivity of unemployment is greater, the greater is its absolute level. This is because when unemployment is high, unemployment benefit carries a greater weight in the household's calculation of the expected wage.

(3) The benefit-sensitivity of unemployment is higher the higher is the replacement ratio.

(4) The benefit-sensitivity of unemployment is higher the more elastic is the active labour supply.

The effects of the introduction of unemployment benefit are illustrated in figure 5.3. The demand and supply curves DD', SS' are exactly the same as before. With a prevailing real wage $\bar{w}_1$, employment is set at F on DD', giving $n_1 = n_1^d$. In the absence of unemployment benefit the expected wage equation is obtained by setting $b = 0$ in equation (5.15). The locus XX' of the expected wage equation intersects the supply curve SS' at H. The expected wage is $\hat{w}_1$, active labour supply is n_{a1}^s, and unemployment is $u_{a1} = n_{a1}^s - n_1$. If the real level of unemployment benefit is now raised to OB then the locus of the expected wage equation rotates about F to YY', which is asymptotic to the horizontal line BB'. The new locus YY' intersects SS' at J to the right of H. The expected wage rises to $\hat{w}_2 > \hat{w}_1$, active labour supply increases to $n_{a2}^s > n_{a1}^s$, and with employment unchanged, unemployment rises to $u_{a2} = n_{a2}^s - n_1 > u_{a1}$.

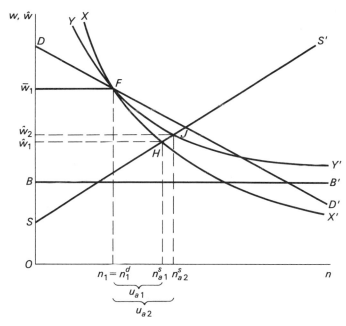

FIGURE 5.3
Effects of unemployment benefit

5.5　MONEY WAGE BARGAINING

This section considers the consequences of relaxing the earlier assumption that wage bargaining is conducted exclusively in money terms. The assumption that unemployment benefits are indexed to the price level is also relaxed. It is assumed instead that workers stipulate for money wages, and that unemployment benefit is fixed in money terms. Money wages cannot be revised during the contract period. This provides a short-run variant of the preceding model, where 'short-run' indicates a time span less than the contract period.

The assumption about money wage bargaining may be interpreted in one of two ways. First, it may be considered as a description of the situation that prevails for the duration of a labour contract, i.e. as a description of short-term behaviour within the contract period. The use of money as a standard of deferred payment reduces transaction costs in the labour market, so it is mutually beneficial for workers and employers to contract with one another in money terms. Given the costs of frequent recontracting, it is convenient to allow each contract to run for a reasonable time, usually about a year. Within the contract period unforeseen changes in price level may cause the real wage to deviate from the level that was anticipated at the time of the agreement. These changes in the real wage will elicit a response from employers which will affect the level of employment.

An alternative interpretation is that workers suffer from money illusion, so that when they recontract they do not take proper account of the changes in prices that have occurred during the previous contract period. This possibility is extensively discussed in the Keynesian literature and, as we have seen, was fully recognized by the Pre-Keynesians too. The Pre-Keynesians, though, would not favour this interpretation, because they believed that workers soon learnt from their mistakes. Pigou, in particular, felt that it would be difficult for a government to exploit money illusion by 'bamboozling' the workers with an engineered inflation.

Analytically, the switch from real wage to money wage bargaining does not affect any of the demand and supply functions derived in the models above. What it does is to change the endogeneity of some of the key variables. Disequilibrium now involves a fixed money wage and not a fixed real wage. This immediately destroys the dichotomy between the real and money sectors referred to in section 4.5. In the real wage bargaining model the real wage determines output, and output determines the price level conditional upon the money supply and the government's fiscal stance. There is no feedback from the price level to the real wage. In the money wage bargaining model the real wage still determines output, and so influences price, but price now feeds back to influence the real wage. The real wage can no longer be determined independently of price: price and the real wage are simultaneously determined. Since monetary variables influence price, they can also influence the real wage, and so affect employment. The assumption of money wage bargaining thus takes us straight from the world of the Pre-Keynesians to the world of Keynes.

If unemployment benefit is ignored then the outcome of a money wage disequilibrium can be derived very simply. Consider again the job search model of section 5.1. Assume that the money wage is fixed at $\bar{W}$, above its full employment level, so that employment is set by firms' labour demand and output by firms' product supply. The product and money markets are perfectly competitive as before. The possibility of bankruptcy is ignored.

The equilibrium of the product market is still characterized by equation (4.29), which is reproduced here for convenience:

$$P=[G+(\tfrac{1}{a}-1)M^s]/y$$

Under real wage bargaining y is determined independently of P in the labour market, but under money wage bargaining labour market behaviour generates an upward-sloping supply curve of output:

$$y=y(\bar{W}/P) \tag{5.18}$$
$$(-)$$

Equations (4.29) and (5.18) are a pair of simultaneous equations which can be solved uniquely for P and y. The solution is illustrated in figure 5.4, which is adapted from the top quadrant of figure 4.3. In the earlier figure the supply of output is totally inelastic with respect to the price level, as indicated by the vertical line HH'. Equation (5.18) indicates that with money wage bargaining, the supply of output is an increasing function of price, as indicated by the curve JJ'. The product market equilibrium condition is represented by XX' as before. The intersection E of JJ' and XX' determines both the price, P_1, and output, y_1.

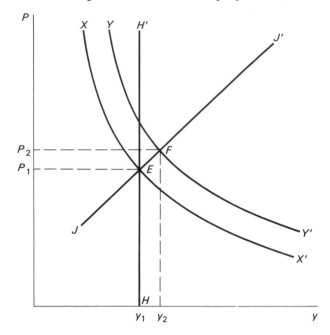

FIGURE 5.4
Price and output determination under money-wage bargaining.

Once price has been determined, employment is given by the labour market equilibrium condition

$$n=n^d(\bar{W}/P) \tag{5.19}$$

Labour supply may be derived from the active labour supply function (5.1) and the equation of the expected wage (5.2):

$$n_a^s=n_a^s(\hat{w})$$

$$(\bar{W}/P)n^d(\bar{W}/P)=\hat{w}n_a^s(\hat{w})$$

When there is money wage bargaining, output and employment can be stimulated by fiscal and monetary measures. For example, an increase in government expenditure, a reduction in taxation, or a higher initial money supply, will all shift out the locus XX'. The new locus YY' intersects JJ' at a new equilibrium F, associated with a higher price, $P_2>P_1$, and a higher output, $y_2>y_1$.

The introduction of unemployment benefit fixed in nominal terms complicates the analysis quite considerably, as the payment of benefits has implications for the money supply. The moral of the exercise is quite straightforward, however. Unemployment benefit tends to stimulate employment because it increases houshold nominal incomes; it also increases the money supply, and so leads to higher prices and a lower real wage. Thus employment will be higher when unemployment benefit is paid than when it is not. It does not follow, though, that unemployment itself will fall, for the payment of benefits will also stimulate labour supply. Whether unemployment increases or not will depend upon a number of factors, including the elasticities of labour demand, the demand for money balances, and labour supply.

5.6 SUMMARY

Pre-Keynesian writers were very familiar with the operation of casual labour markets, in which the worker's attachment to the market is governed by the expected wage. Their insights into labour market operation can be captured by a synthesis of the theories of disequilibrium and job search. This chapter has effected such a synthesis.

The theory has a number of important implications.

(1) When the real wage is too high, labour supply will be discouraged by the reduced prospects for finding work. The reduction in employment induced by a high real wage may therefore be partly compensated by a reduction in labour supply. Thus unemployment may not be as high as it would otherwise be.

(2) The impact of a real wage cut on labour supply depends crucially upon the wage elasticity of labour demand. If the wage elasticity of demand is less than unity then a real wage cut will reduce expected wage income and so reduce labour supply. If, on the other hand, the wage elasticity of demand is greater than unity then a real wage cut will raise expected wages and so increase labour supply. In the latter case, a real wage cut, though it stimulates employment, may have little effect in reducing unemployment. Although unemployment will be reduced in percentage terms, in absolute terms it may remain unchanged, or even increase.

(3) The sensitivity of unemployment to unemployment benefit

increases with the level of unemployment. This is because unemployment increases the weight attached to unemployment benefit in the calculation of the expected wage. For a similar reason, the benefit sensitivity of unemployment tends to be greatest when the replacement ratio is high.

(4) The sensitivity of unemployment to unemployment benefit is lower when there is money wage bargaining than when there is real wage bargaining. The payment of unemployment benefit, financed by a budget deficit, stimulates aggregate demand and so raises money prices. When the money wage is fixed this reduces the real wage and so stimulates labour demand. If, on the other hand, the money wage is linked to money prices, then there is no stimulus to labour demand. When the money wage is fixed, therefore, the increase in labour supply induced by higher unemployment benefit is to some extent offset by increased labour demand, and so the increase in unemployment is lower than it would otherwise be.

6

Structural Disequilibrium

6.1 INTRODUCTION

This chapter presents a simple model of structural unemployment inspired by the Pre-Keynesian analysis summarized in chapter 3. The model is essentially a multi-sectoral version of the aggregative models introduced in chapters 4 and 5, and uses similar notation. The model has rigorous microeconomic foundations, and provides a convenient framework for the appraisal of Pre-Keynesian employment policies in chapter 7.

Three variants of the model are presented. The first variant is extremely simple and is introduced merely to elucidate some of the general features of structural models of unemployment. It assumes a closed economy, totally immobile labour, and utilizes the orthodox version of disequilibrium theory which ignores job search. This model is analysed in sections 6.2–6.4. The second variant, discussed in sections 6.5 and 6.6, retains the closed economy assumption but assumes mobile labour and takes account of job search. The final version of the model, presented in section 6.7, extends the analysis to an open economy. Between them, these models provide a reasonably comprehensive treatment of the determinants and effects of structural unemployment, as perceived by the Pre-Keynesian economists.

6.2 THE BASIC MODEL

It is assumed for simplicity that there are just two industries: a new one (indexed $j=1$) which is expanding, and an old one (indexed $j=2$) which is contracting. In the context of the 1920s, the new industry may be identified as motor cars and the old industry as textiles. In some applications of the model the industries are assumed to use similar skills but to be located in different places—the 'new' industry in the 'centre' of the economy and the 'old' industry on the 'periphery'. In other applications the industries are assumed to be located in the same area but to use different skills. Employers have no scope for adjusting either the location of production (e.g. they need to be close to raw material sources) or the skills required (i.e. technology and the mode of production are fixed).

The second interpretation is probably more plausible than the first. The assumption of the geographical immobility of industry may be quite reasonable in respect of the declining industry—for even if it could in principle relocate elsewhere, it would almost certainly be uneconomic to move the capital stock for this purpose, and even less economic to use new capital stock—but it is less plausible in respect of the expanding industry. Certainly, the evidence suggests that expanding industries are in general more footloose than declining ones.

The assumption that the two industries use different, and non-substitutable skills, has much more to recommend it. It is an extreme version of the 'stylized fact' that in inter-war Britain many of the new industries used a somewhat different mode of production from the older industries. By and large, work in the new industries required precision, routine and the monitoring of machinery rather than the application of manual effort. These demands could not be met without retraining workers recruited from the older industries.

Each industry consists of the same fixed number of identical profit-maximizing firms, employing just one variable factor of production: labour. Each firm produces a consumer good under positive but continuously diminishing marginal returns. There is no free production. Each firm in the jth industry demands n_j^d units of labour and supplies y_j^s units of the product.

It is assumed to begin with that the economy is closed. Consumers regard the products of the two industries as perfect substitutes in consumption. Units of the two goods are chosen so that their (constant) marginal rate of substitution is unity. Both product markets are perfectly competitive, so that both goods are traded at the same uniform money price, P. These assumptions about the product market are, of course, very strong. They rule out the possibility that the output of one of the industries is an input to the other. They also rule out the possibility of complementarities in consumption. The assumptions are, however, quite crucial in simplifying the analysis and permitting presentation of the results in diagrammatic terms.

The total number of individuals is equal to the total number of firms. The representative individual has preferences defined over total consumption, labour supply and money balances. Money balances are demanded in order to economize on the transaction costs of acquiring consumer goods; individual utility varies directly with the ratio of nominal money balances to nominal expenditure on consumption.

In the absence of barriers to labour mobility the individual would be prepared to divide his labour supply between the two industries (e.g. by alternating its work between them)—see section 6.5. But because of barriers to labour mobility one group of individuals is constrained to work in one industry and the rest in the other. To simplify matters it is assumed that half of the individuals are attached to each industry. In the light of earlier assumptions this implies that in each industry the number of firms and the number of individuals are equal.

There are no government bonds. Nominal *per capita* government expenditure is fixed exogenously at G. All taxation is lump-sum personal income taxation and is fixed exogenously at the nominal *per capita* level T. The nominal *per capita* money stock at the beginning of the period is M.

It is assumed that the profits of the jth industry are distributed in full to the households who are attached to that industry, and that households correctly anticipate their profit income. This does not mean that the households attached to an industry cooperate in running it; it is merely a simplifying assumption about the distribution of profit rights (i.e. equity holdings) within the economy as a whole, and is of little consequence for the main results.

In the jth industry there is a basic money wage $\bar{W}_j$ which sets a floor to the actual money wage W_j. Under real wage bargaining the basic wage is indexed to the price level, whereas under money wage bargaining it is not. If there is an excess demand for labour in any industry then employers bid up the wage above the basic wage in order to eliminate the excess demand (the consequences of relaxing this assumption are considered in section 6.3 below). Under no circumstances, however, will workers bid down money wages below the basic wage in order to eliminate an excess supply.

Of all the assumptions made, perhaps the most counterintuitive is that the same fixed number of identical firms and individuals is attached to each industry. The rationale of such assumptions was explained in section 4.1. The assumption is made to facilitate consistent aggregation: it is quite inessential so far as the main results are concerned. The assumption enables the macroeconomic relations between firms and individuals to be analysed in terms of the microeconomic relations between a representative pair of firms— one from each industry—and a representative pair of individuals. All macroeconomic relations are simply scaled-up versions of the microeconomic relations between these representative units. This enables the main results to be illustrated using simple notation and simple diagrams.

The representative firm in industry j maximizes nominal profit

$$\Pi_j = P y_j^s - W n_j^s \tag{6.1}$$

subject to the production technology

$$y_j^s = \gamma_j(n_j^d) \tag{6.2}$$

This determines labour demand, product supply and real profit as continuously decreasing functions of the real wage $w_j = W_j/P$:

$$n_j^d = n_j^d(w_j) \atop (-) \tag{6.3}$$

$$y_j^s = y_j^s(w_j) \atop (-) \tag{6.4}$$

$$\pi_j = \pi_j(w_j) \atop (-) \tag{6.5}$$

Let c_j^d be the consumer demand of an individual attached to the jth industry, n_j^s his ordinary labour supply, M_j^d his demand for nominal money balances, and M_j his initial money stock. The individual maximizes the utility function

$$u_j = c_j k_j^\alpha - \varphi(n_j^s) \tag{6.6}$$

where φ', $\varphi'' > 0$, $0 < \alpha < 1$ is a fixed parameter, and

$$k_j = M_j/P c_j^d \tag{6.7}$$

subject to the budget constraint

$$P c_j^d + (M_j^d - M_j) + T = W_j n_j^s + \Pi_j \tag{6.8}$$

which indicates that the sum of consumer expenditure, saving and tax payments must equal the sum of wage and profit income. The first-order conditions for a constrained maximum of (6.6) subject to (6.7) and (6.8) give the individual's labour supply and his demands for consumption and money balances:

$$n_j^s = n_j^s(w_j) \tag{6.9}$$

$$c_j^d = (1-\alpha)x_j \tag{6.10}$$

$$m_j^d = \alpha x_j \tag{6.11}$$

where $m_j^d = M_j^d/P$ and x_j is a measure of post-tax real wealth:

$$x_j = w_j n_j^s + \pi_j + (M_j - T)/P \tag{6.12}$$

The special form of these demand and supply functions was explained in section 4.3.

The government budget constraint asserts that the government budget deficit must be financed by an increase in the money supply:

$$M^s = M + G - T \tag{6.13}$$

A general equilibrium exists when all four markets in the economy clear: the two labour markets, the market for the perfectly substitutable final products, and the money market:

$$n_j^d = n_j^s \qquad (j=1,2) \tag{6.14}$$

$$\sum_{j=1}^{2} c_j^d + G/P = y^s = \sum_{j=1}^{2} y_j^s \tag{6.15}$$

$$\sum_{j=1}^{2} M_j^d = M^s \tag{6.16}$$

Only three of these four equations are independent because of Walras' Law (see section 4.5). Substituting equations (6.3)–(6.5) and (6.9)–(6.13) into equations (6.14)–(6.16) gives three independent equations which determine the equilibrium real wages, w_j^e, and the money price level, P^e. The real wages are determined entirely by real factors—technology and households' taste for leisure—and price is determined by the 'Quantity Theory' equation

$$P^e = [G + (\tfrac{1}{\alpha} - 1)M^s]/y^e \tag{6.17}$$

Substituting the real wages w_j^e back into the labour demand and product supply functions (6.3) and (6.4) determines equilibrium employment and output, n_j^e, y_j^e, in the two industries.

Figure 6.1 illustrates an equilibrium between a pair of representative firms and a pair of representative individuals—one from each industry—but by a simple scaling-up of quantities it also represents the equilibrium of the industries as a whole. Equilibrium in the new industry is shown in the left-hand quadrant and equilibrium in the old industry in the right-hand quadrant. The two industries are

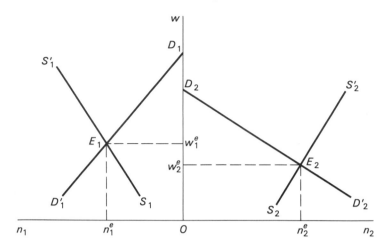

FIGURE 6.1
Full employment equilibrium in a closed two-sector economy

shown back-to-back: the real wage is measured along the vertical axis Ow, employment in the new industry is measured along the horizontal axis On_1, and employment in the old industry along the horizontal axis On_2.

Since by assumption both products are perfectly substitutable on a one-to-one ratio, the value of output in each industry is commensurate with the physical output. Labour demand in the new industry is given by the marginal physical product schedule D_1D_1' and labour demand in the old industry by the corresponding schedule D_2D_2'. Equilibrium in the new industry occurs at the intersection E_1 of D_1D_1' and S_1S_1', and a simultaneous equilibrium occurs in the old industry at the intersection E_2 of D_2D_2' and S_2S_2'. As shown, the equilibrium wage in the old industry, w_2^e, is below that in the new industry, w_1^e, indicating the relatively weak economic position of the labour attached to the old industry. The equilibrium employments are respectively n_1^e and n_2^e. In the new industry the total output is measured by the area $OD_1E_1n_1{}^e$, the real wage bill is $Ow_1^eE_1n_1^e$ and real profit is $D_1E_1w_1^e$. Likewise in the old industry the total output is measured by the area $OD_2E_2n_2^e$, the real wage bill is $Ow_2^eE_2n_2^e$ and real profit is $D_2E_2w_2^e$. The aggregate output of the economy is measured by the area $n_1^eE_1D_1D_2E_2n_2^e$.

6.3 ALTERNATIVE REGIMES

Structural unemployment occurs when the wage in one of the industries is too high relative to the wage in the other.

Suppose to begin with that nominal wages are rigid both upwards and downwards. Under these conditions the money wage relativity fixes the real wage relativity and if this differs from the equilibrium relativity then unemployment is liable to occur.

Unemployment need not be purely structural, though, even when the relativities are wrong. If the *average* money wage is very high relative to the money supply then conventional Keynesian unemployment may occur: individuals' desires to accumulate money balances leads to a failure of consumer demand, prices fall and, with money wages fixed, real wages rise to above their equilibrium level. Firms demand less labour than individuals wish to supply, and unemployment occurs in both industries.

Conversely, it is possible that unemployment may not occur at all, even when the relativities are wrong, if the average money wage is very low relative to the money supply. Individuals' holdings of money balances will be excessive, and attempts to divest these balances will stimulate consumer demand. High product prices, coupled with low money wages, may lead to excess demand for labour throughout the economy.

Altogether there are six possible regimes which may prevail when the economy is out of equilibrium.

(I) General unemployment: there is unemployment in both industries because on average money wages are too high.

(II) General excess demand for labour: there is an excess demand for labour in both industries because on average money wages are too low.

(III) Structural unemployment in the new industry: there is unemployment in the new industry and either full employment or excess demand in the old industry.

(IV) Structural unemployment in the old industry: there is unemployment in the old industry and either full employment or excess demand in the new industry.

(V) Structural excess demand in the new industry: there is excess demand for labour in the new industry and full employment in the old industry.

(VI) Structural excess demand in the old industry: there is excess demand for labour in the old industry and full employment in the new industry.

In all these regimes some form of quantity rationing is experienced in the labour markets. In one or both of the markets either individuals' supply of labour is constrained by the firms' demand, or the firms' demand for labour is constrained by the individuals' supply (though both constraints are never binding at once).

A constraint on an individual's labour supply spills over on to his demands for consumer goods and money balances (see section 4.3). Suppose for example that the money wage in industry j is too high, so that each individual experiences an employment constraint n_j in the labour market. It is assumed that the individual continues to signal the notional labour supply (6.9), though his effective labour supply is reduced to n_j. Because his wage income is now reduced, he will demand fewer consumer goods and fewer money balances than before.

In the case of a constraint on a firm's labour demand the spill-overs are more complicated. A constraint on labour demand affects product supply and also profit. Profit affects the non-wage income received by individuals and this in turn affects consumer demand and the demand for money balances.

Suppose, for example, that the money wage in industry j is too low, so that each firm in industry j experiences an employment constraint n'_j in the labour market. The firm continues to signal the labour demand (6.3) but its actual employment is only

$$n'_j < n_j^d(w_j) \qquad\qquad (6.18)$$

It follows from the production function (6.2) that the actual supply of output is only

$$y'_j = y_j(n'_j) \qquad\qquad (6.19)$$

which is less than the supply of output that would otherwise prevail. Profit is reduced to

$$\pi'_j = y'_j - w_j n'_j \qquad\qquad (6.20)$$

and individuals attached to industry j experience a reduction in their income. This reduces consumer demand, lowers the money price level, and so raises the real wage. This in turn encourages households

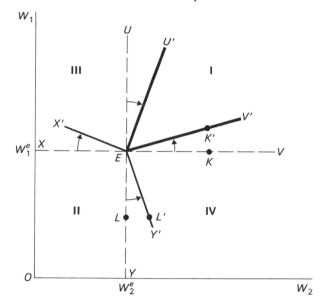

FIGURE 6.2
A classification of regimes in a closed two-sector economy

to increase their labour supply and so helps to alleviate the employment constraint on firms.

Figure 6.2 illustrates the way in which different permutations of employment constraints are associated with the different regimes of the economy. The diagram is drawn conditional upon the money supply and government expenditure and taxation. It assumes that the money price level is endogenous and maintains the product market in equilibrium.

The combination of money wages required for general equilibrium is illustrated by the point E. In the absence of spill-over effects, all points above the horizontal line XEV correspond to an excess supply of labour in the new industry, and all points below it to an excess demand. All points to the right of the vertical line YEU correspond to an excess supply of labour in the old industry, and all points to the left of it to an excess demand. Regime I (general unemployment) therefore corresponds to the set of points in the quadrant UEV to the north-east of E, regime II (general excess demand) to the quadrant XEY to the south-west of E and regimes III and IV to the respective quadrants UEX and VEY to the north-west and south-east of E. Regimes V and VI correspond to points along the respective lines *EY and EX* (the lines *EU* and *EV* are included in the regimes *III* and *IV* respectively).

Spill-over effects cause the quadrants variously to rotate, expand or shrink. Consider, to begin with, a point such as *K,* where the money wage in the old industry is too high, but where, in the absence of spill-overs, the new industry would be in equilibrium. The high money wage discourages firms in the old industry from demanding labour and supplying output. The lack of demand for labour means that individuals attached to the old industry experience an employment constraint. Their real incomes are reduced and they cut back their consumer demand. At the same time they attempt to run down their money balances. Consumer demand actually exceeds product supply in the old industry because employees are financing consumption by attempted dissaving. The product price rises and this stimulates product supply and labour demand in the new industry. Thus the equilibrium wage in the new industry rises. The new industry is no longer in equilibrium at *K,* but at *K'* instead.

Applying this argument to all points on *EV* shows that spill-over effects cause *EV* to rotate anti-clockwise into the north-east quadrant to *EV'*. A similar argument, with the role of the industries reversed, establishes that spill-over effects rotate the line *EU* clockwise to *EU'*.

Consider now a point such as *L,* where in the absence of spill-overs the money wage in the old industry is in equilibrium and there is excess demand for labour in the new industry. The excess demand constrains the employment, and hence the output, of the firms in the new industry. This in turn reduces the income distributed to the workers attached to the new industry. Workers attempt to dissave, and so—in spite of lower incomes—there is an excess demand for the consumer product which can only be eliminated by a rise in money prices. This spills over to stimulate the demand for labour in the old industry. To restore equilibrium in the old industry the money wage must therefore rise. The old industry is therefore no longer in equilibrium at *L* but at *L'* instead. This is illustrated by the fact that the spill-over causes *EY* to rotate anti-clockwise to *EY'*.

A similar argument, with the role of the industries reversed, shows that the spill-over effects rotate the line *EX* clockwise to *EX'*. The net result of all these rotations is that in the wage-space, the area of regime I (general unemployment) contracts, the area of regime II (general excess demand) expands, and the areas of regimes III and IV (structural unemployment) rotate. Regimes V and VI are represented by the lines *EY* and *EX* which rotate to *EY'* and *EX'* respectively.

So far it has been assumed that money wages are rigid both upwards and downwards. It will be assumed throughout the rest of this chapter that in each industry the money wage is flexible upwards in response to excess demands. In this case an excess demand in any market will be eliminated by wage inflation; competition between employers in the industry will cause the wage rate to 'drift' up above the basic wage. Money wage adjustments will transfer any point in the regimes II, III, IV into a point on the locus $U'EV''$ which bounds these regimes from above. The locus represents points at which one of the industries is at full employment while the other experiences unemployment. Thus observable money wage combinations are confined to the boundary and the interior of the segment $U'EV'$.

This analysis has important implications for the role of monetary policy in an economy suffering from structural imbalance (cf. Barro and Grossman, 1976, ch. 5). In the simple model above monetary expansion is effected by government expenditure. Suppose to begin with that the economy is in regime I, with unemployment in both industries—though concentrated chiefly in the old one. Government expenditure raises final product demand, forcing up prices and encouraging firms to expand employment and output. The additional employment has a multiplier effect in raising personal incomes. It also encourages increased saving, but this is easily accommodated because the stock of money in circulation is rising at the same time.

The increased product demand will be distributed between the two industries in such a way that the ratio of their marginal productivities remains constant (this is because relative money wages, and hence relative real wages, do not change). There is a certain level of government expenditure, however, at which the new industry will become fully employed. Beyond this point additional labour supply will not be forthcoming. If money wages are flexible upwards then monetary expansion will generate wage inflation in the new industry.

For very large expansionary measures, full employment may be achieved in both industries. Beyond this point further government expenditure will be purely inflationary and supply response will be zero. The inflation–unemployment trade-off for a structurally un-balanced economy is represented by the schedule *GHJK* in figure 6.3. Movement along the schedule from *G* is generated by expansionary policy. Low levels of government expenditure move the economy along a mildly inflationary path to *H,* reducing unemployment in both industries. More substantial government expenditure moves the economy on to the segment *HJ* where the new industry is at full employment and 'wage drift' begins to occur. Very large government expenditure moves the economy on to the segment *JK* where unemployment is eliminated in both industries and further expansion is absorbed entirely by wage and price inflation.

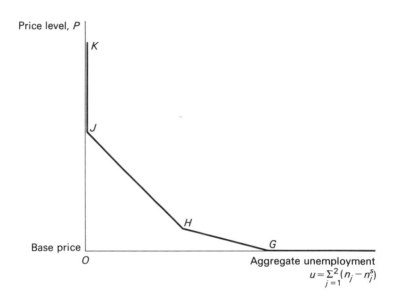

FIGURE 6.3
A Phillips curve generated by expansionary policies applied to a structurally unbalanced economy

The schedule *GHJK* resembles in many respects the familiar Phillips curve (see e.g. Jackman, Mulvey and Trevithick, 1981). The Phillips curve is often explained in purely macroeconomic terms, by arguing that an excess supply of labour depresses the average level of money wage settlements. One of the main strengths of the derivation above is that it turns the heterogeneity of industries to advantage by explaining the form of the curve in terms of *differential* inflation rates and unemployment rates (see also Corry and Laidler, 1967, and Vanderkamp, 1968).

6.4 STRUCTURAL DISEQUILIBRIUM UNDER REAL WAGE BARGAINING

The discussion in the previous section was predicated upon money wage bargaining, but, as emphasized earlier, the Pre-Keynesian economists preferred to assume real wage bargaining. The assumption of real wage bargaining considerably simplifies the analysis because it means that the spill-over effects between industries are neutralized. A change in the real wage in one industry affects the money price level, just as a change in the money wage does. An increase in the real wage, for example, reduces product supply. It also cuts product demand, by reducing the income of households attached to the industry. The reduction in demand is less than the reduction in supply, however, because the households will attempt to maintain their consumption by running down their money balances. As a result, money prices will be bid up. The important point is that with real wage bargaining the money wage in the other industry is indexed to the price level. The money wage will therefore adjust to leave the real wage unchanged and hence output and employment in the other industry will be unaffected. Since real wage bargaining eliminates inter-industry spill-overs, it effectively reverses the rotation of the regime boundaries illustrated in figure 6.2.

Using the real wage bargaining assumption it is possible to restate simply the gist of the Pre-Keynesian debate over the relationship between structural unemployment and vacancies (see section 3.5). The form of structural unemployment visualized by Pigou is illustrated in figure 6.4. It is assumed that initially there is no wage differential between the two industries, so that the weaker position of the declining industry is not reflected in the relative wage. It may be, for example, that trade unions in the weaker industry are attempting to maintain a relativity that existed before the industry went into decline. To simplify the diagram it is assumed that this relativity is unity. At the uniform wage w', unemployment A_2A_2' in the old industry is matched by an equal number of unfilled vacancies A_1A_1' in the new industry. Employment in both industries is below the equilibrium level. It is low in the new industry because of labour supply constraints and in the old industry because of labour demand constraints.

Structural Disequilibrium

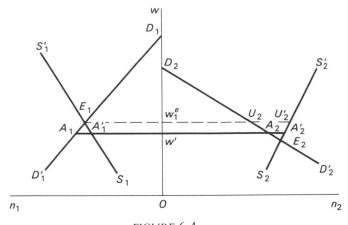

FIGURE 6.4
Structural wage adjustments

If wages are flexible upwards then competition between employers in the new industry will bid up the wage to w_1^c, eliminating the labour supply constraint and restoring employment to its equilibrium level. This gives the kind of situation visualized by Clay, in which wages in the old industry are lower than wages in the new industry, but are not low enough, with the result that unemployment is concentrated in the low-wage industry.

It is possible, though, that trade unions in the old industry will attempt to maintain relativities by forcing up the wage in the old industry to w_1^c. Employment in the new industry is unaffected, but unemployment in the old industry is worsened considerably. The new industry remains in equilibrium at E_1, but the old industry experiences unemployment of $U_2 U_2' > A_2 A_2'$.

The possibility emphasized by Pool, that the equilibrium real wage in the new industry would be consolidated into the basic wage, does not directly affect the level of unemployment illustrated in the figure; it simply strengthens the barriers to mobility that underlie the structural problem that is being modelled in the first place. It may be added as a rider, however, that if the equilibrium wage in the new industry is consolidated into the basic wage then it is more probable, in practice, that trade unions in the old industry will attempt to maintain the original relativity.

The simple diagrammatic analysis gives a powerful illustration of how Pre-Keynesian theory can be formulated in disequilibrium terms. The downward rigidity of the real wage captures the 'stylized fact' that in the declining industry the real wage is too high. The wage is too high, not in absolute terms, but relative to productivity in the industry. This productivity in turn depends upon two main factors: the technology and working practices of the industry, and consumer's valuation of its output (relative to the output of the expanding industry). The analysis does not imply that the real wage is higher in the declining industry than in the expanding industry: it may well be lower, but it is simply not low enough. During the inter-war period, wages in the declining industries fell relative to wages in the expanding industries, but this did not prevent the contraction of employment in the declining industries. The disequilibrium model suggests that it was resistance to further reductions in wages in the declining industries that contributed to the rising unemployment in those industries. This resistance may not, in itself, have been the cause of the decline, but it certainly exacerbated it.

6.5   LABOUR MOBILITY

This section explores the connection between structural unemployment and labour mobility. The analysis is based upon the concept of job search introduced in section 5.1. The job search concept is tailormade for the analysis of labour mobility—indeed it is best known to modern economists from theories of rural–urban migration (Harris and Todaro, 1970). The theory has also been used to analyse migration between the union and non-union sectors of an economy; in this context, Pigou's original insights, described in section 3.3, have been recently rediscovered by a number of writers (Collier and Pemberton, 1981; Minford, 1981; Pemberton, 1981).

In a multi-sectoral economy where wage rates are generally too high, mobile workers have a choice of labour pools to join. Each labour pool is attached to a particular industry: it consists of a collection of unemployed workers who either search around for work, or wait for employers to approach them (e.g. they stand in a hiring line). Individuals cannot belong to more than one pool at a time, though they may alternate between them. Individual decisions on which pools to join determine labour migration between different sectors of the economy. Migration decisions are influenced both by wage relativities and by the relative sizes of the pools in the different sectors. Migration leads to an equilibrium distribution of the work-force which has important implications for the sectoral incidence of unemployment.

The job search model is derived by relaxing the assumptions about labour supply made in section 6.2. Households are no longer attached to particular industries; they are everywhere identical. The representative household has a utility function

$$u = c^d k^\alpha - \sigma(n_{a1}^s, n_{a2}^s) \tag{6.21}$$

where n_{aj}^s is the active labour supply to the jth industry and σ is a twice-differentiable strictly quasi-concave function implying substitutability rather than complementarity between labour supplies, i.e. the partial derivatives of σ satisfy the conditions

$$\sigma_1, \sigma_2, \sigma_{11}, \sigma_{22}, \sigma_{12} > 0, \quad \sigma_{11}\sigma_{22} - \sigma_{12}^2 > 0 \tag{6.22}$$

Note that the subscript j has now been dropped in respect of household consumption c, and the money balance ratio, k.

Implicit in this formulation is the idea that the representative household can divide its time between the two labour pools, but is averse to spending all of its time in any one of the pools and none of its time in the other. The intuition underlying the assumption that labour supplies are substitutes rather than complements is that as the amount of work supplied to one industry increases the marginal dis-utility of work in the other industry increases too. This is reflected in the sign restriction on the cross-derivative σ_{12}. The condition is analogous to the cardinalist concept of substitutability favoured by Auspitz, Lieben, Edgeworth, Pareto and Pigou. It differs, however, in that the restriction is applied only to the function σ and not to the function u itself; as is well known, a cross-derivative sign restriction on u is not invariant with respect to an arbitrary monotone transformation of the kind admissible in ordinal utility theory.

This formulation of the household utility function is intended to capture the fact that in the real world some people prefer to work in one industry and other people in another, so that a change in relative wages will induce some people to switch industries, but that a small change in relative wages will affect only a small number of people who are at the margin of indifference between work in the industries concerned. A change in regional wage differentials, for example, will encourage some workers to migrate, but will not induce migration amongst the workers who are most strongly committed to the region in which they live.

The budget constraint of the representative household is

$$Pc^d + (M^d - M) + T = \sum_{j=1}^{2}(\hat{W}_j n_{aj}^s + \Pi_j) \tag{6.23}$$

where $\hat{W}_j$ is the expected money wage in industry j. Maximising (6.21) subject to (6.23) gives the household demand and supply functions

$$n_{a1}^s = n_{a1}^s(\hat{w}_1, \hat{w}_2) \tag{6.24}$$
$$(+) \ (-)$$

$$n_{a2}^s = n_{a2}^s(\hat{w}_1, \hat{w}_2) \tag{6.25}$$
$$(-) \ (+)$$

$$c^d = (1-\alpha)x' \tag{6.26}$$

$$m^d = \alpha x' \tag{6.27}$$

where $\hat{w}_j$ is the expected real wage in industry j and x' is a measure of post-tax real wealth:

$$x' = \sum_{j=1}^{2}(\hat{w}_j n_{aj}^s + \pi_j) + (M-T)/P \tag{6.28}$$

It is worth noting that the wage-sensitivities of the labour supplies are determined solely by the second derivatives of labour disutility, σ. Differentiating the first-order conditions for a maximum of (6.21) with respect to the expected wages shows that

$$\partial n_{ai}^s/\partial \hat{w}_j = \sigma_{ij}/(\sigma_{11}\sigma_{22} - \sigma_{12}^2) \qquad (i, j = 1, 2) \tag{6.29}$$

The simplicity of this result is due once again to the absence of income effects on labour supply.

Job search behaviour of the kind described here is relevant only when there is an excess supply of labour, and so attention will be focused at the outset on just three regimes. In two of these regimes one of the labour markets is at full employment while the other experiences unemployment. In the third regime both markets experience unemployment. In all of these regimes the expected real wage in each market satisfies the equation

$$w_j n_j^d + a_j = \hat{w}_j n_{aj}^s \tag{6.30}$$

where a_j is the real unemployment benefit payment in industry j:

$$a_j = b(n_{aj}^s - n_j^s) \tag{6.31}$$

In each of the three regimes

$$n^s_{aj} \geqslant n_j = n^d_j \tag{6.32}$$

so that substituting (6.31) into (6.30) gives

$$(w_j - b)n^d_j(w_j) = (\hat{w}_j - b)n^s_{aj}(\hat{w}_1, \hat{w}_2) \tag{6.33}$$

When there is real wage bargaining the values of w_1 and w_2 are fixed, so that (6.33) constitutes a pair of simultaneous equations which can be solved for the expected wages $\hat{w}_j$. Suppose to begin with that unemployment benefit is ignored (it is discussed later in section 6.6). The expected wage combinations giving equilibrium in industry 1 are illustrated in figure 6.5 by the locus $Z_1 Z'_1$, likewise the expected wage combinations giving equilibrium in industry 2 are illustrated by the locus $Z_2 Z'_2$. Under the assumed conditions both loci are upward-sloping from left to right, with $Z_2 Z'_2$ sloping more steeply than $Z_1 Z'_1$. The equilibrium expected wages w^E_1, w^E_2 are determined at the intersection Y of $Z_1 Z'_1$ and $Z_2 Z'_2$.

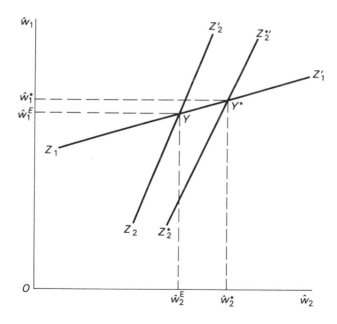

FIGURE 6.5
Determination of a structural unemployment equilibrium with labour mobility

It is readily established that wage adjustments are stabilizing in a Walrasian sense. Imagine that there is an auctioneer who quotes trial expected wages for each industry. From the trial expected wage the representative household calculates its active labour supplies, while the auctioneer himself calculates how much labour supply would have to be attracted to each industry if the expected wage he has quoted were to prevail. The auctioneer's calculations lead him to 'pseudo-demands' for job seekers in each industry. He compares these with the active labour supplies and if there is an excess of pseudo-demand over supply then the expected wage quote is revised upwards; conversely if there is a shortfall of pseudo-demand with respect to supply then the expected wage quote is revised down-wards. In the diagram, points above $Z_1 Z_1'$ attract an excessive active supply of labour to industry 1 and tend to depress the expected wage $\hat{w}_1$. Points to the right of $Z_2 Z_2'$ attract an excessive active supply of labour to industry 2 and tend to depress the expected wage $\hat{w}_2$. It follows that any trial wage combination in any segment of the wage-space sets up adjustments in the direction of the equilibrium Y.

It is, of course, unrealistic to assume that in practice there is a Walrasian auctioneer. Indeed, the inspiration for recent develop-ments in disequilibrium theory came from the rejection of the idea of a Walrasian auctioneer. In the absence of an auctioneer, stability cannot be guaranteed. 'Cobweb' effects may emerge, in which an excessive initial allocation of labour to one industry depresses the average wage so much that, with stationary expectations of the future wage, there is a massive exodus of labour to the other industry, where a similar problem then arises the following period. This process could well generate explosive oscillations in the allocation of labour between industries and in the expected wage relativity. The fact that such oscillations do not normally occur may be ascribed to personal inertia, which reduces the speed with which households react to changes in the expected relative wage.

Despite its dynamical limitations, the model has considerable practical relevance. In particular it explains how regional unemploy-ment differentials can persist in the face of quite significant levels of interregional migration. This is illustrated by the following example.

Suppose that industry 1 is a prosperous industry, while industry 2 is in decline. Workers, however, are strongly attached to the declining industry because of its traditional craftsmanship and work organization. Initially real wages in both industries are too high, but most of the unemployment is concentrated in the declining industry. The real wage in the declining industry is then marginally reduced to w_2^* in order to stimulate employment. Differentiating equation (6.33) and setting $b=0$ shows that unemployment in the declining industry will fall at a rate

$$du_{a2}/dw_2 = n_2^d[\{(1-\eta_2^d)\,(\hat{\eta}_{12}^s\hat{\eta}_{21}^s\hat{w}_2 + \hat{\eta}_{22}^s(1+\hat{\eta}_{11}^s)\hat{w}_1)/(\psi\hat{w}_1\hat{w}_2)\} + (\eta_2^d/w_2)] \quad (6.34)$$

where

$$\psi = (1+\hat{\eta}_{11}^s)\,(1+\hat{\eta}_{22}^s) - \hat{\eta}_{12}^s\hat{\eta}_{21}^s$$

and

$$\hat{\eta}_{ii}^s = (\partial n_{ai}^s/\partial \hat{w}_i)(\hat{w}_i/n_{ai}^s)$$

$$\hat{\eta}_{ij}^s = - (\partial n_{ai}^s/\partial \hat{w}_j)(\hat{w}_j/n_{ai}^s) \qquad\qquad (i,\ j=1,\ 2;\ j\neq i) \qquad (6.35)$$

The implications of equation (6.34) are most easily considered in diagrammatic terms.

As noted in section 5.3, the effect of a wage cut on the expected wage depends upon the elasticity of labour demand. If the elasticity is less than unity then the expected wage will fall. Geometrically, the locus Z_2Z_2' will shift to the left and the expected wage in both industries will fall. The expected wage in the declining industry will normally fall farthest, and this will tend to reduce the relative expected wage, and so encourage labour to migrate out to the prosperous industry.

If, however, the elasticity of demand in the declining industry is greater than unity then the expected wage will rise. Geometrically, the locus Z_2Z_2' will shift to the right, say to $Z_2^*Z_2^{*'}$, giving a new equilibrium Y^* where both expected wages are higher than before. As illustrated, the expected wage relativity has now moved in favour of the declining industry, and this will stimulate inward migration of labour. Although labour demand has increased, labour supply has increased also, and so unemployment will fall by less than employment has been increased. In the prosperous industry unemployment has fallen too, since labour demand is unchanged but labour supply has been reduced. In an extreme case the exodus of labour from the prosperous industry may be sufficiently large that the main effect of employment creation in the declining industry is to reduce unemployment in the prosperous industry, with unemployment in the declining industry remaining virtually unchanged.

6.6 UNEMPLOYMENT BENEFIT AND STRUCTURAL ADJUSTMENT

Unemployment benefit can influence the relative incidence of unemployment on different groups of workers. This is because unemployment benefit is normally paid at a standard rate throughout the economy whilst workers attached to different industries or different regions receive different rates of wages. The effect will be different, of course, if an earnings-related supplement is paid, but this qualification has little relevance to inter-war Britain. When unemployment benefit is paid at a standard rate, the replacement ratio is highest in the low-wage industries. Evidence that unemployment is high in low-wage occupations is sometimes used to support the view that unemployment benefit is a major cause of unemployment.

Differentiating equation (6.33) with respect to b shows that

$$du_{ai}/db = \sum_{j=1}^{2} (\partial n_{ai}^s/\partial \hat{w}_j) d\hat{w}_j/db \qquad (i, j = 1, 2) \tag{6.36}$$

$$d\hat{w}_i/db = [n_i^d u_{aj} \hat{\eta}_{bij}^s + n_{aj}^s u_{ai}(1 + \hat{\eta}_{bjj}^s)] / \theta \qquad (i, j = 1, 2, j \neq i) \tag{6.37}$$

with

$$\theta = (1 - \hat{\eta}_{b11}^s)(1 + \hat{\eta}_{b22}^s) n_{a1}^s n_{a2}^s - \hat{\eta}_{b12}^s \hat{\eta}_{b21}^s n_1^d n_2^d \tag{6.38}$$

$$\hat{\eta}_{bii}^s = (\partial n_{ai}^s/\partial \hat{w}_i)(\hat{w}_i - b)/n_{ai}^s.$$

$$\qquad (i, j = 1, 2, j \neq i) \tag{6.39}$$

$$\hat{\eta}_{bij}^s = -(\partial n_{ai}^s/\partial \hat{w}_j)(\hat{w}_j - b)/n_{ai}^s$$

Since the elasticities (6.39) are always positive, it follows from equation (6.37) that an increase in unemployment benefit will increase the expected wage if $\theta > 0$. Inspection of equation (6.38) shows that since own-expected wage elasticities normally exceed cross-expected wage elasticities, the condition $\theta > 0$ is usually satisfied. The increase in the expected wages creates a tendency for unemployment in both industries to rise. The distribution of unemployment between industries will, however, be affected by the migration of labour induced by the movement in the relative expected wage. The expected wage is likely to increase most in the low-wage industry, and is likely to increase more the higher the rate of unemployment there. A low-wage industry with initially heavy unemployment is therefore likely to attract inward migration, which will further concentrate unemployment upon it. Thus a rise in unemployment benefit may exacerbate inequalities in the incidence of unemployment between industries by making low-wage industries with heavy unemployment relatively more attractive than they were, and so encouraging labour to migrate to them. This supports the view that, in inter-war Britain, unemployment benefit may have exacerbated the structural unemployment problem by encouraging labour not to move from the declining industries or, in some cases, perhaps, by encouraging those who had already moved away to return to them.

6.7   STRUCTURAL DISEQUILIBRIUM IN AN OPEN ECONOMY

The Pre-Keynesian economists recognized that the structural problems of the British economy were intimately connected with its decline in international competitiveness during the inter-war period—as reflected, for example, in its falling share of world trade. Modelling fully the disequilibrium of an open economy involves a number of complexities which would be outside the scope of the present book (see e.g. Dixit, 1978; Neary, 1980; Johansson and Lofgren, 1981; Steigum, 1981; Lorie and Sheen, 1982). The present analysis has a very limited objective: to extend the model of section 6.4 to the case where the products of the two industries are internationally traded.

It is assumed that the declining industry (industry 2) produces a good which is sold exclusively for export, and that the new industry (industry 1) produces an import-substituting good. This is intended as a stylized picture of the inter-war British economy. Domestic consumers have no taste for the exported good and consume only the import-substituting good. There is real wage bargaining in both industries, where the real wage is defined, of course, with respect to the domestically consumed good. It is assumed that the exported good is slightly differentiated from the exported products of other countries, due, for example, to the good-will (or ill-will, perhaps) attaching to the country of production. It is suggested, for example, that goods with a 'Made in Britain' label are perceived slightly differently abroad from goods made elsewhere.

It is assumed that exchange risk is negligible, so that it is reasonable to postulate a version of purchasing power parity in which the relative price of the export good in terms of the import good is determined, independently of monetary factors, by tastes and technology alone. Because of the differentiated nature of the product, the demand for the export good, y_2^d, is a decreasing function of the relative export price, λ:

$$y_2^d = y_2^d(\lambda) \tag{6.40}$$
$$(-)$$

(In the case where export markets are perfectly competitive λ is parametric; by redefining the units of the export good it is then possible to normalize λ to unity, and the extension of the model to an open economy becomes completely trivial.)

Export supply is determined by the maximisation of the profit of the representative firm:

$$\Pi_2' = P_1 \lambda y_2^s - W_2 n_2^d \tag{6.41}$$

The labour demand and product supply functions derived from (6.41) are

$$n_2^d = n_2^d(w_2/\lambda) \tag{6.42}$$
$$(-)$$

$$y_2^s = y_2^s(w_2/\lambda) \tag{6.43}$$
$$(-)$$

where $w_2 = W_2/P_1$ is the export industry real wage. Since labour is now once again assumed to be immobile between sectors, the supply of labour to the export industry depends only upon the export industry real wage:

$$n_2^s = n_2^s(w_2) \tag{6.44}$$
$$(+)$$

Substituting equations (6.40) and (6.42)–(6.44) into the equilibrium conditions for the labour and product markets in the export industry gives a pair of simultaneous equations for the real wage and the terms of trade:

$$n_2^d(w_2/\lambda) = n_2^s(w_2) \tag{6.45}$$
$$y_2^d(\lambda) = y_2^s(w_2/\lambda) \tag{6.46}$$

Equilibrium in the import-substituting industry labour market determines that industry's real wage:

$$n_1^d(w_1) = n_1^s(w_1) \tag{6.47}$$

where $w_1 = W_1/P_1$. Equilibrium in the import-substituting industry product market gives the familiar price equation

$$P_1 = [G + (\tfrac{1}{a} - 1)M^s]/\gamma' \tag{6.48}$$

where γ' is the total value of output in terms of the domestically consumed good:

$$\gamma' = \gamma_1 + \lambda\gamma_2 \tag{6.49}$$

The condition for the stability of equilibrium in the export industry is

$$1 + \left(\frac{\gamma_2^d \eta_\gamma^d}{\gamma_2^s \eta_\gamma^s} \right) \left(1 + \frac{n_2^d \eta_n^d}{n_2^s \eta_n^s} \right) > 0 \tag{6.50}$$

where the elasticities

$$\begin{aligned}
\eta_n^d &= -(dn_2^d/d(w_2/\lambda))w_2/\lambda n_2^d \\
\eta_\gamma^d &= -(d\gamma_2^d/d\lambda)\lambda/\gamma_2^d \\
\eta_\gamma^s &= -(d\gamma_2^s/d(w_2/\lambda))w_2/\lambda\gamma_2^s
\end{aligned} \tag{6.51}$$

are all positive. It follows that the condition (6.50) is always satisfied.

Equilibrium in the export industry is illustrated in figure 6.6. Labour market equilibrium is represented by the locus NN'; points below NN' correspond to an excess demand for labour, and points above it to an excess supply. Product market equilibrium is represented by the locus YY'; points to the left of it correspond to an excess demand for the product, and points to the right of it correspond to an excess supply. The locus YY' cuts NN' from below, indicating that the stability condition is satisfied. Full employment equilibrium is at the intersection E of NN' and YY', giving the full employment real wage w_2^c and the full employment terms of trade λ^c.

Suppose now that the real wage in the export industry is set too high at $w_2^* > w_2^c$. Firms reduce output and employment, creating a scarcity of the export good which is reflected in a marginal improvement in the terms of trade. Workers are forced off their supply curve (6.44), and unemployment prevails. Geometrically, the equilibrium point moves away from E along the product market locus to F, which lies above the labour market locus NN'. The effect of a high

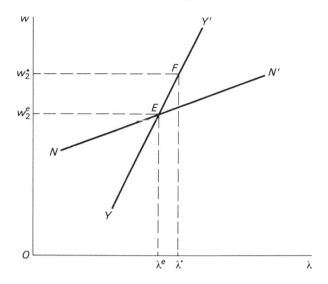

FIGURE 6.6
Equilibrium in an export industry

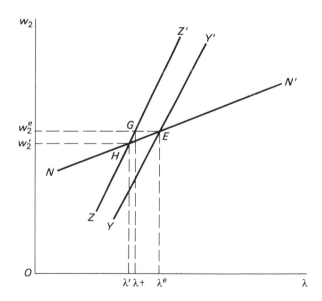

FIGURE 6.7
Effects of a decline in export demand

real wage, therefore, is to simultaneously reduce exports, create unemployment and improve the terms of trade.

A change in world trading conditions will be reflected in a shift in the product market locus YY'. Suppose, for example, that there is a move toward protection in traditional export markets. The demand curve (6.40) will shift inwards, so that less is demanded at any given price. In figure 6.7 the product market locus YY' shifts to the left to ZZ', indicating that the new full employment equilibrium H involves a lower real wage, w_2', and a deterioration in the terms of trade to λ'. If the real wage fails to adjust then the deterioration in the terms of trade will be partially arrested at $\lambda\dagger$, and the economy will move instead to G, where the real wage is still w_2' and unemployment prevails.

It is important to note that because real wage bargaining is assumed, this behaviour is invariant with respect to the exchange rate regime. Given the assumptions made earlier, the relation between real wages, unemployment and the terms of trade is the same whether the exchange rate is fixed or floating. If domestic currency is convertible at a fixed exchange rate then an increase in the money supply is neutralized by a once-for-all currency outflow. As domestic prices rise the demand for imports increases, and a balance of payments deficit ensues. The export of currency reduces the domestic money supply until prices have been restored to their original level; this occurs when the money supply too is back at its original level. If, on the other hand, the exchange rate is floating, then the increase in the money price level is neutralized, not by the export of currency, but by a depreciation of the exchange rate coupled with a rise in money wage rates; the former neutralizes the effect on the terms of trade while the latter neutralizes the effect on the real wage.

It is not difficult, in principle, to extend this analysis to an economy in which labour is mobile. The model becomes more complex because in each industry the labour supply is affected by the expected wage in the other industry. The implications of this interdependence were explored in sections 6.5 and 6.6, and the results derived there still apply even when the products are tradeable. An extension of the formal model does not provide any new insights. Changes in the pattern of international demand impact upon the export industry through the export product market. This feeds through to employment in the export industry, which in turn affects the expected wage. The change in the expected wage alters the wage relativity and induces labour migration. The interaction of the change in employment and the change in the supply of labour causes changes in the aggregate level and in the structure of unemployment.

6.8 SUMMARY

This chapter has used a two-sector model to examine the causes and consequences of structural unemployment under a variety of assumptions. It has been assumed throughout, however, that the outputs of the two sectors are substitutable. Substitutability reflects either the nature of consumer tastes in the domestic market (when the economy is closed), or the opportunities for exchanging export goods for import goods (when the economy is open).

Under money wage bargaining, changes in product prices generate spill-over effects between industries, but these effects are neutralized under real wage bargaining. This means that when there is real wage bargaining, the problem of structural unemployment can be analyzed on an industry-by-industry basis. An economy in which real wages in some industries are much more out of line with productivity than in others has a structural problem. The question of whether there are labour shortages elsewhere in the economy is not necessarily relevant.

Immobility of labour exacerbates structural problems. The Pre-Keynesians were inclined to assume that immobility was caused by obstacles to movement outside the worker's control. But immobility may simply reflect worker's preferences for the kind of employment offered in declining industries. In the latter case workers may be reluctant to migrate out of the industry when labour demand contracts, and if they do migrate out, they may migrate back again if labour demand temporarily expands. In this case fluctuations in demand may well be accompanied by migration flows, but over the cycle the level of unemployment will remain persistently higher in the declining industries. This shows that long-run strong structural problems can persist even in the face of substantial short-run migration flows.

7

Policies for Structural Unemployment

7.1 INDUSTRIAL TRANSFERENCE

This chapter discusses four of the Pre-Keynesian policy prescriptions
for structural unemployment:

(1) industrial transference;
(2) employment subsidies;
(3) selective protection; and
(4) rationalization.

It compares these policies with the Keynesian policy of selective
regional investment which was advocated in the thirties by Austin
Robinson.

Industrial transference seems, at first sight, to be an obvious
remedy for structural unemployment. Cannan (1928, 1930) certainly
had no doubts on this score:

The true remedy for long-term unemployment always applied throughout
history, and always effectual, is . . . redistribution of labour-force between
the different occupations. When there are more people offering to do some
particular kind of work than can be employed in it without reducing the
advantages much below that of other occupations, surely the obvious and
certain remedy is a redistribution of labour-force in the shape of a decrease
of the number of persons offering to work in the depressed trade and an
increase of persons working in the others. In most cases the redistribution
required is not very great and sudden, and it is consequently carried out
almost imperceptibly by the non-replacement of the persons who drop out
of the industry owing to death or old age or any other reason. But
sometimes, as now certainly in the case of coal, the required redistribution
is so great and sudden that it necessitates the transfer of some individuals
from the depressed industry to others (Cannan, 1930, pp. 50–1).

The benefits of industrial transference are illustrated in figure 7.1,
which is based upon figure 6.4. Suppose that the skill levels required,

and the general agreeableness of work, is the same in both industries. If a uniform wage were set at the level $\bar{w}$ then the unemployment in the old industry would be matched by an equal number of vacancies in the new industry. If surplus labour A_2A_2' is transferred from the old industry to the new, then the potential loss of output in the old industry is measured by the shaded area $H_2A_2F_2H_2'$, while the potential gain of output in the new industry is $H_1A_1GH_1'$. Since labour is more productive in the new industry than in the old, there is a net increase in output. In the left-hand quadrant of the figure the area $H_1F_1A_1'H_1'$ corresponds to the loss of potential output in the old industry, and so the net potential gain is measured by the area $F_1A_1GA_1'$. In fact, since the labour transferred from the old industry would quite probably have remained unemployed, there may be no loss of output in the old industry whatsoever. In this case the gain from industrial transfer is measured by the whole area $H_1A_1GH_1'$.

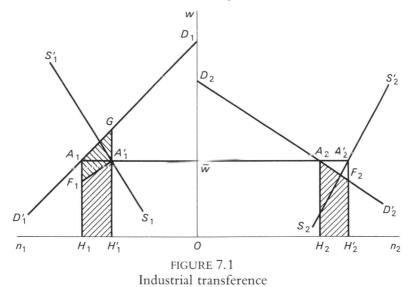

FIGURE 7.1
Industrial transference

As noted earlier, advocates of industrial transference tended to assume that the only obstacles to mobility were market failures—lack of information about vacancies, barriers to change of residence because of the non-price rationing of housing, underinvestment in training of employers who are unable to 'lock in' their employees, and so on. Most advocates of transference gave only cursory consideration to the possibility that immobility may reflect personal preferences (though Pigou was a notable exception to this).

Job evaluation may suggest that work in two industries is equivalent, but it may not be rated as such by the people concerned. Workers in the old industry may be strongly attached to families and friends, or be committed to the trade and its pattern of work organization. This is very likely to be true of older workers with long and continuous service in the industry, who may prefer premature retirement—with the prospect of occasional recall—to regular employment in another industry. The strength of this attachment may also be influenced by the unemployment benefit system. As noted earlier, because unemployment benefit is paid at a uniform rate across all industries, the replacement ratio is highest in the low-wage industries, which tend, as Clay noted, to be also the most depressed ones. The Pre-Keynesians were, however, reluctant to recommend a reduction in unemployment benefit on these grounds, although they were adamant that benefits should not be paid for long to workers who refused to contemplate taking work outside their usual trade or district (on this particular point see the trenchant remarks of Beveridge (1931)).

The transfer of people who are strongly attached to the old industry may induce a long-term loss of welfare which must be set against the potential gain in real output. Indeed, if dissatisfaction with work in the new industry causes effort to diminish, the potential increase in real output may not be achieved. There is no guarantee, therefore, that a policy of subsidizing industrial transfer, or placing people who are eligible for transfer under duress to comply with the policy, will on balance improve social welfare. It may do so, but more needs to be known about the reasons why people resist voluntary transfer, before a definite judgement can be reached.

7.2 EMPLOYMENT SUBSIDIES

If industrial transference is ruled out then an obvious alternative is a selective employment subsidy for the depressed industry. Pigou (1927a), in conjunction with Ramsey, developed a simple model of employment subsidies which anticipates some recent work by Layard (1981), Layard and Nickell (1980) and others.

Suppose that the new industry is in equilibrium but that in the old industry the real wage is too high. Following Pigou, assume that the labour supply in the old industry is totally inelastic, as indicated by the schedule S_2S_2' in figure 7.2. At the prevailing real wage w_2' unemployment is A_2A_2'. The wage would have to fall to $w_2^e < w_2'$ to achieve full employment at E_2. Suppose that unemployment benefit is paid at a rate $b < w_2^e$, financed out of employers' profit, and that a subsidy $s = w_2' - w_2^e$ is offered on each employee. The introduction of the subsidy will shift the demand for labour D_2D_2' up to F_2F_2' and restore full employment at A_2'. Output in the industry will rise on average by $w_2' + (1/2)s$ per additional person employed. The additional income is distributed between the newly employed workers, who each receive $w_2' - b$ more, and the employers who save on average $b - (1/2)s$ on each additional employee. As Pigou points out, both employers and employees gain provided that $s < 2b$, i.e. provided that the rate of subsidy is less than twice the unemployment benefit rate.

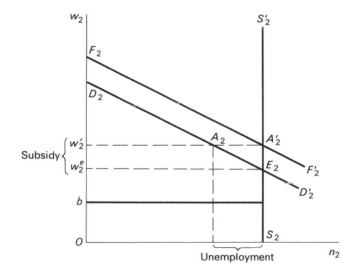

FIGURE 7.2
Effects of an employment subsidy

Pigou assumes that the subsidy is financed out of a tax on profits in the same industry. In this case it makes no difference to the representative employer whether the subsidy is paid only on the marginal worker or on intramarginal workers too—i.e. on workers who would be employed even in the absence of the subsidy. The amount the employer pays in taxes is recouped immediately in the form of a subsidy. If, however, the burden of taxation falls outside the industry, then there is a strong case for reducing the burden by confining the subsidy, where practical, to marginal workers only. Pigou does not consider this possibility.

Pigou is fairly cautious in recommending subsidies as a practical measure. His results, he points out, assume that there is no industrial mobility of labour, so that everyone who is put to work in the subsidized industry would otherwise be idle. If there is mobility, however, selective subsidies will attract workers to the most heavily subsidized industries, or at least discourage people from leaving them, and so help to perpetuate the structural problem. Pigou therefore argues for a non-selective subsidy which will not distort the long-run allocation of labour between industries. This argument overlooks, however, that a uniform rate of subsidy will do nothing to alter the effective wage differentials (i.e. differentials net of subsidy) facing employers, and therefore do nothing to alleviate the specifically structural aspects of unemployment. Uniform subsidies will reduce unemployment in the depressed industries only at the expense of wage inflation in the prosperous fully employed industries.

Pigou's chief concern is that selective subsidies will lead to strategic lobbying by special-interest groups. This seems to be a development of Marshall's view that the subsidization of an industry leads to the replacement of cost-minimizing firms by grant-maximizing firms. Subsidies weaken the market discipline on collective bargaining, and create a continuous upward spiral of rates of subsidy and consequently, of rates of taxation.

At the present time the relatively distressed engineering and ship-building industries would certainly demand more favourable treatment than, say, the railway industry. As the demand for the products of any industry fell off and distress became more pronounced, higher subsidies, both absolutely and relatively to those ruling in other industries, would always be called for. Such pleas would often be acceded to. As a consequence, too many people would be set to and kept at work in some industries and too few in others. Extraordinary strength and competence on the part of the Government would be needed to prevent a policy of wage subsidies from acting in this way. If these were not forthcoming the resulting social loss might well be large. There is also a second serious danger. If the Government were in a position to control the wage demands of the workpeople as well as the amount of the subsidies, and if it were absolutely impervious to political pressure, the adoption of the above policy would not lead to any change in the rate of wages demanded. In practice, however, once the policy was adopted and, as a result of it, unemployment reduced to a low level, there would be a strong temptation to workpeople to demand higher wage-rates, while employers, hoping to recoup themselves from an increased subsidy, might not resist these demands very strenuously. In this way both wage-rates and the rates of subsidy would be subjected to a continuous upward pressure. This tendency, which would exist even in a stationary State, would be accentuated in the actual world; for in times of boom wages would tend, as now, to go up; and when subsequently, depression came, there would be a powerful demand, very likely on the part of employers and workpeople acting together, for an addition to the subsidy to prevent them from falling again. The annual revenue required to provide the subsidy would thus tend to grow larger and larger continually. This is a serious matter. To adopt the subsidy plan is to set foot without adequate support on a very steep and slippery incline (Pigou, 1927a, p. 365).

7.3   SELECTIVE PROTECTION

Although protection was a political issue during the Great Depression, there seems to have been little agreement over what kind of protection was required. Some people wanted protection for import-substituting industries. Agriculture, for example, was experiencing severe competition from the agribusiness interests established in developing countries using the British capital exported before World War I. But agricultural products are wage-goods, and protection of agriculture has obvious implications for the standard of living of the poorer paid. Others wished to protect the staple export industries which were experiencing severe competition from newly industrializing countries in overseas markets. But how does one protect an overseas market? In the British case the most widely advocated solution was to strengthen imperial economic ties. Finally there were those who sought to protect infant industries, such as motors and 'white goods' (household electrical durables), from American domination.

By and large the Pre-Keynesian economists were not disposed to recommend protection: they were too aware of the welfare losses incurred by reciprocal 'beggar my neighbour' policies. Pigou, however, gave some attention to the protection issue, possibly because he had made an academic study of the subject some years earlier (Pigou, 1906).

The analysis of protection under conditions of structural unemployment is not an easy matter, and it is therefore appropriate to quote Pigou in full, beginning with his preliminary observations.

Classical doctrine points out that foreign trade is not a one-sided but a two-sided operation, and that, subject to certain qualifications connected with international borrowing, the real issue is not whether British labour or foreign labour shall be employed in making motor-cars for Englishmen, but whether British labour shall be employed in the manufacture of these cars or in the manufacture of export goods with which to buy them from abroad. We have a choice, the argument runs, between obtaining these motor-cars by making them or by making cotton goods to exchange for them. If, apart from fiscal interference, we should have chosen the exchange method, presumably that is the one which pays us best; and, therefore, to prevent us from having resort to it will do us hurt. . . . This argument is plainly valid if we assume that wage-rates are adjusted to demand and supply conditions. . . . If, however, it be admitted that wage-rates are not fully adjusted to demand and supply, but, through collective bargaining or authoritative state action, are set at levels which, even in a stationary state, would involve some measure of unemployment, the above argument is no longer watertight.

. . . Let the people of the country be composed of two groups, equipped respectively to make food and motor-cars. The motor-car makers insist on a 'living wage' at a level which, in existing conditions, involves a number of potential motor-makers being unemployed, and the food-makers on a wage which, while giving full employment to all present food-makers, will not allow of any motor-makers migrating to their industry. To focus the ideas, suppose that one-half only of the people attached to the motor-making industry are in work; the other half being sustained with food in return for a service rendered, by the rest of the population. The food-makers meanwhile obtain half the motor-cars they want, say 100,000 a year, by exchanging food with domestic motor-makers and the remaining half by exchanging it with foreigners. Suppose that in these conditions the Government decide to forbid the importation of foreign motor-cars. The food price of motor-cars will go up, and the food-makers are therefore not likely to want as many of them as before. But, in order to get the clearest possible case, let us imagine that their demand is absolutely inelastic and that they *must* have 200,000 cars a year, whatever the price. They will then buy the whole 200,000 from the domestic motor-makers, all of whom will now be employed at their higher living wage. They will obviously be much better off than before. The food-makers will be worse off than before, in that they have to pay a higher food-price for their motor-cars; but they will be better off in that they no longer need to contribute toward the support of unemployed motor-makers. Conditions can easily be conceived in which the extra cost of their cars is less than the savings they make in this way: so that they and the motor-makers are *both* better off than they would have been had the importation of foreign motors been permitted. Even if the conditions are less favourable, and the food-makers are worse off than before, it may still well happen that their loss (measured in terms of satisfaction) is less than the motor-makers' gain: so that the community as a whole—food-makers and motor-makers together—are advantaged by the policy of import restriction. It is clear, therefore, that if wages are set at an uneconomically high level, i.e. at a level too high to admit all would-be wage-earners to be employed even in a stationary state, that policy will in certain conditions alleviate unemployment and not inflict any counter-balancing hurt (Pigou, 1927a. pp. 360–1).

Pigou's argument seems somewhat contrived. Despite his heroic assumptions the underlying model is still fairly complex, and remarks such as 'Conditions can easily be conceived . . .' and 'It is clear, therefore . . .' do not, in this context, carry much conviction. His extreme assumption that food-makers continued to demand 200,000 cars a year begs the question of whether they can afford to do so. In particular, if food-makers resist a cut in their real wage then unemployment may spread to the food industry. Under such conditions the main effect of protection could be simply to transfer the burden of unemployment from one industry to the other.

Pigou himself admits that the argument must be heavily qualified.

It goes without saying that it [i.e. protection] cannot be used to reduce unemployment in industries that make goods for export, nor yet in those which, while manufacturing for the home market, are not subject to foreign competition. Moreover, even in home industries which are subject to this competition, it would often do more harm than good. Thus against the extreme case of a perfectly inelastic demand for motor-cars on the part of food-producers we may set the opposite extreme case of a perfectly elastic demand. In that case to stop imports of motor-cars would add nothing to employment in the home motor-making industries, while it would damage the food-producers both by preventing them getting half the cars they want, and, by destroying without compensation a market for their output, thus creating unemployment among them. It appears, therefore, that a good case for restricting competitive imports as a means of alleviating unemployment can only be made out in respect of commodities for which the home demand is considerably urgent or inelastic. A delicate discrimination would be needed, for which neither available data nor the economic education of governing persons are at present adequate (Pigou, 1927a, pp. 361–2).

In contrast to his earlier argument, Pigou's counter-argument has a very simple logic. This logic can be illustrated by a modification of the model developed in section 6.7. Suppose that the old good is consumed domestically and that the new good is produced solely for export (this reverses the role of the industries assumed earlier). If the home country is small relative to the rest of the world then the two goods will exchange in competitive international markets for a parametric price. This parametric price may be normalized to unity; in this case each unit of the new good is equivalent to one unit of the old good when transformed through foreign trade.

Under free trade the domestic relative price of the two goods will be the same as their international relative price, namely unity. Suppose now that in the old industry the real wage (expressed in units of the wage good—which is the old good itself) is too high, so that unemployment prevails. To protect the industry an import quota is introduced. This creates an artificial scarcity of the old good and raises its price relative to the new good in the domestic market. Since, however, the real wage in terms of the old good is fixed, employers in the old industry are no better off than before, their demand for labour remains unchanged and unemployment is not reduced. In the new industry the domestic price of the new good has fallen and so, therefore, has the marginal value product of labour expressed in units of the wage good. Demand for labour contracts and either the real wage falls or labour in the export industry becomes unemployed. In either case, not only are people attached to the old industry no better off than before, but people attached to the new industry are actually worse off than before.

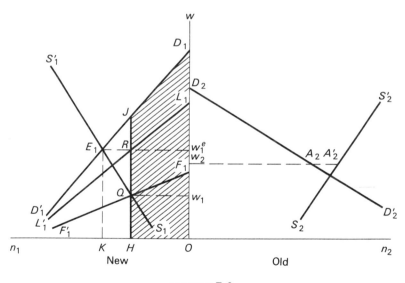

FIGURE 7.3
Effects of protection

The situation is illustrated in figure 7.3. The right-hand quadrant shows that initially there is unemployment A_2A_2' in the old industry due to a too high real wage w_2. In the left-hand quadrant the demand curve D_1D_1' expresses the marginal product of labour in the new industry in units of the old–industry output. The output of the new industry is entirely exported in exchange for imports of the old product measured by the area OD_1E_1K.

Suppose now that imports of the old product are restricted to a level measured by the shaded area OD_1JH. It is assumed that domestic exporters must now compete for import licences, and that the domestic price of the new good will fall until the excess demand for licences has been eliminated. Alternatively, it could be assumed that a tariff is imposed, set at a rate which generates the same yield as the import licences. In either case it is assumed that the government spends the proceeds on purchases of the old product. The imposition of quotas or tariffs on the old product reduces the domestic price of the new product. The fall in the domestic price shifts down the demand for labour. If the real wage is flexible downwards then demand falls to F_1F_1' and equilibrium is achieved at Q. Wage income in the industry is much lower: it is measured by the area Ow_1QH instead of by the area $Ow_1^cE_1K$ as before. Profits too are lower; they are measured by the area of the triangle w_1QF_1, instead of by the area $w_1^cD_1E_1$ as before. The bulk of the income in the new industry accrues to the government; competitive bidding for import licences accounts for income measured by the area F_1D_1JQ.

If the real wage is inflexible then the domestic price of the new product will fall much less. The demand curve shifts down to L_1L_1', with the result that firms produce at R; they employ OH workers at the initial wage w_1^c. Both real wage income and profits are higher than before, and the real income appropriated by the government is correspondingly reduced. The total income and output generated by the industry is unaffected by the wage inflexibility because the constraint on industry output is set by the import quota. Wage inflexibility, in this case, simply serves to redistribute income in favour of labour (and incidentally in favour of the employers also).

It is clear from this analysis that protection has very limited scope in alleviating structural unemployment. Relative to employment subsidies it performs very badly indeed. Subsidies are particularly effective in import-substituting industries, as compared to exporting industries, as it is less likely that the benefits of the subsidy will accrue to foreign rather than domestic consumers. As Pigou remarks

. . . it is clear that the subsidy device is applicable over a much wider range than the device of excluding imports that compete with home produce. It [i.e. the subsidy device] will lessen the volume of unemployment in all conditions, not merely in some conditions; and so long as it is confined to industries whose products are not exported, it will correspondingly increase the real income of the country (Pigou, 1927a, p. 364).

It might be added that where export demand is infinitely elastic at the prevailing world price, a subsidy to an export industry will benefit the home country and not the rest of the world, so that in this case Pigou's concluding qualification is unnecessary.

7.4   RATIONALIZATION

Rationalization was widely canvassed as a solution to unemployment in the depressed industries. Rationalization was defined by H. S. Jevons (1931) in terms of five essential features.

(1) Amalgamation or unified control of companies and elimination of weak concerns, so as to secure control of the market, and thus facilitate on the basis of monopoly profits the raising of the large amounts of new capital necessary;
(2) Specialisation of plants and their re-equipment so as to reap the maximum economies of large-scale production, both in respect of machinery and of organisation; and the building of large new plants for products in the manufacture of which the utmost economy can be reached only in this way;
(3) The planning of each plant for continuous production with specialised machines and tools;
(4) Specialised management, largely functional, including careful buying, grading and mixing of raw materials;
(5) Perfection of manual operations on the basis of time and motion studies, with necessary instruction (Jevons, 1931, pp. 4–5).

At first sight the emphasis on monopoly in (1) suggests that rationalization could actually be a hindrance rather than a help to employment, as it could result in a restriction of output in the depressed industry through higher prices. Monopoly has the further disadvantage that it tends to create monopsony power in the labour market whenever the supply of labour to the monopolized industry is less than perfectly elastic. This monopsony power provides an additional incentive for the employer to restrict employment and output.

Employment may also be reduced because of the increase in capital-intensity, and the exploitation of economies of scale in work organization, which arise when the small-scale plants are replaced by fewer highly mechanized plants.

On what grounds, then, can rationalization be recommended as a cure for structural unemployment? Its advocates sought to apply it mainly to export industries. Their intention seems to have been to create a captive market for the industry by protecting the home market, and if possible overseas imperial markets too. These markets would generate sufficient monopoly profits to cover the fixed costs of establishing large-scale production. Additional output would be sold on unprotected world markets at the competitive price. Economies of scale would allow this additional output to be produced at low marginal cost. Thus if overseas competition was intensive, output could be 'dumped' abroad.

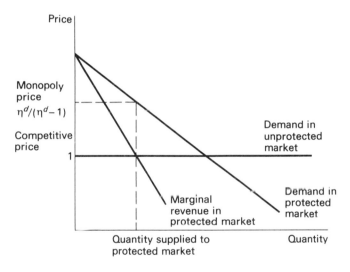

FIGURE 7.4
Price discrimination under rationalization

The employment-creating effects of rationalization depend crucially upon price discrimination. The situation is illustrated in figures 7.4 and 7.5. It is assumed that only the product of the new industry is consumed domestically. The old product is exported to two different markets—a protected imperial market where the domestic producer enjoys a monopoly, and a competitive unprotected market where a parametric relative price of unity prevails. Suppose that it is always economic to supply some output to the competitive market. When this condition is satisfied the marginal cost of each unit supplied to the monopolized market is equal to its price in the competitive market, namely unity. The profit-maximizing strategy in the monopolized market is therefore to mark up the competitive price by a factor inversely related to the price elasticity of demand, η^d; in fact since the competitive price is unity the monopoly price is $\eta^d/(\eta^d-1)$. This result is illustrated graphically in figure 7.4.

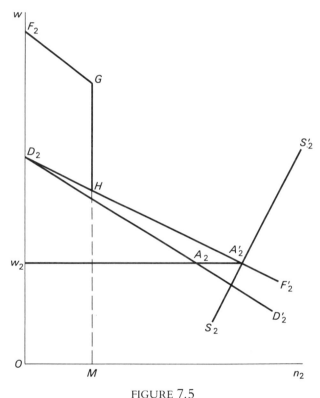

FIGURE 7.5
Rationalization as a solution to structural unemployment

Monopoly pricing enhances the marginal value product of labour in the old industry. Figure 7.5 shows that the effect of rationalization is to shift up the marginal value productivity of labour in a discontinuous fashion. Prior to rationalization, the marginal value product is given by the schedule D_2D_2'; after rationalization it is given by the schedule F_2GHF_2'. The premium price set in the protected market generates a revenue (in units of the new commodity) measured by the area D_2F_2GH. This additional revenue is used to pay the interest and depreciation charges on new capital equipment. To simplify matters it may be assumed that this capital equipment is produced and financed by the countries in the protected overseas market, and that the interest and depreciation charges just exhaust the monopoly revenue obtained. The monopoly revenue does not, therefore, contribute directly to domestic real income.

The contribution of the monopoly revenue is indirect. The capital purchased using the monopoly revenue improves labour productivity and shifts out the competitive marginal value product of labour schedule from D_2D_2' to D_2F_2'. The diagram is contrived so that the resulting increase in the demand for labour is just sufficient to achieve full employment at the prevailing real wage w_2.

The benefits of rationalization depend crucially, however, on two conditions being satisfied. The first is that the monopoly revenues are used to purchase capital equipment, and that the installation of new capital equipment is in turn associated with an increase in the productivity of labour. The second is that the increased output of the export industry can be absorbed by the rest of the world without any diminution of the export price, and that no other country simultaneously attempts to supply world markets with additional output of the same product.

Advocates of rationalization do not, on the whole, appear to have considered these qualifications very seriously. Henry Clay (1929a,c) for example, was a strong advocate of rationalization for the textile industry. His main preoccupation, however, was with a short-run policy of staving off bankruptcy among small firms. Much of his advocacy is concerned with what Jevons dismisses as 'financial reconstruction'; writing down book assets, carrying through amalgamations and raising new capital. He assumes that the incentives exist for the managers of a newly formed monopoly to exploit competitive opportunities in unprotected markets, rather than to just sit back and enjoy the profits from protected ones. Other economists, who were more sceptical of rationalization, believed that offering monopoly privileges to near-bankrupt firms would simply perpetuate the practices that had led toward bankruptcy in the first place.

Even if the rationalized industry did sell aggressively in unprotected markets there is always the danger of retaliatory action. World recession leads to excess capacity in the export industries of many countries, and if several decide to rationalize then the increased supply may cause the competitive price to fall dramatically. There are two problems here: first, the rationalizing countries will protect their own domestic and imperial markets, so that the size of the open competitive market will shrink. The second is that the open market will receive increased supplies from several sources, and the resulting fall in prices may cause other countries to introduce protection in the interests of their import-substituting industries.

Under these conditions the exploitation of economies of scale may create market instability. To lower its marginal cost in order to compete effectively at a lower price each firm must increase its output, but the individual increases in output collectively lead to a still lower price. International instability may be restored only when some of the rationalized firms go bankrupt!

7.5   SELECTIVE INVESTMENT

A rather disappointing aspect of Pre-Keynesian theory is the lack of consideration given to industrial relocation through selective investment. Although they touched upon the issue, it seems that the Pre-Keynesians were preoccupied with the idea of moving the workers to the jobs rather than with moving the jobs to the workers. This could be interpreted as reflecting an old-fashioned hierarchical view of society in which workers are servile to capital. Alternatively, it may have reflected an appraisal of the relative costs of moving labour and capital — although no explicit assessment of these costs appears in their published work.

There was, however, a contemporary analysis of structural unemployment, published by Austin Robinson; although inspired by Keynesian ideas, it is a useful adjunct to the Pre-Keynesian literature. Keynes himself normally took a strictly macroeconomic view of employment problems (see section 1.4). It is true that in the late 1930s Keynes expressed surprise that some sectors of the economy were so resistant to a general reflation. But while Keynes, in his policy discussions, recognized the importance of bottlenecks and other structural factors, he never successfully incorporated these concepts into his theoretical analysis. Austin Robinson, however, took structural unemployment just as seriously as the Pre-Keynesian economists. He did not subscribe to Keynes' view of the early 1930s that a general reflation would cure unemployment in the depressed areas. Anticipating the analysis of section 6.4, he notes that

A financial and industrial policy which, if applied uniformly to the country as a whole, might attract workers out of the derelict areas or restore prosperity within them, would almost certainly produce exaggerated conditions of boom and slump in the more prosperous parts of the country . . . (Robinson, 1935, p. 189).

Robinson argues in favour of selective policies, which include government expenditure on 'useful works', subsidizing the provision of facilities for new industries, and negotiating special wage bargains for local employers.

Robinson's argument for selective investment rests upon a pioneering application of the regional income multiplier (this seems to be a Keynesian multiplier rather than an 'economic base multiplier' of the kind that had been used earlier). He argues that

The failure of the old staple industries has led to such secondary unemployment and to such diminution of local real incomes that those industries which provide commodities other than primary necessaries, the minor luxuries of the full employed salaried or skilled worker, cannot flourish in the market conditions of the North. If there could be such restoration of these incomes that investment could profitably be made in these industries, and if they could be built up on a local market to serve not only that market but distant markets as well, then the effects of public works need not be as ephemeral as they are supposed . . . to be (Robinson, 1935, p. 190).

He continues

Public works are most efficacious where the system in which they are expected to produce their results is most nearly closed. But the economy of Tyneside or of a South Wales coal valley is very far from being closed. The exceedingly interesting inquiry into the conditions in Brynmawr, conducted under the leadership of the Society of Friends, would appear to indicate that approximately 60 per cent of expenditure in that derelict town is on goods imported into the town, approximately 40 per cent on goods and services produced in the town. If this ratio would apply to investments of income as well as to the average of the whole, and if all additional income were spent and none saved or used to repay debts, then £100 of direct income from public works would yield only some £67 of local secondary incomes. That is three men put into employment would employ indirectly only two more. Clearly South Wales as a whole, or the North-east Coast as a whole, is far more nearly self-sufficient than a single small town. The amount of secondary employment in the whole area may be substantially greater and induce further secondary employment in the small towns themselves. Nevertheless, it remains true, I think, that when account has been taken of probable savings and debt repayments and of increased actual payments of rents the local secondary employment is likely to be comparatively small. This is the more likely where incomes are increased after a period of severe depression and local sources of supply for the newly demanded goods are insuficient, so that they are brought in from the already prosperous areas (Robinson, 1935, p. 191).

Robinson's calculation of secondary employment effects are consistent with the use of an income multiplier equal to the reciprocal of unity *minus* the propensity to save *plus* the propensity to import.

Finally it is interesting to note that Robinson's emphasis on the propensity to import into an area ties in with the dependence of depressed areas upon a few staple industries. Not only are such areas the most vulnerable to depression brought on by structural change, but they are also the most difficult to revive through local investment because the lack of a broad industrial base means that they have a high propensity to import. This point links Robinson's analysis to an earlier analysis of structural unemployment by G. C. Allen (1930). Allen emphasized the importance of industrial diversity in an area and explained on this basis the ability of one of Britain's oldest industrialized areas—the West Midlands—to thrive during the depression. He argued that industrial diversity not only spreads the risks of fluctuations, or of decline in specific industries, but also provides a broad spectrum of component and service industries which will in turn attract new industries (e.g. motor-cars). Such diversity, he claims, also builds up an entrepreneurial spirit amongst employers, and encourages adaptability in the labour force, who are constantly aware of the opportunities for switching to alternative (and possibly higher-paid) occupations. The movement into 'new' industries in the Midlands began in the late nineteenth century, and it was the subsequent growth of these industries in the early part of the twentieth century that enabled the Midlands to weather the slump with so little difficulty.

7.6   SUMMARY: AN EVALUATION OF ALTERNATIVE POLICIES

The implication of the preceding discussion is that there is no single cure for structural unemployment.

Industrial transference can be recommended when the mobility of labour is clearly impeded by market failures. For example, it may be useful to improve information flows by creating a national job index to link up the vacancy files of different employment exchanges, or to subsidize visits to factories in prosperous industries and areas, so that those who are interested in moving can do so more easily. Analogous measures could be adopted to facilitate long-distance house-moving and to encourage firms to offer more training to people with obsolete skills. It is important, though, to allow individuals to select themselves for transference, and not, for example, to confine transference subsidies to the long-term unemployed. Transference will be successful in the long run only if those who are most suitable for transference are the ones who transfer. Transference of the most suitable workers still helps those who do not want to transfer, as their departure has a 'knock-on' effect in creating local vacancies which those who do not wish to transfer can fill.

Employment subsidies can be strongly recommended as a short-term measure. Like any ameliorative measure, however, they are liable to create difficulties in the long run. Selective subsidies reduce the incentive for individuals to transfer out of declining industries. Non-selective subsidies avoid this problem, but only at the expense of encouraging wage inflation in the expanding industries. Subsidies have to be financed out of taxation, and the collection of taxes may distort incentives and lead to a misallocation of resources elsewhere in the system. However, the cost of the subsidy will normally be less than the saving in benefit payments to the unemployed.

Selective protection is, under almost all conditions, inferior to a selective subsidy. The strongest case for protection arises when it forms an element of a wider policy of rationalization. The protection of an export industry against import substitutes can be justified on the grounds that discriminatory pricing is necessary to achieve efficient and profitable production under increasing returns to scale. Subsidies would do just as well if only the domestic market were protected. If, however, foreign markets can be protected through imperial influence then protection may be preferable so far as the interests of the home country are concerned.

The Keynesian policy of selective investment may be considered either as a long-term strategy for developing a new industrial base with the aid of public funds, or as a short-term policy for ameliorating unemployment. An intelligent policy will, in fact, cover both aspects.

In the second respect the closest parallel is with the selective employment subsidy. A detailed evaluation of the merits of investment and employment subsidies is outside the scope of this book. In theory the balance of advantages normally lies with the subsidy meausre, though on administrative grounds investment would seem to be the most expedient.

The relative long-term merits of the two measures depend very much upon the kind of investment that is contemplated. If it consists of 'digging holes in the ground' then the additional output of the subsidized industry is likely to be of greater value than the product financed by the investment. If on the other hand the investment is in useful infrastructure of a kind which private industry could not normally provide then the balance of advantage may be reversed. In the light of earlier discussion, infrastructure investments which encourage industrial diversity will be particularly advantageous.

8

The Pre-Keynesian Theory
and the Keynesian Revolution

8.1 INTRODUCTION

This chapter attempts to answer the question 'If Pre-Keynesian theory was really as cogent as it appears in retrospect, why has it not been more influential?' The eclipse of the Pre-Keynesian theory seems to have begun about 1930, and was very rapid. By 1939 the theory had been practically obliterated from the economic literature.

The eclipse of the Pre-Keynesian theory is explained partly by the personalities of the Pre-Keynesian economists and partly by the nature of the theory itself. In both these respects, the contrast with Keynesian theory is quite striking. Once the social and political role of economic theorizing is considered, it is not difficult to see how Pre-Keynesian theory was thrust into the background by the economic crisis of 1929–33, and by the failure of the Pre-Keynesians to develop an effective short-run policy response. It was finally discarded in the aftermath of the Keynesian revolution. Not only was it intellectually discredited, but it seemed to have become irrelevant once Britain's structural problems were temporarily disguised by the rearmament boom.

8.2 THE FORMULATION OF THE THEORY

Pre-Keynesian theory is very much concerned with British conditions, and it retained its ascendency in Britain so long as the major concern of policy was the high level of unemployment in Britain relative to the rest of the world. Little attempt was made to generalize the theory to explain structural unemployment in other countries whose economic performance was also relatively poor. It is true that during the slump it was noted that the staple industries in which Britain had excess capacity were also the industries in which

other countries tended to have excess capacity too. On these grounds
the Pre-Keynesians were pessimistic about the prospects for reviving
the export trade of Britain's staple industries without substantial cuts
in costs. On the other hand, the structural theory had to be modified
quite substantially if it was to account for unemployment in, say, the
US, where the depression in agriculture was of far greater economic
significance than in Britain. It is unfortunate that the Pre-Keynesians
were so narrow in their outlook that they allowed themselves to
become preoccupied with the problems of the British economy. It is
reasonable to suppose that had they applied the theory more widely,
it would have become much better known.

The Pre-Keynesians also failed to emphasize the generality of the
theoretical techniques that they employed. In chapters 4–6 it has been
shown that Pre-Keynesian theory involves a pioneering application
of disequilibrium concepts. The Pre-Keynesians themselves,
however, did not emphasize this departure from equilibrium
assumptions; indeed, it is quite possible that Clay for example, did
not fully appreciate that this was what was involved. It is only with
the benefit of hindsight that one can recognize the full extent of the
Pre-Keynesian theoretical contribution. By failing to draw attention
to the generality of the disequilibrium approach the Pre-Keynesians
reinforced the view that they were merely commenting upon
unfortunate rigidities in the otherwise perfectly functioning economic system.

If Pre-Keynesian theory was very 'British', Keynesian theory, by
contrast, was of almost universal application during the period of the
slump. Although Keynes had initially developed his argument for
reflation with special reference to the British economy, the onset of
the slump gave his ideas an international relevance, which he was
quick to exploit. The collapse of the world payments system created
a world-wide demand for liquidity, generated rapid price deflation,
and made mass unemployment an international problem. Governments reacted by pursuing beggar-my-neighbour trade policies in an
attempt to safeguard jobs, which in practice meant the export of
unemployment. Business confidence was damaged and investment
curtailed. As a result, the dissimilarities in national economic
performance manifest during the 1920s were submerged during the
slump. In developing the *General Theory*, Keynes kept his assumptions closely in line with prevailing international conditions. He
explained the exceptional demand for liquidity by arguing that
interest rate expectations are regressive towards some normal rate.

Restrictions on international trade were reflected in his assumption of a closed economy; this assumption, in turn, made it possible for Keynes to exaggerate the size of the national income multiplier by ignoring import leakages. The crisis of business confidence was reflected in his assumption of a continuing decline in the marginal efficiency of capital.

Keynes himself was not backward in claiming generality for his theory. He argued not only that his methods were new, but that his theory subsumed all previous theories of employment and money as a special case; theories which could not be subsumed in this way were said to be incorrect. At the time, the universality of the phenomena he was analysing made his claim for generality seem valid. In retrospect, however, Keynes' formal model of the *General Theory* seems to be rooted in phenomena which were specific to the slump period 1929–33. His assumption of regressive interest rate expectations, for example, conforms with the very steep yield curve which prevailed during this period: even when the short-term interest rate was as low as 0.5 per cent, the long-term rate remained above 2 per cent. However, with the exception of the period of Dalton's low-interest rate policy after World War II, the same phenomenon has not recurred again.

It may be concluded that the Pre-Keynesian economists failed to demonstrate properly the generality of their theory. They understated the originality of their method of analysis, and in discussing its applications they took a very insular view. As a result, when the world economy entered the slump, and mass unemployment ceased to be a purely 'British' problem, interest in the Pre-Keynesian theory began to lapse.

8.3   POLICY IMPLICATIONS OF THE THEORY

The Pre-Keynesians had serious difficulty spelling out the policy implications of their theory. Part of the problem is that the theory is concerned with the medium run rather than the short run, so that its practioners cannot promise immediate results from their policies (see section 8.7). Furthermore the predictions of the theory are basically pessimistic, and suggest that even in the medium run no easy or painless remedy is to hand (see section 8.8 and chapter 11). Even so, the Pre-Keynesians were peculiarly inept in putting across the policy implications of their theory. This seems to be largely a matter of personality.

The Pre-Keynesians, and Pigou in particular, viewed economics as a moral science. Pigou had learnt utilitarian ethics from Henry Sidgwick at Cambridge. He believed implicitly in the diminishing marginal utility of income; according to Pigou, economic policy should be directed to the attainment of a social optimum in which the marginal utility of income spent by each individual is equal. So far as is known, he never abandoned this view, but simply ignored the criticism to which it was subjected from the 1930s onwards.

Pigou's writings have an underlying unity because he always sought to relate his discussion of policy to this basic philosophical position. Unfortunately, it also gives an air of unreality to much of his discussion. Distributional issues dominate, and very little space is given to administrative or political feasibility of the measures under consideration.

His moral outlook make Pigou a staunch internationalist. In common with Clay, he was reluctant to recommend any policies — such as import controls — which represented a step backwards away from this ideal. He seems to have had a sentimental belief that international trade would lead nations to better mutual under-standing, and perhaps eventually to political unification.

The Pre-Keynesians were also critical of governments and poli-ticians. Their distrust of government was linked to the fact that government was national rather than international. The strengthen-ing of government almost inevitably meant the strengthening of powers to pursue nationalistic policies. Extensive government involvement also led to bureaucracy. Bureaucrats were less sensitive to the wishes of the people than were private entrepreneurs because they were not subject in the same way to the disciplines and incentives of the market place. These considerations weighed more heavily with Cannan and Clay than they did with Pigou. By and large, the Pre-Keynesians supported the powers of government that existed in 1920 or thereabouts, but felt that by then matters had gone far enough. Further redistribution of income through subsidized education and health care, unemployment benefits and progressive income taxation would seriously damage incentives. At the same time, the Pre-Keynesians were certainly not advocates of *laissez-faire*; Cannan — who was the most right-wing — was aware from his historical studies, that none of the major classical economists, from Adam Smith to John Stuart Mill, had recommended such a policy.

Dislike of politicians was shared by both Cannan and Pigou. Cannan loved to debunk the absurd generalizations of orators on the hustings, and Pigou was disgusted with politicians' subservience to lobbies and vested interests.

Their moral idealism and distrust of government inhibited the Pre-Keynesians in their development of a policy. They were reluctant to recommend additional government measures, particularly discretionary or selective measures about which there was certain to be lobbying. Their dislike of politicians made it difficult for them to communicate with them. These problems are well illustrated by the tenor of Pigou's testimony on unemployment to the Macmillan Committee in 1930, to which the chairman understandably took offence. Having explained to the committee the theoretical advantage to a nation from selective import controls (see section 7.3.), Pigou asserts that they should never be applied because of the practical certainty of political abuse.

Lord Macmillan (Q.6501): Are we to forego that advantage to the nation which you are satisfied will occur, because of the possibility of political abuse?

Pigou (A.6501): I should say yes; and I should also say that the Government would certainly choose the wrong objects for putting a tax on.

Lord Macmillan (Q.6502): That is a criticism of Governments generally?

Pigou (A.6502): Yes.

Lord Macmillan (Q.6503): It is a pity that we should be deprived of a remedy because politicians happen to make use of it as a political thing?

Pigou (A.6503): That would be the position.

Later on Pigou was given a chance to outline measures that he would consider more suitable for remedying unemployment.

Lord Macmillan (Q.6646): Will you imagine for a moment that you are not giving evidence, but that you are a member of this Committee, and that you are framing in your mind recommendations which you would like to see at the end of the Report with the responsibility attaching to that, knowing that they might possibly receive effect — what recommendations would you make?

Pigou (A.6646): Well, that is a rather difficult question. . . .

Lord Macmillan (Q.6648): You have given us certain views on the financial position of this country. You have made an analysis of the causes to which we have listened with great interest. We naturally ask you: Have you any remedy? Have you anything to recommend which you think it would be safe to adopt? It would be quite fair if you were to say 'No, I cannot tell you.' But if you say that, will it not be a little difficult for us to

find something that you cannot find, with all your specialised knowledge?
   Pigou (A.6648): Well, I have been thinking of my function rather as trying to make an analysis, but I could, of course, suggest remedies.

His suggestions, however, made on the spur of the moment, were rather feeble, and his chance was gone. Pigou attempted to retrieve the situation by submitting later a written note, though what effect this had on the Committee is difficult to say.
   Pigou's final remark quoted above indicates that, in his middle and later life, analysis always took precedence over policy. He believed that his role as witness was to help the Committee members think the unemployment problem through; once this had been done, the appropriate remedies would suggest themselves. With Keynes the exact opposite applied: policy came first and analysis later. Keynes had hit upon suitable employment policies by the late 1920s, but did not publish his full theory until 1936. Keynes was the exact opposite of Pigou in other ways too.
   He did not share Pigou's philosophical idealism. His social philosophy seems to be quite naive (Johnson, 1975, pp. 120–1): to maintain the established order under new and difficult circumstances — to repel the socialist challenge by giving capitalism a more acceptable face.
   But if Keynes' social philosophy is naive, his politics are very sophisticated. Because of his experience as a civil servant and adviser, he speaks the language of the political establishment, and uses his debating skills to undermine and to ridicule the arguments of his opponents. The measures he advocates are always within the realm of practical politics, even if his recommendations do not always prevail.
   While Keynes goes along with free trade as an ideal, he is also familiar with the practicalities of international political relations, and is not afraid to recommend nationalistic policies as a short-run expedient. Indeed, Keynes could be quite jingoistic at times. In his Halley Stewart Lecture for 1931 he argued that the recovery of the British economy should be put before the recovery of other nations, even if this involved imposing tariffs at their expense.

It is a necessary preliminary to world recovery that this country should regain its liberty of action and its power of international initiative. I believe, further, that we alone can be trusted to use that power of initiative, when once we have regained it, to the general advantage. I agree with those who think that many of the difficulties of recent years were due to the fact that the creditor balance available to finance new international investment had

largely passed out of our hands into the hands of France and the United
States. And I therefore welcome, and indeed require as an indispensable
preliminary to a world recovery, that there should be a material strengthen-
ing of the creditor position of Great Britain (Keynes, 1932, pp. 80–1).

He enlarges upon this theme later:

In France . . . they think that if everyone had behaved as they have,
everyone would have as much gold as they have. Their own accumulations
are the reward of virtue, and the losses which the rest of us have suffered are
the penalty of imprudence. They wish to go on to the grim conclusion.
There is nothing to do with them but to wait for their conversion by the
grinding pressure of events. . . . In the United States it is almost
inconceivable what rubbish a public man has to utter today if he is to keep
respectable. Serious and sensible bankers, who as men of common sense are
trying to do what they can to stem the tide of liquidation and to stimulate
the forces of expansion, have to go about assuring the world of their
conviction that there is no serious risk of inflation, when what they really
mean is that they cannot yet see good enough grounds for daring to hope
for it. In this country opinion is probably more advanced. . . . What we
have to fear here is a timidity and a reluctance to act boldly. When once we
have regained a power of initiative we must use it without hesitation or
delay for expanding purchasing power ourselves and for helping others to
expand. *We* must set the example (Keynes, 1932, pp. 87–8).

The Pre-Keynesians did not reply to rhetoric of this kind. No doubt
they would have considered it distasteful. So far as Keynes was
concerned, of course, he was simply following the 'high social duty'
of preaching reflation. If the Pre-Keynesians had perceived a similar
kind of duty to preach structural adjustment then they would have
been forced to think through their policies more carefully, and their
ideas would have reached a wider audience.

8.4   THE APPARENT FAILURE OF INDUSTRIAL TRANSFERENCE

One of the main elements in Pre-Keynesian policy was industrial
transference. Systematic measures to promote industrial transference
began in 1927–8 with an agreement to limit the recruitment of labour
to the coal industry, the establishment of Juvenile Unemployment
Centres and the formation of the Industrial Transference Board
(Hancock, 1962; McCrone, 1969). The Board had a general brief to
promote labour mobility: amongst other things, it subsidized the
direct and incidental expenses involved in rehousing the migrant

worker, and arranged short training courses when necessary. It soon became apparent, however, that industrial transference was making little impact on unemployment. In the peak year for transference — 1929 — a mere 32,000 adults and 6,500 juveniles were transferred under the scheme. Estimates suggest that over half the transferees returned home within 2–3 years of moving. Transferees in later years experienced increasing difficulty in holding their new jobs, and this was ascribed by the Ministry of Labour to the deteriorating quality of the men transferred. Although the scheme continued in operation up to World War II, the initiative in promoting structural adjustment passed to the Special Areas Commissioners in 1934, who acquired an increasingly wide range of weapons to move the work to the workers, as well as move workers to the work.

There seems little doubt that the unwillingness of labour to move, and the unsuitability of the assisted migrants, was a serious disappointment to the Pre-Keynesians. They had pinned their hopes on the view that subsidies would overcome the frictions which they saw as the main deterrent to mobility. They had failed to take proper account of the attitudes of potential migrants. In retrospect, it seems that the failure of the industrial transference scheme was due, at least partly, to two unfortunate aspects. The first is the 'adverse selection' arising from the emphasis of the scheme on transferring the unemployed. It might have been better to encourage those already in employment to transfer, on the grounds that they were likely to be more 'employable' elsewhere, and that their transfer would have a knock-on effect benefiting the local unemployed who could step into their jobs. The second aspect is the timing of the scheme, which began shortly before the onset of the slump temporarily eliminated new vacancies in even some of the prosperous industries.

The Pre-Keynesians clearly found it difficult to sympathize with the unemployed who refused assisted transference. A distinct hardening of the Pre-Keynesians' attitude to unemployment can be detected around 1930–1. This is reflected in Beveridge's emphasis upon the increasingly large 'administrative factor' in unemployment.

Those of us who twenty years ago were concerned in the launching of unemployment insurance had no doubt as to the reality or the bitterness of unemployment. We thought it wicked that a civilised community should leave men to struggle helplessly and alone in the grip of economic forces, should take no measures either to prevent unemployment or to provide for it. But prevention seemed more important than provision, and the danger that provision might stand in the way of prevention was never absent from our minds. . . . Insurance itself was framed in such a way as to give employers and trade unions and individual workmen a sense of financial responsibility for the unemployment fund and motives and rewards for helping to make work regular. With insurance went measures to prevent unemployment both outside the insurance scheme and embodied in it.

Those were our plans and hopes; what has happened to them? Of the measures for preventing unemployment, external to the insurance scheme some have come to nothing — there has been no decasualisation and no systematic planning ahead of public work. . . . The measures embodied in the insurance scheme itself — rebates and refunds of various kinds, proportioning of benefit to contributions, differentiating of premiums by risk — have all been swept away. Unemployment insurance has become just unlimited unemployment relief, just paying for unemployment, or any idleness that can pass itself off as unemployment, out of an apparently bottomless purse. As the £120,000,000 stream pours out from the insurance fund, industries and individuals adapt themselves to it more and more, to get their share with others. . . .

Insurance against unemployment marks in itself a great advance in civilisation; it is a just use of social power to drive needless fear and suffering from the world. But insurance as we have it today is not doing that alone. It is making human life in some ways not better but worse; it is playing down to the slackness and carelessness of human nature, not playing up to what is best in it (Beveridge, 1931, pp. 47–9).

The social philosophy underlying this view is that ultimately the economic role of state insurance can only be to help individuals to help themselves. It is for this reason that prevention takes precedence over provision. But there was another view, in the ascendant at the time, that provision should come first: that the economic role of the state was to secure full employment at 'standard' rates of wages and that the unemployed were simply unfortunate victims of the capitalist system. 'The truth is', said Keynes 'that we stand mid-way between two theories of economic society.' In explaining the failure of industrial transference, the Pre-Keynesians fell back upon the old social philosophy and, in the view of the younger generation of the time, seem to have disqualified themselves from serious considera-tion as a result. Although structural problems continued to give cause for concern — shortages of skilled labour became apparent soon after rearmament began (Allen and Thomas, 1937, 1939) — the new philosophy regarded them as the result of a failure to plan properly, rather than a failure of incentives. The old philosophy still had its adherents (e.g. Fisher, 1945) but it exerted little influence until its revival in the 1960s.

8.5   CHANGING IDEOLOGIES

The onset of the slump revitalized the issue of alternative economic systems — whether capitalism or socialism was the more suitable for a mature industry economy such as Britain. It was an intellectual debate which had little impact on the ballot box or on the shop-floor. Radical intellectuals argued that capitalism had failed, while the more conservative replied that because of increasing government intervention it had not been allowed to work.

At the time the academic debate began to take off, about 1931, the Pre-Keynesians were a fading intellectual force. Cannan had retired and Clay had entered the Bank of England. A growing reputation was being earned by Lionel Robbins, Cannan's eventual successor at the London School of Economics (after the departure of Allyn Young). A young libertarian ideologue, Robbins embraced the strictly subjectivist stance of the Austrian school, and recommended his students to read up the subjective theory of value and distribution in the original German (using special editions that he had reprinted for the purpose). He was one of the pioneers of ordinal utility theory, which denied the practicality of interpersonal comparisons of utility of the kind favoured by Pigou. As indicated earlier, the rise of subjectivism was a challenge that Pigou chose simply to ignore.

Where unemployment was concerned, Robbins took up the extreme position that the mild monetary expansion of the 1920s was the major cause of the slump. Credit expansion, he urged, had stimulated excessive private investment. Drawing inspiration from Hayek (1931, 1933), he argued that not only was the aggregate volume of investment too high but that the speculative mania generated by monetary expansion had led to a maldistribution of investment between industries. As the supply price of new capital goods rose through crowding out in the product market, so expected profits from investments failed to materialize and speculators realized their mistakes. Short-term interest rates rose as unprofitable enterprises attempted to refinance themselves; but the only long-term solution lay in the liquidation of these ill-conceived investments.

Contrary to Clay, who saw bankruptcy as a short-term threat to employment, Robbins saw bankruptcy as a necessary prelude to long-term recovery:

Nobody wishes for bankruptcies. Nobody likes liquidation as such. If bankruptcy can be avoided by sound financing nobody would be against such measures. All that is contended is that when the extent of mal-investment and over-indebtedness has passed a certain limit, measures which postpone liquidation only tended to make matters worse (Robbins, 1934, p. 75).

Robbins thus perceived a short, sharp depression as a necessary antidote to the speculative excesses of a boom engineered through monetary expansion. The only alternative to a short, sharp, depression was a longer and ultimately more painful one — which was exactly, according to Robbins, what Britain was enduring in the early 1930s. According to Robbins, only the discipline of the Gold Standard would deter governments from currency mismanagement. Mismanagement included any attempt by governments to use monetary expansion to alleviate the effects of rigidities elsewhere in the system. Gold movements must be allowed to produce their full effect throughout the whole economy, and this meant that money wages and all other costs must vary in response to the flow of gold.

During the early 1930s, Robbins' free market dogma became the main alternative to the Keynesian reflationary stance. Keynes himself developed into an advocate of welfare capitalism, recommending permanently high levels of government spending to avert the threat of stagnation. Economic opinion thus became divided upon political lines, and the Pre-Keynesians — with their somewhat nebulous political stance — were forced into the background.

8.6   KEYNES' ATTACK ON THE 'CLASSICS'

There is no standard work epitomizing Pre-Keynesian theory. Pigou was the person best equipped to write such a book, but instead he wrote *The Theory of Unemployment* (1933) — a taxonomy of the subject which makes the reader wonder how anyone could write anything so tedious and abstract in the midst of an economic crisis. Pigou incorporated the most relevant parts of his structural theory of unemployment into the later editions of *The Economics of Welfare*, where they were buried in the middle of over 800 pages of dense economic analysis. The academic world is rarely set alight by material incorporated in a new edition of a standard text — however distinguished the author, and however widely read the text.

Pigou's book provided an easy target for Keynes, however, who treated it as if it were indeed an epitome of Pre-Keynesian thinking.

Building on this foundation, Keynes erected a superstructure of false ideas which he then described as the theory of the 'classical school'. To someone who has not read Pre-Keynesian theory, Keynes' description of his departure from the 'classical' theory of the labour market (Keynes, 1936, ch. 2) can appear original and perceptive. To someone who has read Pre-Keynesian theory this description is simply a mixture of bad scholarship and technically incompetent theorizing. Anyone who doubts this should read Pigou's original review (Pigou, 1936) and his subsequent reappraisal (Pigou, 1950).

Some biographers have recognized the problems posed by Keynes' bad scholarship, though others are less than frank about it — notably Harrod (1951). Moggridge (1975, p.75) notes that 'Keynes's working habits were such that he did not *normally* pay attention in a formal sense to the work of his predecessors before making up his mind. Granted this work was often part of his stock of mental capital, but it was unlabelled as to source. Only after he had made up his mind would the predecessors get acknowledgement or blame.' (See also Davis and Casey, 1977; Patinkin, 1978, 1982.) Moggridge suggests that Keynes' shortcomings may have been exaggerated because the importance of his work, together with his love of controversy, led to his sources being scrutinized more carefully than usual.

On the other hand, given the importance that Keynes attached to the *General Theory*, it seems reasonable to expect that he would make special efforts to check his sources. It is difficult to believe that Keynes was unfamiliar with Pre-Keynesian theory, because he was an editor of the journal in which much of the Pre-Keynesian work was published, and was closely connected with Pigou. Pigou's own explanation was stated bluntly in his review of the *General Theory*:

When, in 1919, he wrote *The Economic Consequences of the Peace*, Mr Keynes did a good day's work for the world, in helping it back towards sanity. But he did a bad day's work for himself as an economist. For he discovered then, and his subconscious mind has not been able to forget since, that the best way to win attention for one's own ideas is to present them in a matrix of sarcastic comment upon other people. This method has long been a routine one among political pamphleteers. It is less appropriate, and fortunately less common, in scientific discussion. Einstein actually did for Physics what Mr Keynes believes himself to have done for Economics. He developed a far-reaching generalisation, under which Newton's results can be subsumed as a special case. But he did not, in announcing his discovery, insinuate, through carefully barbed sentences, that Newton and those who had hitherto followed his lead were a gang of incompetent bunglers (Pigou, 1936, p. 115).

The rather peevish and petulant tone of this review probably worked to Keynes' benefit, in fact, for everyone naturally read Keynes' book if only to find out what had so upset Pigou. And when they had read the book, and relished the sarcasm, they found it much more exciting than reading the turgid tome by Pigou.

It is also necessary to draw attention to the impact of Keynesian thinking on US economists. As already noted, the Pre-Keynesian economists were preoccupied with the problems of the British economy, so that their analysis attracted little interest in the US. Furthermore the English monetary theory of D. H. Robertson (1926) had little impact in the US, where the influence of Irving Fisher was paramount. Unlike Robertson, Fisher was primarily concerned with a full employment economy, and so his theory was hopelessly inadequate to deal with the slump; US economists turned instead to Keynes, who was already well known for his works on international financial policy (Keynes, 1919, 1922). Lack of familiarity with the Pre-Keynesian literature meant that the collective wisdom encapsulated in Keynes' writings was taken by some US economists as being the product of Keynes' own original thought. Furthermore Keynes' criticisms of 'classical' economics seemed quite appropriate to Fisher's theory: there was little doubt that 'the cap fitted'. Hence Keynes' US interpreters — Dillard, Hansen, Klein, Metzler, Samuelson and others — had no reason to doubt Keynes' caricature of Pre-Keynesian economics.

8.7   THE SHORT RUN

The Pre-Keynesian theory is a medium-run theory rather than a short-run theory (it cannot really be called a long-run theory since little attention is given to capital accumulation). Politicians and governments are interested in the short-run—particularly when confronted with a crisis like the onset of the slump. The Wall Street Crash led to world-wide financial instability: prices fell and short-term interest rates rose as firms attempted to borrow in order to stave off bankruptcy. The major policy issue very quickly became whether governments should reflate in order to raise prices and restore business confidence. This in turn was linked to two other issues. The first was whether monetary expansion engineered through the banking system would be sufficient to raise prices, or whether money should be put directly into circulation through increased expenditure on public works. The second issue was whether countries could reflate independently without risking a balance of payments crisis, and if not, whether it was justifiable to impose tariffs and/or to abandon the Gold Standard as a temporary measure.

The case for public works was widely accepted in academic circles in both Britain and the United States (Davis, 1971; Hutchison, 1978; Stein, 1969). In Britain, Cannan was one of the few leading economists to demur. In the United States the influential Chicago school argued that public expenditure should be regulated to compensate for variations in private expenditure over the trade cycle. Even the very conservative Irving Fisher accepted the need for monetary expansion to remove the threat of additional bankruptcies. In both countries it was largely financiers and conservative politicians who opposed public works. Possibly they felt that unchaining the Leviathan of state would have further adverse effects on business confidence, and might prove the thin end of the wedge where socialistic policies were concerned. It must also be recognized that some of them, at least, represented a rentier class who would suffer serious losses from reflationary policies which raised commodity prices and reduced the value of fixed-interest debt.

On the second issue, academic opinion was much more divided. In Britain, Keynes argued that the restoration of the Gold Standard in 1925 had been mishandled, and he attributed the uncompetitive position of British labour since 1925 to a too-high exchange rate. The Pre-Keynesians were included to dismiss this argument on the grounds that with real wage bargaining workers could immunize their living standards against the exchange rate: with real wage bargaining the monetary adjustments induced by exchange rate changes are effectively neutralized. It does appear, however, that the combination of downward money wage rigidity and a fixed exchange rate was a factor in the persistence of too-high real wages between 1925 and the early 1930s. Even if they had accepted Keynes' interpretation, however, it is doubtful if the Pre-Keynesians would have supported Keynes' policies. Their strongly internationalist stance encouraged them to accept the balance of payments as an effective constraint on the scale of additional public works.

In contrast to Keynes, who was a vociferous advocate of reflation, linked with protectionist safeguards, the Pre-Keynesians did not have a clear-cut short-run policy stance. By and large, the Pre-Keynesian idea of a short-run policy was a medium-run policy carried out very quickly. This was the gist of Pigou's recommendations to the Macmillan Committee (when he finally got round to writing them up):

The Immediate Emergency

(1) Serious efforts should be made to check the flow of new recruits into industries—coal, cotton, engineering and so on—that are abnormally depressed. If, for example, in one part of the country, more coal miners are needed, they should be obtained from among existing coal miners in other districts.

(2) Young men in these industries should be encouraged, and, if need be, assisted to move out of them to industries of better prospects.

(3) The government should put in hand and should encourage local authorities and public utility companies to put in hand enterprises of a useful character, even though they are likely to yield a return substantially below current rates, and even though guarantees of interest involving a cost to the Treasury are necessary.

(4) The Bank of England and the banking system should not hesitate to allow the volume of bank deposits to expand so that the money needed to finance these undertakings will not need to be withdrawn from other forms of expenditure.

(5) The whole purpose of this policy, so far as it relates to employment will be defeated if wage earners seize the occasion provided by a fall in the unemployment figures to insist on higher wages. It is *impossible* to increase employment if every stimulation of the demand for labour is balanced by new wage requirements.

(6) The above policy should be regarded as a temporary one designed to enable present real wage rates to be maintained without abnormal unemployment during the interval that must elapse before growth of capital equipment and improved technique, in company with the contraction in the annual supply of new labour that will result, a few years hence, from the low birth rate of the war period, allows normal employment to be maintained at existing real wage rates without special government intervention (Pigou, 1931, p. 93).

The first two points spring directly from the structural view of unemployment, and the next two endorse reflation as a remedy for the additional unemployment created during the slump. The last two points qualify Pigou's support for reflation: it should be only temporary because in the longer run it will stimulate higher money wage demands.

While Pigou acknowledged the role of 'Keynesian' policies, Keynes himself paid no attention to the structural aspects of unemployment and ignored Pigou's concern about the long-run implications of his policy. He was preoccupied by the short-run constraint imposed by money wage rigidity. Lecturing on the Harris Foundation in Chicago in 1931 Keynes remarks

Will not the social resistance to a drastic downward readjustment of salaries and wages be an ugly and a dangerous thing? I am told sometimes that these changes present comparatively little difficulty in a country such as the United States where economic rigidity has not yet set in. I find it difficult to believe this. But it is for you, not me, to say. I know that in my own country a really large cut of many wages [money wages?], a cut at all of the same order of magnitude as the fall in wholesale prices, is simply an impossibility. To attempt it would be to shake the social order to its foundation. There is scarcely one responsible person in Great Britain prepared to recommend it openly (Keynes, 1931, p. 31).

He adds later, 'while most people probably accept this view, I doubt if they feel it with sufficient intensity' (Keynes, 1931, p. 34).

Given money wage rigidity, Keynes is able to derive the government expenditure multiplier, which provides the basis for a simple technique of short-term budgeting. Budgetary policy is something that politicians and administrators can easily understand. The need to balance a budget is an irksome constraint on administrators and a vote-loser for politicians (except for those, noted earlier, who represent the rentier class), so that a budgetary theory which advocates a deficit will soon attract a following.

But problems begin to arise when a short-run policy is applied on a long-run basis. Keynes judged that during the 1930s the British economy could be reflated without inducing a substantial increase in money wages, and he seems to have been broadly correct. Pigou's anxieties about wage inflation seemed unfounded at the time, but even so he reiterated his fears in his review of *The General Theory*. Applying the theory of monopoly to trade unions, he warns

. . . even if Mr Keynes' full employment were established, wage-earners would still have a choice between policies that promote respectively higher real wages plus less employment and lower real wages *plus* more employment. It is not necessarily in their own interest, or even in the general interest, that they should prefer the second type of policy. In any event, the choice belongs, neither to the banks nor to the State, but to them. If they opt for the first type of policy—and experience shows that they do opt for it to some extent—the establishment of full employment in Mr Keynes' sense would not prevent the level of employment from being substantially less than that normal to a boom (Pigou, 1936, p. 131).

During the 1930s the relatively high level of unemployment, coupled with surprisingly good industrial relations, seem to have prevented the trade unions from forcing the issue in this way. But there is no doubt that the trade unions' leaders at the time perceived the trade-off between wages and employment in exactly the same way as did Pigou. The Trade Union Congress had this to say in 1930:

. . . Professor Jones, who stated in 1925 'that the future would witness a struggle between the Treasury and the trade unions for the final word in the determination of the currency system', is realistic enough to appreciate the nature of the conflict that would ensue were an attack on wages to take place. He says 'In 1925 I predicted a period of serious industrial strife, and my prediction was justified by subsequent events. Failing a rapid reversal in the trend of world prices . . ., I cannot see how we are to avoid, in the near future, difficulties of a similar character. . . . The only alternative seems to be to give up the attempt to reduce the 1929 volume of unemployment to pre-war dimensions and to be content with providing maintenance, without work, for over a million willing workers.

We may say quite frankly that we would prefer this alternative, if the choice had to be made. We would prefer to wait for international action, in the meantime pressing forward the reorganisation of industry while maintaining those unemployed, and preserving the present standard of living for those in employment, rather than have unemployment eliminated immediately at the cost of a degradation in the standard of living of the workers. (Trade Union Congress General Council, 1931, pp. 324–5).

World War II intervened before the full implications of this trade union outlook could be felt, and it was not until recently that the consequences of the attitude became evident in increasing wage demands and increasing unemployment.

8.8   THE UNPOPULARITY OF STRUCTURAL CHANGE

The main thrust of Pre-Keynesian policy is towards the promotion of structural change. It suggests that obstacles to mobility should be reduced. It presents a direct challenge to vested interests in declining industries who may be seeking continuing subsidies for inefficient management and low labour productivity. It is a threat to the social life of established communities in areas where declining industries predominate. It is even a threat to national cultural values, as structural change often involves importing new technologies and working practices—either under licence or through direct invest-ments from overseas. Pre-Keynesian policies are vote-losers. It takes considerable political will to push them through. That political will did not exist in inter-war Britain, and quite possibly it still does not exist today.

Pre-Keynesian policies are medium-run policies, and there are often short-run arguments for putting them off. The main argument (or excuse) stems from the periodic booms which bring even the depressed industries somewhere near to full capacity. Although the booms are only temporary, those attached to the declining industries tend to behave as though they were permanent. In inter-war Britain many of the declining industries were related to the munitions trades—ship-building and heavy engineering, for example—and from the mid-1930s rearmament enabled structural adjustments to be shelved. Industries which had had surplus labour and surplus capacity since 1920 were working close to full capacity again after a spell of nearly 15 years.

The political appeal of Pre-Keynesian policies depends, of course, upon the way in which they are presented, and it has been shown above that in inter-war Britain they were not presented in a particularly attractive way. The attitudes and personalities of the Pre-Keynesian economists made them see only the negative side of the policy issues, and observers could be forgiven for thinking that they were really recommending a return to *laissez-faire*.

8.9 SUMMARY

The eclipse of the Pre-Keynesian theory has been explained in terms of seven factors:

(1) the lack of generality in the formulation of the theory, reflecting a somewhat insular concern with British problems;
(2) failure to develop a coherent package of policies which could be urged upon the government, and a general ineptitude in policy debate;
(3) the Pre-Keynesian response to the apparent failure of the Industrial Transference Scheme;
(4) a switch in the interests of the academic community towards ideological issues such as 'the future of capitalism' and 'the possibility of planning';

(5) Keynes' misrepresentation of Pre-Keynesian theory, and the Pre-Keynesians' failure to reply adequately to his criticisms;

(6) the difficulty of applying Pre-Keynesian theory in the very short run, and

(7) the general unpopularity of policies involving far-reaching structural change.

The first five factors largely reflect the personalities of the Pre-Keynesians, and in particular the ineffectiveness of Pigou in debating with Keynes. The last two factors are inherent in the theory, and are problems that any modern advocate of Pre-Keynesian policies must contend with.

9

The Determinants of Employment and the Real Wage in Inter-war Britain

9.1 INTRODUCTION

This chapter and the next test the relevance of the Pre-Keynesian theory of unemployment to the inter-war British economy. The tests are subject to important limitations due to the shortage of reliable statistical evidence.

Previous work on unemployment has, by and large, examined the determinants of unemployment as a whole rather than considered separately the determinants of employment and labour supply. Within a disequilibrium framework, however, it is clear that these two elements in unemployment merit separate attention (Rosen and Quandt, 1978). In Pre-Keynesian theory, when the real wage is too high, unemployment is set on the short side by the demand for labour. The demand for labour is determined by the real wage independently of conditions affecting labour supply. It follows that statistics of wages and employment should unambiguously identify a labour demand curve. Because of diminishing marginal returns to labour the demand curve will be downward-sloping. If unemployment is persistent, then over time in each industry there should be a negative correlation between employment and the real wage.

Statistical evidence on the relation between employment and the real wage is examined in sections 9.2–9.4 below. A short-run employment function is derived from Pre-Keynesian theory, and estimated using inter-war data. In estimating the employment function the real wage is regarded as parametric. Pre-Keynesian views on the determination of the real wage are examined in sections 9.5 and 9.6. Because of statistical limitations, the interpretation of real wage movements in the inter-war period is somewhat speculative. Nevertheless, movements in real wages are broadly consistent with the explanations advanced by Pre-Keynesian writers.

The predictions of the Pre-Keynesian theory with respect to

labour supply are more complex. In the job search model, for example, labour supply in each industry is governed by migration in response to relative changes in expected wages; these in turn reflect the structure of both actual wages and labour demand. The determinants of labour supply in inter-war Britain are discussed in chapter 10.

9.2 A SHORT-RUN EMPLOYMENT FUNCTION DERIVED FROM PRE-KEYNESIAN THEORY

The Pre-Keynesian view that labour demand is a decreasing function of the real wage has generated a surprising amount of controversy (cf. Thirlwall, 1981). It is, after all, a simple application to the market for labour of the principle of scarcity, as reflected in the first law of demand. Two main objections have been made. The first centres on the fact that firms can be forced off their labour demand curve by short-run fluctuations in product demand. It is well known that when product prices are inflexible, firms may experience a sales constraint (Patinkin, 1965; Barro and Grossman, 1971, 1976). As a result, labour demand may be cut back without any change in the real wage. The sales constraint will persist, however, only so long as the product price remains inflexible. Once the product price adjusts, the firm will return to its labour demand curve.

The second objection is that labour demand could be an increasing and not a decreasing function of the real wage. This view is usually based upon a claim that firms do not produce under conditions of diminishing marginal returns to labour. This claim appears to be supported by statistical estimates of short-run employment functions, which generally indicate that there are increasing rather than diminishing marginal returns (Ball and St Cyr, 1966; Hazeldine, 1981). The Samuelson–Le Chatelier principle suggests that returns to labour will diminish more rapidly in the short run than in the long run. (Samuelson, 1947, p. 36). If the statistical evidence points to increasing returns in the short run, then the Samuelson–Le Chatelier principle suggests that there must be increasing returns in the long run too.

In fact both these objections can be met by only a minor modification of the Pre-Keynesian theory of labour demand. The modification involves the derivation of a short-run Pre-Keynesian employment function which contains the long-run Pre-Keynesian employment function as a special case. This function reconciles short-run sales constraints and increasing marginal returns with a long-run Pre-Keynesian demand for labour. The reconciliation is quite straightforward. It is assumed, to begin with, that firms choose to maintain prices stable in the short run in order to provide a service to consumers (Casson, 1981; Okun, 1981). An integral part of this service is to supply all the consumer demand forthcoming at the quoted price. Since firms cannot predict this demand exactly, it is important for them to build short-run flexibility into the production process.

Flexibility in production can be achieved through intertemporal substitutions of various kinds:

(1) work in progress can be stockpiled during slack periods and depleted during busy periods;

(2) routine maintenance can be deferred by switching maintenance workers to routine production during busy periods (where job demarcation rules allow this) and by switching production workers to 'painting the factory' during slack periods;

(3) labour can be asked to supply additional effort for short periods, either through additional hours of work or through greater intensity of work during a fixed period. Since the effort supplied by an operative often limits the rate of utilization of machinery (Feldstein, 1967), the total effect of additional effort may be quite striking.

These opportunities for intertemporal substitution do not exist to the same extent in the long run. Inventories and work in progress cannot be accumulated indefinitely because of storage constraints, and maintenance cannot be deferred indefinitely because of the increasing risk of breakdown. The intensity of effort cannot be raised for long spells because the effects of fatigue will cumulate over time. It is only in the short run, therefore, that additional output can be achieved for very little additional input. In the long run, the short-run 'debts' of inventory replacement, deferred maintenance and labour recuperation have to be repaid.

For this reason the assumptions underlying the Samuelson–le Chatelier principle do not apply: the factors mentioned above are not fixed in the short run and variable in the long run, but the exact reverse; they are variable in the short run but fixed in the long run. It follows that there may be increasing marginal returns in the short run but diminishing marginal returns in the long run.

The employment function derived below is predicated upon the third kind of intertemporal substitution described above. It is assumed that the employer can meet additional output requirements by temporarily increasing the intensity of work with the consent of the workers, provided that this greater intensity is compensated by much lower intensity of work later on. The lower intensity results when output requirements are temporarily reduced, and labour is 'hoarded' until the anticipated recovery comes. Over the cycle in output, therefore, there is at times a certain amount of 'slack' in the production process; this slack is planned deliberately in order to economize on the costs of adjusting production to varying output targets.

It can be shown that, over the cycle, firms respond to greater demand for output by a combination of increased employment and greater effort per employee, and respond to reductions in demand by a combination of lower employment and lower effort per employee. Because higher employment is associated with higher effort, and the higher effort is not recorded in production statistics, a statistical illusion is created that higher employment generates additional output under conditions of increasing marginal returns.

The formal derivation of the employment function proceeds in two stages. The first stage establishes the properties of the function in the long run; the second stage specifies the dynamics of short-run adjustment (cf. Hendry, 1980).

In the first stage, long-run target employment n^*, is derived from the maximization of long-run profit. It is assumed that in the long run the representative firm hires labour at a parametric money wage W, and sells output at a parametric price P, with no sales constraint. The firm has a log-linear production function relating output, y, to the input of work, z:

$$y = Az^a \qquad (9.1)$$

where $A > 0$ and $0 < a < 1$. Work is the product of the number of employees, n, and the intensity of employees' effort, e:

$$z = ne \qquad (9.2)$$

In the long run the employees' effort is set by implicit contract between employer and employees at a target level e^*:

$$e = e^* \qquad (9.3)$$

The first-order condition for a maximum of long-run profit

$$\Pi = Py - Wn \tag{9.4}$$

subject to (9.1)–(9.3) equates the marginal product of labour to the own–product wage $w = W/P$, and determines the constant–elasticity labour demand function

$$n^* = (\alpha A e^{*\alpha}/w)^{1/(1-\alpha)} \tag{9.5}$$

In the second stage, the firm plans to meet an estimated short-run product demand, $\bar{y}$, by choosing a combination of employment and effort which minimizes short-run costs. It is important for long-run profits that the firm meets this short-run demand in full, otherwise customer goodwill may be lost. A very simple specification of short-run costs is used in which cost is a monotone increasing function of

$$c = (n/n^*) + (e/e^*) \tag{9.6}$$

The cost function (9.6) is specified only up to a monotone transformation because it is concerned with the relative cost of adjusting employment and effort, and not with the absolute costs involved. Absolute costs depend upon other variables, such as the money wage. Since labour as a whole ultimately has to be compensated for both additional employment and additional effort, the wage affects the absolute costs of employment and effort, but not their relative costs.

For a given level of cost, the marginal rate of substitution between employment and effort is independent of actual employment, n, and effort, e, is directly proportional to normal effort, e^*, and inversely proportional to the target employment, n^*. Furthermore when employment is set at its target level n^*, and effort at its normal intensity e^* then the iso-cost elasticity of substitution between employment and effort is unity.

The short-run cost function (9.6) may be regarded as a special case of an adjustment cost function where, in the absence of hiring, employment would be zero. The real world could approximate this situation under two conditions. The first is a fairly untypical case in which the firm is growing very fast, so that initial employment is very small relative to the actual employment required to meet current product demand. The second case is where voluntary labour turnover (i.e. natural wastage) is very high, so that if no hiring were done, employment would diminish close to zero during the course of each period. This is not unreasonable as a description of conditions in some of the industries in inter-war Britain which relied heavily upon the recruitment of casual labour.

The first-order condition for a minimum of adjustment cost (9.6) subject to the demand constraint

$$y = \bar{y} \qquad (9.7)$$

is that effort per employee is directly proportional to the level of employment

$$e = (e^*/n^*)n \qquad (9.8)$$

Notice that in the long-run equilibrium, where $n = n^*$, the optimum level of effort is the target level e^*. In the short run, however, n will not normally equal n^*, and so e will normally deviate from e^*. Thus the effort condition for long-run equilibrium (9.3) is replaced by the short-run condition (9.8). It is the replacement of (9.3) by (9.8) which generates the illusion of increasing returns in the short run. For substituting (9.8) back into (9.1) gives a relation between output and employment of the form:

$$y = A(e^*/n^*)^\alpha n^{2\alpha} \qquad (9.9)$$

The coefficient on n in (9.9) is 2α, which is double the coefficient on n implied by equations (9.1)–(9.3). It follows that if $\frac{1}{2} < \alpha < 1$ then there will be diminishing marginal returns in the long run but there will appear to be increasing marginal returns in the short run.

Substituting long-run employment (9.5) into the short-run equation (9.9) gives the short-run employment function

$$n = [\alpha(Ae^{*\alpha})^{(2\alpha-1)/2\alpha}]^{1/(1-\alpha)} y^{1/2\alpha} w^{-1/2(1-\alpha)} \qquad (9.10)$$

This represents a log-linear employment function in which employment is a function of current output and the current own-product wage. The coefficient on output is $1/2\alpha$ and the coefficient on the own-product wage is $-1/2(1-\alpha)$.

The derivation of the employment function (9.10) is illustrated in figure 9.1. The upper quadrant exhibits the trade-off between effort and employment, while the lower quadrant shows the determination of target employment by the own-product wage. Suppose that initially the firm is in long-run equilibrium with the real wage at w_1. Employment is n_1^*, effort is fixed at e^*, and so the firm produces at X_0. The firm incurs short-run costs in replacing natural wastage: the costs are some monotone-increasing function of OC_0, or equivalently, of OC_0', the intercepts of the 45-degree line C_0C_0' passing through X_0. These costs are the minimal short-run costs, given the effort–employment trade-off Y_0Y_0' associated with the long-run target output.

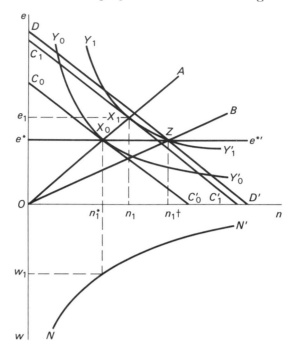

FIGURE 9.1
Derivation of a short-run Pre-Keynesian employment function

Suppose now that there is an exogenous increase in product demand, with prices remaining sticky, so that the effort-employment trade-off shifts out to $Y_1 Y_1'$. If the level of effort were maintained unchanged at e^*, then the firm would need to produce at Z, and employment would increase to $n_1\dagger$. Short-run costs would rise into line with the intercepts OD, OD' of the 45-degree line DD' passing through Z. Adjustment from X_0 to Z will, however, increase the intensity of employment relative to the intensity of effort, as indicated by the fact that the slope of the ray OB through Z is lower than the slope of the ray OA through X_0. The cost-minimizing strategy is to substitute effort for employment along the trade-off locus $Y_1 Y_1'$ until the point of tangency X_1 is reached between the locus $Y_1 Y_1'$ and the iso-cost line $C_1 C_1'$. At this point the intensity of employment relative to effort has been returned to its long-run equilibrium level. The level of employment has been reduced from $n_1\dagger$ to n_1 at the expense of an increase in the intensity of effort from e^* to e_1. Assuming that the real wage, and hence long-run target employment, are unchanged, the firm will therefore recruit n_1 employees. This level of employment is a compromise between the target employment and the level of employment necessary to produce the output with the target intensity of effort. It represents a 'partial adjustment' of employment from the target level determined by the real wage towards the level dictated by the short-run exigencies of demand.

9.3   EVIDENCE ON THE DEMAND FOR LABOUR

The employment function (9.10) can be estimated from either cross-section or time-series data. Both kinds of data have been used in this study. Let there be n industries, indexed $i = 1, \ldots, n$, observed at times $t = 0, 1, \ldots, T$. It is assumed that each industry consists of a fixed number of identical firms, and that each industry has the same coefficient of marginal returns to labour, a, which is constant over time. Each industry has its own productivity factor which varies exponentially with time:

$$A_{it} = A_{i0} \exp (g_i t) \qquad (9.11)$$

where g_i is the trend growth rate of labour productivity in the ith industry. The trend growth is explained by factors such as capital accumulation and technical progress, which are not explicitly modelled by the theory. It is assumed that the target effort in each industry, e_i^*, is constant over time.

Substituting (9.11) into (9.10) and transforming to logarithms gives

$$\log n_{it} = \frac{1}{2a(1-a)} \left[a \log a + 2a - 1) \log A_{i0} e_i^{*a} \right]$$

$$+ \frac{2-a}{2a(1-a)} \ g_i t + \frac{1}{2a} \log y_{it} - \frac{1}{2(1-a)} \ \log w_{it} \qquad (9.12)$$

For cross-section estimation the terms in A_{i0} and e_i^* can be eliminated from industry data by first-differencing with respect to time. This provides an equation relating the logarithmic change in employment to the logarithmic change in output and the logarithmic change in the own-product wage. The only problem is that there is an intercept term involving the trend growth rate g_i which varies across industries. When the changes are measured over a fairly short time interval the bias induced by the trend growth rate may be quite small. This is because it is likely that the changes in output occurring during a short period will be due mainly to fluctuations in output about the trend rather than by trend growth itself. The bias will be more serious over longer periods, for then the correlation between change in output and trend growth may be quite high. This will generate an upward bias in the estimates of the coefficient on current output.

For time-series estimation the equation (9.12) can be used as it stands. Both time-series and cross-section estimates are liable to suffer bias due to errors of measurement in the independent variables. This is particularly true of the wage coefficients, whose least-squares estimates are likely to be biased towards zero because of the substantial measurement errors in the wage statistics.

Notwithstanding these reservations, the data provide convincing support for this short-run variant of the Pre-Keynesian theory. Table 9.1 reports the results of a cross-section study of the changes in employment, output and wages in 38 UK industries over two adjacent periods 1924–30, 1930–35, and over the period 1924–35 as a

TABLE 9.1

Determinants of the growth of employment in 38 UK industries 1924–30–35

Period	Constant	Growth of output	Growth of earnings	Growth of wage index	R^2	DW
1924–30	0.012 (0.026)	0.633 (0.098)*	−0.124 (0.386)	−0.401 (0.581)	60.0	2.21
1930–35	−0.017 (0.027)	0.613 (0.098)*	−0.276 (0.257)	−0.185 (0.486)	54.0	2.02
1924–35	−0.075 (0.036)	1.025 (0.096)*	−0.026 (0.363)	−1.441 (0.485)*	78.0	2.18
1924–30	0.016 (0.023)	0.624 (0.094)*		−0.455 (0.549)	59.9	2.25
1930–35	−0.033 (0.023)	0.609 (0.098)*		−0.257 (0.483)	52.5	1.88
1924–35	−0.075 (0.034)*	1.024 (0.094)*		−1.449 (0.467)*	78.0	2.18

Note: An asterisk denotes that the coefficient is significant at 5 per cent in two-tailed *t*-test.

whole. The data on output and wages are in nominal rather than real terms. The sources of data, the selection of the sample and the general characteristics of the industries are discussed in detail in Appendix A. The substitution of nominal for real variables is valid only if relative product prices are stable over the period concerned. The method of estimation is ordinary least-squares. To simplify the interpretation of the results, logarithmic changes have been approximated by percentage changes.

The coefficients on output in each of the two sub-periods indicate a coefficient of marginal returns to labour of about 0.8. If effort adjustments were ignored the corresponding figure would be 1.6—suggesting strongly increasing returns. The coefficient on output is much higher over the full period, as would be expected if the impact of trend growth were greater over the longer period. This view fits in well with the history of the inter-war period, for 1930 was a year of sharp depression in which many industries suffered a major deviation from trend, whereas 1924 and 1935 were on balance closer to the trend. Thus the inter-industry variations in the growth of output over the sub-periods are less likely to be explained by differences in trend growth than the variation over the full period. The coefficient of marginal returns calculated from the sub-period results may therefore be interpreted as a reasonably unbiased estimate of the true marginal returns. The results therefore support the view that there are diminishing marginal returns with a coefficient of about 0.8.

Two alternative measures of wages were used, one based upon earnings and the other upon basic wage rates. The coefficient on the growth of earnings is statistically insignificant, though it has the right (negative) sign. The coefficient on the growth of wage rates is statistically significant over the full period, and although insignificant over the sub-periods, again has the right (negative) sign. A value $\alpha = 0.8$ would suggest a true value for the wage coefficient of 2.5, but as noted above there is likely to be a serious downward bias in the estimated wage coefficient, and this view is consistent with the estimates reported in the table, which are all below this value. The Durbin–Watson statistics (DW) all suggest that the assumption of a log-linear function form is valid—there is no evidence of deviations from log-linearity. The percentage of the variation in employment explained by the variation in output and wages (R^2) seems reasonably satisfactory for a cross-section study of this kind.

The results of the time-series study are reported in table 9.2. The study concerns five manufacturing industries and uses annual data for 1920–38. The selection of the industries and the limitations of the data are discussed in Appendix B. It cannot be too heavily stressed that time-series analysis on 19 annual observations is liable to encounter a number of pitfalls. A limited amount of 'data mining' had to be done in order to investigate problems connected with serial correlation, but the manner in which the 'mining' was done was strictly controlled in order not to invalidate the significance of the results. The results reported in table 9.2 are not the best-fit results, but merely a representative set which illustrate the kind of results obtained.

TABLE 9.2

Log-linear regressions of employment on output, time and the own-product wage, using annual data for five UK industries, 1920–38

Industry	Constant	Current output	Lagged output	Time trend	Own-product real wage	R^2	DW
Iron and steel	3.335* (0.348)	0.446* (0.075)			−1.341* (0.221)	79.5	0.88†
Mechanical engineering	3.855* (0.459)	0.404* (0.100)			−1.818* (0.206)	85.4	1.19
Electrical engineering	1.890* (0.357)	0.605* (0.604)			−0.129 (0.226)	86.1	0.85†
Ship-building	2.818* (0.261)	0.463* (0.068)			−0.329 (0.165)	77.5	0.72†
Vehicles	1.790* (0.487)	0.644* (0.083)			−0.091 (0.142)	95.6	1.38
Iron and steel	2.675* (0.316)	0.518* (0.062)	0.159* (0.053)	−0.017* (0.005)	−0.441 (0.241)	89.6	0.98†
Mechanical engineering	4.047* (0.376)	0.192 (0.092)	0.151 (0.091)	0.010* (0.004)	−1.729* (0.244)	89.8	2.60
Electrical engineering	4.834* (0.649)	−0.139 (0.115)	0.059 (0.114)	0.052* (0.010)	−1.135* (0.262)	96.9	1.06
Ship-building	3.386 (0.175)	0.323* (0.046)	0.083 (0.047)	−0.027* (0.006)	−0.017 (0.098)	94.4	1.49
Vehicles	1.287* (0.379)	0.675* (0.092)	0.065 (0.089)	−0.004 (0.006)	−0.083 (0.180)	98.1	1.42

Note: An asterisk indicates that the coefficient is statistically significant at 5 per cent in a two-tailed *t*-test. A dagger (†) indicates that there is significant autocorrelation at the 5 per cent level.

A very stable set of coefficients on current output was obtained by regressing employment on output and the real wage, ignoring the time trend. These results are reported in the top half of the table. The output coefficients are not dissimilar to those obtained for the sub-periods in the cross-section study, though on average they are somewhat lower. The output coefficients are significantly positive, and the wage coefficients are consistently negative, though only two of the five are significantly so. The values of R^2 are high (though not so high as to be suspect), but the Durbin–Watson statistics are unsatisfactory, as in three of the five industries they conclusively indicate positive serial correlation.

Eliminating serial correlation proved difficult. Inclusion of the time trend effected a marginal improvement, and so did the inclusion of lagged output. The introduction of additional variables led to some instability in the output coefficients, however. The kind of results obtained are illustrated in the bottom part of the table. The statistical significance of current output is reduced, and in the case of the engineering industry the coefficient changes sign. The time trend coefficients suggest negative productivity growth in iron and steel and ship-building, and positive productivity growth in mechanical and electrical engineering. The coefficients are all significant and seem quite reasonable in the light of the history of the period. The corresponding coefficient in the vehicle industry is negative and insignificant; the probable explanation is that high trend growth of output in this industry has led to multicollinearity between output and employment. The coefficients on lagged output are consistently positive, but only one of them is significant. It can be seen that the coefficients on the real wage are quite robust to the inclusion of additional explanatory variables. They all remain negative, and once again two of the five are significant.

9.4   A COMPARISON WITH OTHER STUDIES

Some readers may feel that these results are unrepresentative of the kind of results produced by other studies of employment and the real wage. There is a widely held belief that previous results have been inconclusive (Bodkin, 1969) or have even rejected the hypothesis of a negative association between employment and the real wage. This view is false, and appears to have arisen from a misunderstanding of early work by Dunlop (1938) and Tarshis (1939).

Dunlop and Tarshis tested Keynes' conjecture that money wages and real wages were negatively correlated over the trade cycle, and rejected it. However, Keynes' hypothesis does not depend only upon the hypothesis that there is a negatively sloped demand curve for labour. It also rests, as Dunlop points out, upon an implicit postulate that money wage increases reflect trade union strength, which in turn depends upon the level of employment. Keynes' hypothesis fails because this implicit postulate is incorrect (Dunlop, 1938, p. 432). On the specific question of employment and the real wage, Dunlop's results are actually consistent with the Pre-Keynesian view (see also Dunlop, 1939). Dunlop summarizes the behaviour of wage rates in the UK 1860–1937 as follows:

Statistically, real wage rates generally rise with an increase in money wage rates, rise during a first period after the peak, and then fall under the pressure of severe wage reductions. Correcting for changes in the terms of trade or for trend does not materially alter these results (Dunlop, 1938, p. 434).

This lag structure indicates that over the course of the trade cycle, rises in real wages synchronize with the downturn in economic activity and reductions in real wages precede the upturns in activity. This is entirely consistent with the view that changes in the real wage induce changes in employment of opposite sign with a lag.

Dunlop's conclusion were corroborated by Tarshis (1939) using monthly data for the US 1932–8. Tarshis showed that in the US too, changes in money wages were positively rather than negatively correlated with changes in real wages. He also identified a negative relation between employment and the real wage, with a correlation coefficient of -0.64. More recently, Neftci (1978) and Sargent (1978) have confirmed the negative association between employment and the real wage for the US economy after World War II. They also show that changes in the real wage lead changes in employment, which is again consistent with the view that employment is adjusting to the real wage (for further evidence on the post-war period see section 11.2).

Hatton (1981) has estimated employment functions for inter-war Britain by adapting conventional models of employment adjustment costs. His data are drawn from broadly similar sources to those of the time-series study reported in section 9.3 above, though because he has studied many more industries, the quality of his data is, on average, slightly poorer. He estimates a log-linear regression of employment on the real wage and several other explanatory variables, and finds that in 14 of the 19 industries there is a negative coefficient on the real wage, which is significant in 11 of the cases.

All of the studies discussed here thus support the view that there is an inverse relation between employment and the real wage. Such a relationship was taken for granted by the Pre-Keynesian economists. It is one of the unfortunate results of the Keynesian revolution that such an obvious relationship should have been questioned, when the evidence in its favour is so very strong.

9.5 THE COURSE OF REAL WAGES IN THE INTER-WAR PERIOD

The disequilibrium approach outlined in chapters 4–6 assumes that the real wage is determined exogenously. The theory does not claim to explain the determination of the real wage, but only to analyse the consequences of a given level of it. It is clear, however, that the Pre-Keynesian economists had definite ideas on the determination of the real wage. This section examines the relevance of these ideas to movements in the real wage in the inter-war period. The next section compares the Pre-Keynesians' view with the views of Keynes himself.

There are good reasons to suppose that behaviour patterns in the labour market changed quite significantly during the inter-war period (see below). It is therefore difficult to specify a model in which the structural parameters are likely to have remained stable throughout the period. Sargan (1964), for example, attempted to estimate modified Phillips-curve relations using quarterly data 1922–38, but found his results unconvincing and unreliable. Somewhat similar problems have been encountered in econometric studies of the labour market in the post-war period—for example, the instability of the unemployment–vacancy relationship and the breakdown of the Phillips curve. It is possible that such instability results from the principal actors in the labour market—trade unions, government and employers—learning to anticipate one another's behaviour. One party learns how to neutralize the effect of another party's strategy; as one party learns that his opponent has changed his strategy, so he modifies his own strategy too.

There are three main aspects of inter-war real wage rates that require explanation. The first is that the level of real wages was on average relatively high compared to the pre-war period. After the war the domestic capital stock was heavily depreciated through intensive utilization (e.g. the railway network) and holdings of foreign assets had been substantially reduced. But real wages, rather than being lower than before the war, were about 13 per cent higher. Pigou and Clay both relied heavily upon the statistical work of Arthur Lyon Bowley and Josiah Stamp, which showed that nominal earnings of fully employed wage-earners rose 94 per cent between July 1914 and December 1924, while according to the Ministry of Labour the cost of living rose 81 per cent during the same period. This was no transitory phenomenon, for according to Bowley's estimates, between December 1924 and December 1929 the real wage rose a further 6 per cent (Bowley, 1930).

The Pre-Keynesians explained this rise by an increase in the power of the trade unions. Modern estimates indicate that in British industry as a whole, trade union membership density (union membership as a percentage of 'potential' membership, as proxied by labour supply) rose from 31.9 per cent in 1913 to a peak of 58.2 per cent in 1920, returned to its pre-war level by 1928 and recovered to 38.3 per cent in 1938 (Bain and Price, 1980, p. 39). High union membership density does not, of itself, imply the aggressive pursuit of wage claims. In the context of the peak in membership in 1920, however, the association seems to hold, for the number of man-weeks lost in strikes was very high, as it was again in 1921. Although the association between membership density, strike activity, and the level of wage settlements does not necessarily imply causation, the evidence is clearly consistent with the Pre-Keynesian explanation of the high real wage.

The second aspect of inter-war real wages is the narrowing of skill differentials compared to the pre-war period. The data in table 9.3 show that in a sample of five industries studied by Rowe (1928), between 1913 and 1920, and again between 1920 and 1926, the wage rates of unskilled workers rose relative to those of semi-skilled workers, and the wages of the semi-skilled rose relative to those of the skilled. These tendencies are confirmed by Routh (1980, p. 124) who shows in addition that between 1913/14 and 1922/4 women's wages rose relative to men's, particularly in the unskilled group. He also shows that foremen and managers improved their position relative to the professional, skilled and semi-skilled groups.

The narrowing of skill differentials can be explained in one of three ways. The first is by the rising strength of the general unions; craft

TABLE 9.3
Relative wages for different skills in
five British industries (1913 = 100)

Industry	Grade	Job	Wage index	
			1920	*1926*
Building	Skilled	Bricklayer	94	104
	Semi-skilled	Painter	105	117
	Unskilled	Labourer	124	121
Coal mining	Skilled	Coal-getter	110	97
	Semi-skilled	Putter and filler	118	96
	Unskilled	Labourer	123	99
Cotton	Skilled	Mule spinner	118	106
	Semi-skilled	Grinder	123	110
	Unskilled	Woman weaver	125	112
Engineering	Skilled	Turner	97	93
	Semi-skilled	Machineman	109	98
	Unskilled	Labourer	120	105
Railways	Skilled	Engine driver	91	117
	Semi-skilled	Guard	104	123
	Unskilled	Goods porter	125	127

Source: Rowe (1928), Table III, p. 48.

unions for skilled workers had long been established in many trades, but general unions recruiting unskilled workers on an industry basis mainly came to prominence after the turn of the century. It is to be expected that when these unions began to 'flex their muscles' they would be able to improve the relative position of the unskilled workers. It is certainly true that during the 1920s the general unions were amongst the most aggressive—in the Triple Alliance, for example—although it was often the older established of them—the coal miners and the dockers, for example—that caused the most disruption. The growth of general unions cannot, however, explain other changes such as the relative improvement in women's wages and managerial salaries.

An alternative explanation is that the changes in relativities reflect the forces of supply and demand. Scientific management placed increasing emphasis upon a small group of 'time-and-motion' men monitoring and evaluating a larger group of people performing repetitive unskilled or semi-skilled work. Where the unskilled work involved dexterity rather than strength, women appear to have been just as suitable (if not more suitable) than men. Increasing demands for foremen and managers, and for unskilled women workers, could explain the relative improvement in the wages of these groups. While this view has much to commend it, the concept of the equilibrium wage which underpins it is incompatible with the disequilibrium implied by the prevalence of mass unemployment. It may explain why women's wages improved relative to men's, but it cannot explain why unskilled men's wages were maintained high when a high proportion of unskilled men were unemployed.

The third explanation is that improvements in the level of unemployment benefit strengthened the bargaining power of trade unions representing the lower-paid workers. The extension of the unemployment insurance scheme in 1920, and the subsequent advance in the real level of benefit, afforded a high replacement ratio for many lower-paid workers. By assuming complete financial responsibility for the unemployed, the government may also have given the impression that it accepted moral responsibility for unemployment too. This could explain why the real wages of unskilled male workers remained high in the face of substantial unemployment. It could also explain why the general unions representing the lower-paid were able to win the support of low-paid workers for the aggressive pursuit of wage claims.

The combination of high union membership density and increased levels of unemployment benefit, emphasized by the Pre-Keynesians, may therefore explain the improvement in the relative wage of unskilled male workers in the face of substantial unemployment. It is unlikely, though, to be the sole explanation of the improvement in unskilled wages as a whole, for the wages of unskilled women, amongst whom unionization was relatively low, rose even faster than those of men. The Pre-Keynesian explanation of relativities is plausible only if the effects of changes in technology and working practices on the labour market are allowed for too.

The third aspect of inter-war wage behaviour concerns short-run fluctuations in the real wage. The Pre-Keynesians explained deviations from trend in the real wage in the same way as did Keynes. They ascribed it to money wage rigidity in the face of fluctuating money prices, which caused the real wage to rise at a time when money prices fell. This interpretation is broadly consistent with the evidence. Figure 9.2 indicates that over the inter-war period the average real wage increased at about 1 per cent per annum. There are two main deviations from this trend: in 1921 and from 1930 to 1934. By comparing the graph of the real wage with the graph of the money wage it can be seen that in both cases the increase in the real wage is caused by money wages being stickier than money prices. In both cases there is a price deflation, but whereas in 1921 the fall in money wages 'catches up' with the fall in money prices by the following year, in 1930 the money wage falls so little that in subsequent years the real wage continues to rise.

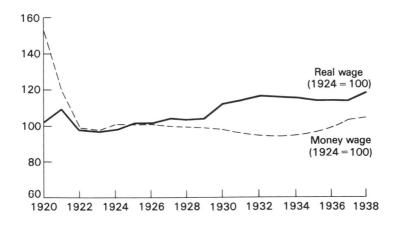

FIGURE 9.2
Time path of real and money wages in Britain, 1920–38.
Source: Mitchell and Deane (1971), table 'Wages 1D', p. 345.

It appears, therefore, that Pre-Keynesian theory is broadly consistent with the history of real wage movements in the inter-war period. The Pre-Keynesian theory is not a comprehensive explanation of real wage movements, because it ignores the impact of changing production methods on wage relativities. But with the limited data available it is impossible to deny that the causes emphasized by the Pre-Keynesians may have had some influence upon real wages.

9.6   CAUSES OF DOWNWARD MONEY WAGE RIGIDITY

It was noted above that Keynes and the Pre-Keynesians—especially Pigou—were agreed that in a deflationary situation downward money wage rigidity would raise the real wage and lead to unemployment. There was, however, an important difference between them regarding the policy implications of this. Keynes argued that if there were domestic reflation then although the cost of living would rise, money wages would not increase until mass unemployment had been eliminated. Pigou denied this: he believed that a rise in prices would soon generate higher wage claims based upon the cost of living. It is of course, impossible to know for certain what would have happened had Keynesian policies been pursued during the slump. The question is, however, of such importance that it merits discussion, even if no conclusive answer can be given.

It is useful to begin by discussing the causes of downward money wage rigidity during 1929–33. Money illusion was, until recently, a popular explanation for money wage rigidity. But while it may be relevant to the mild inflation of the 1950s (see section 11.3 below), it does not seem very plausible in the context of the inter-war period. The inter-war period began with a rapid price inflation (1918–20) followed by a rapid deflation (1920–2). There is no doubt that this violent fluctuation impressed itself heavily upon workers. The failure of money wages to keep up continually with prices was a major factor in the industrial unrest of 1919. It led to arrangements in many industries for wage settlements to be indexed to the cost of living (at one stage over 3 million workers had their wages determined on a 'sliding scale' related to either output price or the retail price index—Fisher, 1926). Most of these arrangements were short-lived because during the subsequent deflation there was pressure to abandon indexation from the same people who had demanded it earlier. With this experience relatively fresh in their memory it is difficult to believe that following the dramatic crash of stock prices on Wall Street in 1929, workers were unaware of the subsequent fall in prices, and its consequence for the real wage.

Another popular explanation of wage rigidity emphasizes workers' concern with their relative wage. If different groups of workers have contracts terminating at different dates then any reduction in the money wage accepted by one group of workers will temporarily reduce their relative wage. By contrast, an increase in the cost of living reduces the wages of all groups in the same proportion, and so leaves relativities unimpaired. On these grounds, it is argued, workers prefer real wage adjustments to be effected through changes in the cost of living rather than through changes in the money wage.

There is, doubtless, a good deal in this argument, but it is, perhaps, easy to overestimate its importance. Workers who are concerned about relativities can stipulate for money wage increases indexed to the wages of some 'leading' group with whom they compare themselves. If they are concerned about temporary disturbances of relativities they can stipulate for their contract period to be altered to coincide with that of the leading group. If, then, the wages of the leading group were cut, the wages of other groups linked to them could also be cut. If this seems implausible, it is probably because the leading group would not allow its wages to be cut anyway, or because the leading group would believe that the other groups would not allow their wages to be cut whatever happened to its own wage. This suggests that while relativities may be important, there are other factors which, quite independently, encourage resistance to cuts in the money wage.

In a historical study of wage negotiations, Dunlop (1938) identifies several arguments against money wage cuts which form part of the tradition of trade union bargaining. Two of these arguments rely heavily upon expectations. The first argument is that because of the natural ill-will between workers and employers, following a wage cut employers will be reluctant to restore money wages when prices return to their original level. Because the fall in money prices is probably temporary, it is suggested that in the long run a cut in the money wage will amount to a cut in the real wage too. (An argument of this kind was considered by Pigou (1905) in a work involving collaboration with the young Keynes.)

The second argument involves extrapolative expectations. A money wage cut, however small, is likely to be the 'thin end of the wedge'. Concession of a small money wage cut may be taken as a sign of weakness by employers, and further more substantial wage cuts will be forced upon the workers. Extrapolative expectations may therefore create a discontinuity in workers' attitudes to money wage changes, which makes them willing to compromise over claims for money wage increases, but intransigent with respect to money wage cuts.

Dunlop also mentions an argument that a cut in money wages reduces purchasing power. He traces the argument back as far as 1739, and notes that it was used particularly to enlist the support of shopkeepers on the workers' side! This crude purchasing power argument was discussed and criticized in section 4.3. The argument is sometimes erroneously ascribed to Keynes. It is interesting to note, however, that in the later part of the *General Theory*, Keynes effected a synthesis of the purchasing power argument and the extrapolative wage expectations argument (Keynes, 1936, ch. 19). He claimed that partial money wage cuts were worse than no money wage cuts because they led to expectations of further cuts in money wages. Expectations of wage deflation raised the real rate of interest, reduced investment, and led to a downward spiral of prices. Such a spiral could undermine confidence in the stability of the currency and even lead to financial collapse. It was considerations such as these which led Keynes to suggest that workers are 'instinctively more reasonable economists than the classical school' (Keynes, 1936, p. 14).

This argument about extrapolative expectations and purchasing power seems a little fanciful. The historical importance of the instability it describes is questionable. So too is the logic, for the argument fails to recognize that prices are regulated not solely by wages but also by the money supply.

The first argument has more to commend it, however; especially in the context of the period 1929–33. The argument assumes that workers perceive the initial fall in prices as temporary, and that there is an antipathy between employers and workers, so that workers anticipate that money wage cuts will not be restored in the long run. It seems quite possible that in 1929 workers failed to interpret the economic situation properly and, while recognizing that a fall in prices had occurred, mistook a long-run fall in prices for a temporary one. Short-run price fluctuations had hitherto been quite common. Many groups of workers could probably remember the mistake they had made in 1919 in thinking that a temporary rise in prices signalled a permanent inflation (hence their stipulation for indexation of wages, which was abandoned very shortly afterwards). Determined not to make the same mistake again, they may have chosen to regard the fall in prices in 1929 as temporary, and to hold money wages fixed whilst waiting for a return to 'normality'. The prevalence of this state of expectation is borne out by the term structure of interest rates (section 8.2) which reflects expectations of an imminent rise in prices and a return of interest rates to their normal level.

The assumed antipathy between workers and employers is borne out by the political and industrial climate of the 1920s. Many trade unions were led by militant radicals, and governments of the time were seriously worried by the threat of Bolshevik-type revolution. Employers' associations were also in aggressive mood, and large-scale lockouts had been used in an attempt to break the power of the most militant unions. At the onset of the slump the bitterness caused by these lockouts, and by the collapse of the General Strike, was still a recent memory. In this climate, workers might well believe that employers would use any strategy, including deception, to resist the eventual restoration of a money wage cut.

If the application of Keynesian policies is considered against the background of such poor industrial relations, it must be doubtful how far reflation would have been successful. Many trade union activists appear to have had Marxist and syndicalist attitudes, and to have viewed wage bargaining as a war of attrition between workers and employers. On this view, each round of annual wage bargains is important, not so much for the level of income secured for that year, as for the progress that is made toward the long-term objective of workers' control of industry. Higher real wages are an instrument in this struggle primarily because they weaken the economic position of the employers, and only incidentally because they make the workers better off. The object of securing high wages this year is that higher wages still can be demanded next year, so that steady progress is made in raising employers' costs to the point where private production is no longer viable. When pursuing this long-term strategy any reduction in wages— whether real or monetary—is a setback which should be avoided if at all possible. This suggests a two-pronged trade union bargaining strategy in which there is no reduction in *either* the real wage *or* the money wage.

This view is supported by Dunlop (1938), who discerns in the history of wage bargaining two distinct sets of arguments: one against reductions in the money wage and the other against reductions in the real wage. Arguments for money wage increases based upon the cost of living have been very common. 'The argument is human: it finds favour with the press, it is useful and effective in generating the support of the membership and those in the trade outside the union, and the basic data are supplied by the Government (as contrasted to profits-data furnished by the employers)' (Dunlop, 1938, p. 426). On the basis of historical evidence, Dunlop maintains that the cost of living is a more important factor in wage negotiations than Keynes is prepared to admit.

The statistical evidence is to a large extent consistent with this view. In the first year after the slump in which the cost of living rose, 1934, average money wage rates rose as well, and continued to rise thereafter. Although the real wage fell slightly between 1934 and 1937—by about 0.5 per cent per annum—this fall was associated with a rise in the cost of living of 2.5 per cent per annum, so that a substantial proportion of the cost of living increase was made up by increases in money wages. In 1938 the real wage advanced to above the 1934 level, so that within 4 years workers had more than caught up with the erosion of their living standards caused by the rise in the cost of living.

This perspective on trade union behaviour may also explain the attitude of union leaders towards mass unemployment. Although mass unemployment may weaken workers' support for militant action, it is at least a symptom that capitalism is being weakened through wage bargaining. It provides a propaganda weapon with which to hasten the eventual collapse of the system. The trade-off emphasized by the economic theory of trade unions—between employment and the real wage—may not be perceived as a trade-off by militant union leaders. Given their objective of hastening the collapse of capitalism, a higher real wage is always to be preferred to a low one. Unemployment is not traded off against the real wage—it is simply a constraint on the size of the wage claim that union members will support by industrial action. It limits the speed with which the objective can be attained, but does not significantly affect the strategy that is used. As indicated above, this strategy appears to be to take advantage of deflation to secure increases in the real wage, and to defend these increases using cost of living arguments during inflationary times.

9.7   SUMMARY

The results reported in this chapter provide striking confirmation of the Pre-Keynesian theory that labour demand depends upon the real wage, and that in inter-war British industries, employment was determined by labour demand. It is shown that the most important anomaly in previous estimates of Pre-Keynesian-type employment functions—namely the existence of increasing returns to employment in the short run—can be explained by positive correlation between employment and effort. This positive correlation is predicted by a simple theory of short-run adjustment costs.

Because of data limitations, and strategic changes in labour market behaviour during the inter-war period, it is difficult to provide a conclusive explanation of movements in the real wage. The limited data available are consistent, however, with the Pre-Keynesian view that the increasing strength of trade unions (as reflected both in membership and strike activity) and the increasing real level of unemployment benefit had an influence on the level of real wages. Downward money wage rigidity was the major factor in the rise in the real wage during the slump. It cannot be inferred, however, that just because the money wage was rigid downward, the real wage would not have been rigid downward too. Contrary to the claims of Keynes, it is quite possible that had reflationary policies been implemented during the slump, trade unions would have used their power to resist the consequent reduction in living standards, and would have stipulated for a compensating increase in the money wage. While reflation might have worked in the short run, it could well have been neutralized by the trade unions in the long run.

10

Labour Supply, Unemployment and Migration in Inter-war Britain

10.1 INTRODUCTION

This chapter examines evidence on labour supply in inter-war Britain. A variety of topics is discussed. Sections 10.2–10.5 test the theory of labour supply presented in chapters 5 and 6. Section 10.6 examines the Pre-Keynesian theory of unemployment in an open economy presented in section 6.7. Sections 10.7 and 10.8 are concerned with the regional distribution of labour supply and the pattern of geographical and occupational migration. Section 10.7 discusses the shift-share analysis of regional unemployment, and section 10.8 summarizes studies of inter-war labour migration.

Labour supply is extremely difficult to measure and, in consequence, the statistical evidence is difficult to interpret. This means that the results obtained are in some cases rather speculative. Subject to this qualification, it is possible to discern a coherent picture of labour supply in inter-war Britain which is broadly consistent with the Pre-Keynesian view. The evidence is not sufficiently conclusive, however, to support the particular emphasis that the Pre-Keynesians placed upon some factors rather than others.

10.2 THE DETERMINANTS OF LABOUR SUPPLY

The determinants of labour supply can be examined using the theory of job search developed in chapters 5 and 6. Suppose that for analytical purposes the economy is divided into two sectors. One sector (industry 1) comprises a single industry while the other sector (industry 2) comprises all the remaining industries. The job search variant of the structural unemployment theory gives active labour supply in industry 1, n_{a1}^{s}, as a function of the expected real wage in industry 1, $\hat{w}_1$, and the expected real wage in industry 2, $\hat{w}_2$:

$$n_{a1}^s = n_{a1}^s(\hat{w}_1, \hat{w}_2)$$
$$\phantom{n_{a1}^s = n_{a1}^s}(+) \; (-)$$

(10.1)

It is assumed for simplicity that labour supply in the rest of the economy (industry 2) is independent of the expected wage in industry 1:

$$n_{a2}^s = n_{a2}^s(\hat{w}_2)$$
$$\phantom{n_{a2}^s = n_{a2}^s}(+)$$

(10.2)

The restriction (10.2) would not necessarily be valid even if a 'small industry' assumption were made, but it is, unfortunately, practically indispensable to any simple test of the theory. Relaxation of the restriction would necessitate an analysis of the simultaneous determination of labour supply in every industry. Although the present state of economic theory and econometric practice make such an analysis perfectly feasible, it is too ambitious to be pursued in the present book.

Given this simplifying assumption, the expected wage in the rest of the economy, $\hat{w}_2$, is determined by the equation

$$(\hat{w}_2 - b)\, n_{a2}^s(\hat{w}_2) = (w_2 - b)n_2^d$$

(10.3)

where b is the real level of unemployment benefit, and n_2^d is labour demand in the rest of the economy. Assuming that the real wage in the rest of the economy is too high, employment, n_2, is determined by labour demand, n_2^d,

$$n_2 = n_2^d$$

(10.4)

and so the solution for $\hat{w}_2$ becomes

$$\hat{w}_2 = w_2 + (b - w_2)u_2$$

(10.5)

where

$$u_2 = (n_{a2}^s - n_2)/n_{a2}^s$$

(10.6)

is percentage unemployment in the rest of the economy.

Labour supply and the expected wage in industry 1 are determined simultaneously by the labour supply equation (10.1) and the expected wage equation

$$(\hat{w}_1 - b)n_{a1}^s = (w_1 - b)n_1^d$$

(10.7)

Assuming that the real wage, w_1, is also too high, employment, n_1, is determined by labour demand, n_1^d,

$$n_1 = n_1^d \tag{10.8}$$

The solution of (10.1) and (10.7) gives labour supply, n_{a1}^s, as a function of the wage bill in industry 1, $w_1 n_1$, the expected real wage in the rest of the economy, $\hat{w}_2$, and the real level of unemployment benefit, b,

$$n_{a1}^s = n_{a1}^s (w_1 n_1, \hat{w}_1, b) \tag{10.9}$$
$$\phantom{n_{a1}^s = n_{a1}^s (}(+)\ \ (-)(+)$$

Eliminating $\hat{w}_2$ from equation (10.9) using equation (10.5) gives

$$n_{a1}^s = n_{a1}^s (w_1 n_1, w_2, u_2, b) \tag{10.10}$$
$$\phantom{n_{a1}^s = n_{a1}^s (}(+)\ \ (-)(+)$$

Notice that the partial derivative of n_{a1}^s with respect to b cannot be unambiguously signed because b affects the expected wages in both industries. The 'normal' impact of b is positive, but if industry 1 has a relatively low unemployment then it could be negative. In the latter case, an increase in b raises the expected wage in the rest of the economy relative to the expected wage in industry 1 and induces labour to migrate out of the industry into the rest of the economy.

10.3   TIME-SERIES ESTIMATES OF THE LABOUR SUPPLY FUNCTION

To estimate the labour supply function (10.10) using time-series data it is necessary to make one or two adjustments. To begin with, it is important to adjust for changes in the population of working age, which were quite considerable over the inter-war period. It is also necessary to allow for changes in taste with respect to labour force participation, since changing attitudes towards female employment, in particular, were reflected in increasing female participation during the period. This factor is captured by introducing a time trend into labour supply. Also, in the light of the discussion in chapter 9, it is assumed that workers expect to supply a normal level of effort, but are willing to tolerate supplying a higher level of effort without additional compensation in the short run. Finally, it is necessary to impose a specific functional form on equation (10.10). It is very difficult to derive a simple functional form directly from a household utility function because of non-linearities in the equations for labour supply and the expected wage. A multiplicative form will, therefore, be imposed quite arbitrarily upon (10.10).

It is desirable at this stage to change the notation slightly. Let the index $i = 1, \ldots, n$ range over individual industries, and let the absence of an industry index indicate that the variable relates to the economy as a whole. Let $t = 0, 1, 2, \ldots$ index time. The estimating equation for labour supply in industry i at time t then becomes

$$n_{ait}^s = A_{0i} w_{it}^{a_{1i}} n_{it}^{a_{2i}} w_t^{-a_{3i}} u_t^{a_{4i}} b_t^{a_{5i}} v_t^{a_{6i}} \exp(a_{7i} t) \qquad 10.11)$$

where

n_{ait}^s is labour supply in industry i at time t,

w_{it} is the real wage in industry i at time t,

n_{it} is employment in industry i at time t,

v_t is the working population at time t,

and a_{ji} ($j = 1, \ldots, 7$) are fixed parameters. Theory suggests the following restrictions:

$$a_{1i} = a_{2i} > 0; \ a_{3i}, \ a_{4i} > 0, \ a_{6i} = 1 \qquad (10.12)$$

The estimating equation (10.11) implies a log-linear regression of labour supply on industry wage, industry employment, the average wage in the economy, average unemployment in the economy, the level of unemployment benefit, working population, and a time trend.

The equation was estimated for five UK industries using annual data 1923–38. The sample period is restricted by the lack of suitable labour supply measurements prior to 1923. Choice of industry was to some extent dictated by the need to match the Ministry of Labour supply data to data on employment and earnings obtained from other sources. The industries chosen were three fairly prosperous industries with relatively low unemployment—electrical engineering, vehicles and printing—and two declining industries with high unemployment—cotton textiles and ship-building. Data sources and statistical methodology are described in Appendix C. A representative set of results is reported in table 10.1.

The time trend variable had to be eliminated because of serious multicollinearity. It proved impossible to distinguish the separate effects of an increase in the working population (captured by v) and an increase in labour force participation and other trend factors (captured by t). The very high partial correlation between v and t was in danger of causing numerical problems in the estimation of the coefficients on the other variables.

TABLE 10.1

Log–linear regressions of labour supply on employment, wages, benefits and working population, using annual data for five UK industries, 1923–38

Industry	Constant	Real wage bill	Industry real wage	Industry employment	Economy real wage	Economy unemployment	Real benefits	Working population	R^2	DW
Electrical engineering	−10.589 (7.603)	0.439* (0.179)			−0.586 (0.694)	0.094 (0.057)	−0.071 (0.234)	4.676* (2.039)	99.0	1.44
Vehicles	−25.015* (8.214)	0.037 (0.306)			−0.476 (0.823)	−0.089 (0.110)	−0.414 (0.265)	8.517* (2.296)	97.7	1.60
Printing	−1.379 (2.788)	0.424 (0.195)			−0.777 (0.376)	0.093* (0.022)	0.008 (0.123)	1.866* (0.740)	97.5	2.33
Cotton	9.344 (8.435)	0.156 (0.154)			−2.744* (0.856)	0.247* (0.082)	0.548 (0.317)	−1.357 (2.291)	92.7	1.71
Ship-building	4.333 (5.992)	0.480* (0.103)			−0.941 (0.691)	0.330* (0.073)	−0.677* (0.214)	−0.334 (1.612)	97.4	2.33
Electrical engineering	−13.763 (6.757)		−0.229 (0.858)	0.523* (0.207)	−0.087 (0.965)	0.069 (0.067)	−0.028 (0.242)	4.578* (2.046)	99.1	1.50
Vehicles	−8.527 (5.459)		−0.579* (0.223)	0.897* (0.259)	1.325 (0.619)	0.002 (0.067)	−0.514* (0.155)	2.171 (1.924)	99.3	1.94
Printing	−1.292 (1.884)		0.005 (0.131)	1.086* (0.224)	0.102 (0.264)	0.091* (0.018)	−0.003 (0.079)	−0.084 (0.681)	99.0	2.53
Cotton	8.160 (12.170)		0.145 (0.848)	0.159 (0.220)	−2.740* (0.906)	0.248* (0.101)	0.546 (0.387)	−1.335 (2.926)	92.7	1.71
Ship-building	−3.095 (6.508)		−0.210 (0.576)	0.426* (0.110)	−1.158 (0.699)	0.348* (0.073)	−0.513 (0.248)	0.965 (1.906)	97.8	2.58

Note: An asterisk indicates that the coefficient is significantly different from zero at the 5 per cent level in a two-tailed *t*-test.

In the regressions shown in the top half of the table the restriction $a_{1i} = a_{2i}$ has been imposed, so that labour supply is regressed upon the real wage bill of the industry rather than upon real wages and employment separately. This restriction is relaxed in the regressions shown in the bottom half of the table.

The magnitude of the coefficient on the real wage bill (or on industry employment) measures the elasticity of labour supply with respect to labour demand. A coefficient of zero indicates that labour supply does not respond at all to labour demand, so that unemployment varies as a 'mirror image' of employment. A coefficient of unity indicates that labour supply responds fully to labour demand, so that unemployment is invariant (in percentage terms) to changes in employment. The coefficients shown in the table are all positive and all less than unity, with one exception in the printing industry which is not significantly different from unity.

The restriction that the coefficients on the industry wage and industry employment are equal is rejected in the vehicles and printing industries. It is interesting to note that when the restriction is relaxed, the coefficients on industry employment are higher in each of the three prosperous industries than they are in the two declining industries. This suggests that labour supply is more elastic with respect to employment in the prosperous industries than it is in the declining industries. A 1 per cent reduction in employment in the prosperous industries calls forth a larger percentage contraction in the labour force in electrical engineering, vehicles and printing than it does in cotton or ship-building. It appears that labour is much less 'attached' to the prosperous industries than it is to the declining industries.

One explanation of this differential attachment is that in growing industries the adjustments involve inflows of labour in response to new vacancies while in the declining industries the adjustments involve outflows of labour that have been made redundant. Employers in growing industries may make more strenuous efforts to fill vacancies than unemployed workers make to find jobs. Thus redundant workers may wait around in the industries where they have lost their jobs until they receive news of vacancies elsewhere (this is confirmed by the sample inquiries reported in section 10.8). Even if workers do not literally remain attached to their old industries, the basis upon which the insured unemployed are classified to industries by the Ministry of Labour may give the impression that they do so.

Another explanation of differential attachment is that the average age of the labour force may be lower in expanding industries. If industries have limited 'ports of entry' which discriminate in favour of young people then the rate of growth of the industry will be reflected in the age distribution of its employees. If young people are more mobile than older people then the workforce in the expanding industries will be more mobile than in the declining industries. Workers will move freely between the expanding industries, but not so freely between the declining industries and the expanding ones. These and other possibilities are considered in detail in the cross-section study reported in the next section.

The coefficients on the industry real wage in the unrestricted regressions are unsatisfactory, especially in the vehicle industry, where a significant negative effect is discerned. The coefficients on the real wage in the economy as a whole are all of the right sign (i.e. negative) in the restricted regressions, but in the unrestricted regressions there is a significant positive sign in the cotton industry. The coefficients on unemployment as a whole accord well with the theory. In both sets of regressions unemployment has a significant positive effect on labour supply in three out of the five industries, indicating that unemployment in the rest of the economy encourages labour to migrate to the industry concerned. There is a wrong sign in only one case, and that is insignificant.

The coefficients on real benefits are erratic in sign and generally insignificant. It is possible that this reflects the theoretical ambiguity in sign noted earlier. Theoretical considerations suggest that the coefficient on the benefit variable should be positive in high-unemployment industries and negative in low-unemployment industries. This is borne out, for example, by the large positive (though insignificant) coefficients in cotton, and the large negative coefficients in vehicles. But the results for shipbuilding are quite inexplicable on these grounds: there is a significant negative effect even though unemployment is very high.

The coefficients on working population cannot be easily interpreted because of the elimination of the time trend, for reasons noted earlier. Suffice it to say that all the significant coefficients are positive, and that the coefficients are largest in the fastest-growing industries. This is compatible with the view that the working population constrains labour supply most in the growing industries.

On the whole, the coefficients on the 'quantity' variables—industry employment, and unemployment in the economy as a whole—are very much in accord with the theory. However, the coefficients on the 'price' variables—the industry real wage, the real wage in the economy as a whole, and the real level of unemployment benefit—are not consistently of the correct sign.

It should be emphasized, though, that the number of degrees of freedom available in these time-series is very small—nine or ten for each industry, depending upon whether or not the parameter constraint is imposed. Given the relatively low variance of the 'price' series, it is perhaps too much to hope that the evidence would be conclusive. Fortunately, further light is shed on the unresolved issues by the cross-section analysis reported below.

10.4 CROSS-SECTION ESTIMATES OF THE LABOUR SUPPLY FUNCTION

The major problem in estimating the labour supply function (10.11) from cross-section data is that the parameters vary across industries. Estimation is possible only if restrictions are imposed upon their cross–industry variation. The effects of variations in the parameters A_{0i}, a_{3i}, . . ., a_{6i} can be eliminated by focusing upon proportional variations in labour supply over time, thus:

$$(n^s_{ait}/n^s_{ait-1}) = \exp(a_{7i})\,(w_{it}/w_{it-1})^{a_{1i}}(n_{it}/n_{it-1})^{a_{2i}} \tag{10.12}$$

Of the remaining parameters, particular interest attaches to a_{2i} which measures the elasticity of labour supply with respect to employment. Intuitively, the lower is this elasticity, the more rigidly is labour 'attached' to the ith industry.

It has been suggested in the previous section that the value of a_{2i} varies directly with the rate of growth of the industry, g_i. The higher is the growth rate, the more likely is labour supply adjustment to involve entry in response to new vacancies instead of exit in response to redundancy. An industry with a high growth rate is also more likely to have a youthful labour force, which is more mobile between industries. The average length of work experience in the industry will also tend to be smaller, and this will inhibit the development of a strong commitment to the working practices in the industry.

Attachment to an industry may be reinforced by a number of other factors. The standardization of technology, for example, creates a stable climate in which traditions can be established, and the existence of such traditions may encourage workers to resist adjustment and change.

A high level of trade union membership may reinforce attachment. The trade union rule book codifies traditions and reinforces their observance. Severance of employment may be economically damaging for a worker, particularly if he should ever wish to work in the industry later on.

In the context of inter-war Britain, trade union membership and observance of traditional working practices were of most relevance to craftsmen. Where unskilled workers are concerned, the existence of casual hiring practices may encourage attachment. Casual hiring practices offer the unemployed a reasonable chance of re-employment—at least on a temporary basis—for unlike decasualized markets, existing employees do not enjoy job security. The regular turnover of labour in a casual market means that unemployment takes the form of frequent spells of unemployment for everyone, rather than long spells of unemployment concentrated upon just a few. The risks of attachment to casual labour markets are therefore lower than the risks of attachment to decasualized labour markets, for though employment is insecure, the unemployed have much better prospects of recurrent spells of employment.

Finally, the degree of attachment may be influenced by the geography of production in an industry. When an industry is located in an area with a very diverse production base then unemployed workers have the chance of re-employment in other industries in the same area (assuming these other industries can retrain the workers or use their existing skills). On the other hand, when an industry is located in an area with a narrow production base, local opportunities for re-employment are much smaller. The unemployed must seek work in different localities. Because of the well-known obstacles to geographical mobility, unemployed workers are more likely to remain attached to an industry when the only alternative is geographical migration. The industries most likely to be located in areas with a narrow production base are extractive industries—particularly when the resources are concentrated in isolated parts of the country, remote from the main agglomerations of manufacturing and service activity.

These considerations suggest that the elasticity of labour supply a_{2i} is an increasing function of the growth rate of the industry, g_i, and a decreasing function of the standardization of technology, s_i, the trade union membership density, m_i, the extent of casualization in the labour market, c_i, and the extent of geographical concentration of production in isolated areas with a narrow industrial base, d_i. If a linear functional form is assumed then the elasticity function becomes

$$a_{2i} = b_0 + b_1 g_i - b_2 s_i - b_3 m_i - b_4 c_i - b_5 d_i \tag{10.13}$$

where $b_0, \ldots, b_5 > 0$ are fixed parameters, uniform across all industries. It is assumed for simplicity that the wage elasticity a_{1i} is constant and uniform across all industries, independently of the employment elasticity, and that the working population elasticity is uniform too:

$$a_{1i} = a_1; a_{7i} = a_7 \tag{10.14}$$

Substituting equations (10.13) and (10.14) into (10.12) and taking logarithms gives the estimating equation

$$\log (n_{ait}^s/n_{ait-1}^s) = a_7 + a_1 \log (w_{it}/w_{it-1}) + b_0 \log (n_{it}/n_{it-1})$$
$$+ b_1 g_i \log (n_{it}/n_{it-1}) - b_2 s_i \log (n_{it}/n_{it-1}) - b_3 m_i$$
$$\log (n_{it}/n_{it-1}) - b_4 c_i \log (n_{it}/n_{it-1}) - b_5 d_i \log (n_{it}/n_{it-1}) \tag{10.15}$$

Equation (10.15) was estimated using cross-section data on 27 industries for 1920, 1924, 1930 and 1935. The data sources and the methodology are described in Appendix D. When the full equation was estimated the coefficient on the industry wage consistently took the wrong sign. The problem encountered with the industry wage variable in the time-series study proves even more serious in the cross-section study.

The most likely cause of the negative coefficient on the wage variable is an identification problem. It seems that the industry wage is not truly exogenous, as assumed by disequilibrium theory, but is to some extent influenced by competitive forces. An increase in labour supply relative to demand tends to depress the industry wage, and so the determination of the industry wage is not independent of labour supply.

It was, indeed, recognized by Clay that relative wages fell in industries experiencing the greatest unemployment (see section 3.5) and the present results are compatible with this view. His explanation of unemployment was that wages in the industries concerned did not fall far enough. It is not that wages are totally inflexible, but that they do not adjust completely to shifts in labour demand. The inflexibility of the wage is only a 'stylized fact', used by the theory to capture the sluggishness of the wage-adjustment process.

In interpreting statistical estimates of the labour supply function it is therefore necessary to recognize that the industry wage is to some extent endogenous. A full treatment of the endogeneity issue is outside the scope of the present inquiry. The strategy that has been adopted is to drop the industry wage from the set of exogenous variables, and to estimate the impact of the remaining variables by discarding the information contained in the industry wage. It must be left to future research to estimate simultaneously the determination of labour supply and the industry wage.

A representative set of regression estimates is reported in table 10.2. There are six explanatory variables: industry employment, an 'industry growth' variable, and four 'industry characteristics' variables. The estimates shown relate to six different periods. An obvious feature of the table that calls for some comment is that the constant term is consistently larger for periods starting from 1920 than for periods beginning in 1924 and 1930. This is a consequence of the way that labour supply in 1920 has been estimated. As noted earlier, reliable labour supply statistics are available only from 1923 onwards, and so the figures for 1920 have been estimated using the very crude assumption that unemployment was the same (in percentage terms) in each industry. The arbitrary convention was adopted that unemployment was in fact zero, and the estimates of the constant term indicate that this underestimates average unemployment in 1920 by about 4 per cent. The assumption that unemployment rates were the same in all industries receives some support from this evidence, for given that unemployment was in general very low, most industries were likely to be close to 'full employment'. Because of the log-linear specification, the arbitrary assumption of zero unemployment has no implications for any of the estimated coefficients except the constant term.

The coefficient on industry employment is, as predicted, significantly positive, and in four of the six cases is significantly less than unity also. This corroborates the view that labour supply adjusts less than proportionately to labour demand.

The industry growth factor is positive in five out of six cases, though significantly so in only one case (1930–35). It was during this period that the elasticity of labour supply with respect to employment was the lowest of all. This result suggests that inter-industry differentials in the elasticity of labour supply became most important in the 1930s. It is possible that by this time the most mobile labour had migrated out of the declining industries into the growing ones, so that the least mobile labour had become concentrated in the declining industries and the most mobile labour in the growing ones.

TABLE 10.2

Estimation of labour supply function from cross-section of 27 UK industries, various periods 1920–35

Period	Constant	Change in employment factor	Industry growth factor	Standardization factor	Trade union factor	Casualization factor	Geographical factor	R^2	DW
1920–24	−4.508* (0.011)	0.784* (0.103)	0.100 (0.128)	0.076 (0.139)	−0.181 (0.123)	−0.109 (0.098)	−0.041 (0.097)	92.5	2.06
1924–30	0.031 (0.015)	0.896* (0.122)	0.334 (0.343)	0.045 (0.081)	−0.100 (0.095)	−0.085 (0.094)	0.146* (0.071)	93.3	2.52
1930–35	−0.004 (0.014)	0.513* (0.162)	1.200* (0.536)	0.043 (0.136)	0.096 (0.167)	0.152 (0.162)	−0.146 (0.125)	79.6	1.58
1920–30	−4.464* (0.018)	0.916* (0.077)	−0.054 (0.109)	−0.018 (0.108)	−0.174* (0.084)	−0.155 (0.084)	0.092 (0.060)	94.1	1.64
1924–35	0.048* (0.011)	0.769* (0.055)	0.323 (0.173)	0.078 (0.040)	−0.003 (0.048)	−0.002 (0.048)	−0.055 (0.038)	98.2	2.18
1920–35	−4.445* (0.016)	0.828* (0.049)	0.024 (0.101)	0.043 (0.065)	−0.095 (0.054)	−0.087 (0.057)	−0.055 (0.045)	97.0	1.73

Note: An asterisk indicates that the coefficient is significant at the 5 per cent level in a two-tailed t-test.

The emergence of inter-industry differentials in labour mobility becomes, on this view, an integral part of labour market adjustment through inter-industry migration.

The coefficients on the industry characteristics variables are, on the whole, insignificant. The casualization factor and the trade union factor have the predicted negative effects in five of the six cases, though only the trade union factor is significant, and that only once, over the period 1920–30. In view of the fairly limited degrees of freedom involved, it may be suggested that casualisation and trade union membership possibly have a small effect on the elasticity of labour supply, but that the evidence so far is inconclusive.

The coefficient on the standardization of technology factor is on the whole positive, rather than negative as the theory suggests. Finally, the geographical factor has little or no impact on the elasticity of labour supply. This suggests that spatial factors were less important in constraining migration than the theory might suggest. The result could also be explained, however, by the limitations of the index used, which captures geographical effects only indirectly by ascribing geographical characteristics to industries. A more convincing analysis of geographical factors is presented in sections 10.7 and 10.8.

10.5   THE INTENSITY OF LABOUR SUPPLY, AND INTER-INDUSTRY VARIATION IN THE RATE OF UNEMPLOYMENT

It is important not to confuse the *elasticity* of labour supply, a_{2i}, with the *intensity* of labour supply, as measured by the parameter A_{0i}. A low value of a_{2i} indicates that labour supply does not respond much to variations in the level of employment. A low value of A_{0i}, on the other hand, indicates that labour supply is low relative to the level of employment—in other words, that there tends to be little unemployment in the industry.

At any given point in time the values of the two parameters are unconnected. Over time, however, they may be connected if the trend of employment in the industry is either increasing or decreasing. If employment is steadily rising then a low value of a_{2i} implies that labour supply will not rise as fast as employment, and over time this will come to be reflected in a lower intensity of labour supply, A_{0i}. Conversely, if employment is steadily declining, and a_{2i} is low again, then labour supply will rise relative to employment and so A_{0i}

will rise over time. Thus if the elasticity of labour supply, a_{2i}, is low (i.e. less than unity) then over time the intensity of labour supply, A_{0i}, will be inversely related to the growth rate of the industry. If, on the other hand, the elasticity of labour supply is high (i.e. close to unity) then the intensity of labour supply will be independent of the growth rate of the industry. Since the previous results suggest an elasticity of less than unity, it seems likely that the intensity of labour supply will be highest in the slowest-growing industries, or—put more simply—the rate of unemployment will be highest in the declining industries.

The intensity of labour supply may be influenced by other factors besides the rate of growth of the industry. Factors such as the degree of casualization of the labour market, which influence the elasticity of labour supply, may also influence its intensity. Casual labour markets are most common in industries where there are short-run fluctuations in the demand for labour. In such industries the problems of matching labour supply to labour demand are particularly acute, and the solution involves maintaining a pool of labour readily assembled for short-term hirings. Thus casual labour markets are associated with high steady-state rates of unemployment, equivalent to a labour supply of high intensity. Coal-mining, cotton textiles and ship-building, for example, used casual methods of hiring in the inter-war period, and amongst the declining industries it is these that report some of the highest levels of unemployment. Perhaps the most striking instance of the impact of casualization is the building industry which, despite being one of the boom industries of inter-war Britain, experienced persistently high unemployment (between 12 and 20 per cent most of the time) (Richardson and Aldcroft, 1968). Almost certainly this reflects the volatility and localization of the demand for building labour and the limitations of the market institutions (such as the employment exchanges) for matching supply to demand.

There are a number of reasons for believing that several of the other factors which influence the elasticity of labour supply may influence its intensity too. A rough-and-ready test of this hypothesis can be obtained by regressing labour supply upon wage rates, employment and industry characteristics. To avoid heteroscedasticity, and to reduce the risk of spurious correlation arising from the fact that industry employment is a random variable, it is desirable to normalize the estimating equation by industry employment. Assuming a log-linear relation between labour supply, wages and employment, this gives an estimating equation of the form

$$\log 1/(1-u_{it}) = b_0 + b_1 \log w_{it} + b_2 \log n_{it} + b_3 g_i + b_4 m_i$$
$$+ b_5 s_i + b_6 c_i + b_7 d_i \tag{10.16}$$

where u_{it} is unemployment in the ith industry at time t.

The results are reported in table 10.3. Theory predicts that the coefficient on the wage, b_1, should be positive and that the coefficient on employment, b_2, should be small and negative (this is a consequence of the normalization procedure). The table reveals that the coefficients on the wage are generally unsatisfactory, just as before. The coefficients on employment conform with the theory in two out of the three cases, but their level of significance is very low.

The coefficients on the industry growth factor have consistently the correct sign, although they are insignificant (but only marginally so). It appears that the fastest-growing industries have the lowest unemployment. The coefficients on the standardization factor are consistently negative, but of very low significance. The trade union factor, the casualization factor and the geographical factor all have consistently positive effects, with the casualization factor being the most significant. These results conform with theory. They suggest that the intensity of labour supply—and hence unemployment—is increased by casual hiring practices, by high trade union membership density and by geographical isolation of the industry.

10.6   UNEMPLOYMENT IN AN OPEN ECONOMY

This section attempts to test the open–economy variant of the Pre-Keynesian theory presented in section 6.7. It is assumed that manufacturing industry produces an export good which is exchanged on world markets for an imported wage good. The representative manufacturing firm faces a parametric export price and a parametric wage (both expressed in units of domestic currency). Labour is the only variable input.

The short-run employment function (9.10) can be estimated from annual data on UK manufacturing industry 1920–38. The own-product wage is measured by the ratio of the money wage to the export price level. The results are reported in table 10.4. There is strong support for the Pre-Keynesian employment function. The coefficient on the own-product wage is negative and strongly significant, and the significance is quite robust with respect to the

TABLE 10.3

Influence of industry characteristics on unemployment in a cross-section of 27 UK industries, 1924–35

Date	Constant	Wage	Employment	Industry growth factor	Standardization factor	Trade union factor	Casualization factor	Geographical factor	R^2	DW
1924	0.097 (0.338)	0.024 (0.073)	-0.014 (0.020)	-0.084 (0.065)	-0.016 (0.025)	0.007 (0.022)	0.020 (0.023)	0.024 (0.024)	38.6	1.50
1930	0.618 (0.312)	-0.091 (0.068)	0.002 (0.020)	-0.108 (0.062)	-0.014 (0.024)	0.046* (0.021)	0.035 (0.023)	0.039 (0.024)	68.7	1.78
1935	0.160 (0.338)	0.022 (0.073)	-0.008 (0.021)	-0.123 (0.066)	-0.021 (0.026)	0.030 (0.023)	0.050* (0.024)	0.051 (0.025)	71.0	1.83
1924	0.144* (0.025)			-0.073 (0.061)	-0.010 (0.022)	0.007 (0.021)	0.014 (0.018)	0.032 (0.018)	37.1	1.53
1930	0.175* (0.025)			-0.117 (0.062)	-0.015 (0.023)	0.043 (0.021)	0.051* (0.018)	0.022 (0.018)	55.4	1.66
1935	0.225* (0.026)			-0.124 (0.063)	-0.019 (0.023)	0.030 (0.022)	0.045* (0.019)	0.058* (0.019)	70.7	1.85

Note: An asterisk indicates that the coefficient is significant at the 5 per cent level in a two-tailed t-test.

introduction of additional explanatory variables. The coefficient
indicates that a 1 per cent reduction in the own-product wage will
increase employment by just over one-third of 1 per cent. This
suggests, for example, that a 30 per cent reduction in the own-
product wage would be necessary to stimulate employment by 10
per cent.

TABLE 10.4
Log-linear regressions of employment on output, time and the
own-product wage, using annual data for UK manufacturing industry,
1920–38

Constant	Current output	Lagged output	Time trend	Own-product real wage	R^2	DW
6.044*	0.542*			−0.343*	93.8	0.87†
(0.168)	(0.035)			(0.032)		
6.548*	0.471*	−0.005	0.005	−0.352*	95.5	1.25
(0.530)	(0.083)	(0.078)	(0.008)	(0.135)		

Note: * indicates that the coefficient is statistically significant at 5 per cent in a two-tailed *t*-
test. † indicates that there is significant autocorrelation at the 5 per cent level.

The coefficient on current output is approximately 0.5. In the
context of the theory this implies short-run production under nearly
constant returns, which is fairly reasonable for manufacturing
industry as a whole. The coefficients on lagged output and the time
trend are entirely insignificant.

The determinants of labour supply for manufacturing industry as a
whole may be examined by adapting the analysis presented in section
10.2. Theory predicts that labour supply to manufacturing industry
will be an increasing function of the real wage, employment, the real
level of unemployment benefit, and the population of working age.
Because the manufacturing sector is so large, unemployment in the
rest of the economy cannot be regarded as exogenous, and so the
unemployment variable which appeared before is suppressed. Since,
by assumption, wage goods are imported, the price of consumables
is proxied by the import price index.

Representative estimates derived from log-linear regressions are
reported in table 10.5. The results indicate that the real wage has the
predicted positive effect on labour supply, though the effect is
significant in only one case. The elasticity of labour supply with

TABLE 10.5

Log-linear regressions of labour supply on various explanatory variables,
using annual data for UK manufacturing industry, 1923–38

Constant	Real wage	Employment	Real benefit	Working population	Time trend	Import price	R^2	DW
-2.352	0.087	0.445*	-0.074*	0.738	0.003		99.6	2.91
(1.868)	(0.046)	(0.058)	(0.031)	(0.471)	(0.004)			
-3.424*	0.109*	0.470*	-0.077*	0.988*			99.6	2.87
(0.473)	(0.026)	(0.037)	(0.030)	(0.202)				
-3.431	0.103	0.471*	-0.078*	0.997*		-0.005	99.6	2.87
(0.513)	(0.111)	(0.039)	(0.034)	(0.273)		(0.103)		

Note: An asterisk indicates that a variable is statistically significant at 5 per cent in a two-tailed *t*-test.

respect to employment is stable at just below one-half, indicating that labour supply adjusts less than fully to labour demand. This bears out the results reported in the industry studies. The problem of multicollinearity between working population and the time trend, first noted in the industry studies, recurs here also. It is impossible to distinguish properly between the effects on labour supply of an increase in the population of working age and an increase in the proportion of this population participating in the workforce. The time trend is insignificant, and when it is eliminated the coefficient on working population becomes very close to unity. This accords remarkably well with the predictions of the theory.

The coefficient on real benefit, however, consistently takes the wrong sign. It is significantly negative, suggesting that an increase in unemployment benefit reduces rather than increases the labour supply. The significance of the benefit variable is unaffected by the removal of the time trend. One possible explanation is that the benefit variable is capturing an element of money illusion in short-run labour supply. To test this hypothesis the import price index was introduced as a separate explanatory variable, but it proved totally insignificant.

Another possible explanation of the sign of the benefit coefficient is that benefit levels are fixed by government with reference to the level of employment. If for political reasons the government responds to a reduction in employment by raising benefit levels then the reduction in labour supply may appear to be induced by the rise of benefit. This implies that in the regressions above the benefit variable is assuming part of the role which should be assumed by the employment variable. If this is correct then the coefficient on the employment variable will understate the true influence of employment on labour supply.

On the face of it, these results are very different from the results obtained by Benjamin and Kochin (1979, 1982) who found that unemployment benefit had a strong positive association with unemployment. Certainly the interpretation of the results above does not support Benjamin and Kochin's interpretation of their own results, which is that unemployment benefit had a positive effect upon labour supply. The interpretation is, however, consistent with an alternative interpretation of Benjamin and Kochin's results, which is that unemployment benefit had a negative association with labour demand (Benjamin and Kochin, 1978, p. 454). A correlation of this kind is discernible in the data, and Cross (1982, pp. 383–4) has argued that politicians may have allowed real benefits to rise in response to increasing unemployment by way of a tacit refusal to index the nominal value of benefits to prices. If this interpretation is correct then the positive association between unemployment benefit and unemployment may have been induced, not by the positive effect of unemployment benefit on labour supply, but by the negative effect of labour demand on the benefit level.

It is important not to stretch this argument too far, however, for there are other reasons why Benjamin and Kochin's results may be misleading. For example, they begin their sample period in 1920 and, as Ormerod and Worswick (1982) note, the significance of their results is considerably reduced if this observation is eliminated. There is, in fact, good reason for eliminating this observation, because the statistics of labour supply are not so reliable prior to 1923. The sample period in the present study commences in 1923 and, as Ormerod and Worswick show, the impact of unemployment benefit is statistically insignificant in Benjamin and Kochin's model over the sub-period 1923–38. We may tentatively conclude that there is no evidence of a substantial positive effect of unemployment benefit on labour supply during the inter-war period. Any effect that is present is strongly outweighed by a countervailing positive association, which could be due to a government policy of raising real benefits in response to declining employment.

10.7 REGIONAL INEQUALITY AND INDUSTRIAL STRUCTURE

This section considers to what extent regional inequalities in unemployment in inter-war Britain are attributable to differences in industrial structure. Can the high level of unemployment in South Wales, for example, be explained entirely by the narrow industrial base of the South Wales economy, and the preponderance of declining industries there? Or is the converse true? Is the decline of the iron industry, for example, due to the fact that it is located predominantly in declining regions such as South Wales and the North-east? Or are both factors at work to some extent? Is the decline of certain regions accounted for partly by their industrial structure and partly by factors specific to the region?

It was noted in section 3.5 that the concept of economic structure can be applied not only to industries but also to regions. In the structural model developed in section 6.2, the two industries may be interpreted as the same industry operating in two different regions. The growing region may be one whose infrastructure is spontaneously improving, and where the skills and attitudes of the labour force facilitate productivity gains. The declining region may be one whose infrastructure is not being renewed, where skills are no longer acquired by entrants to the labour force and where attitudes to work inhibit productivity improvements. Under such conditions the existence of a national basic wage, implemented without reference to regional differentials in productivity, will cause labour demand to contract in the declining region as jobs are transferred to the growing region instead.

Another factor could be that changes in the geographical distribution of population and wealth place certain regions further from the main centres of product demand. Such changes could, in principle, explain not only the worsening position of the peripheral regions of Britain with respect to the British market, but also the worsening position of Britain as a whole with respect to the growing markets of continental Europe, North America and the Pacific region. On the other hand, the influence of freight transport costs on the location of production during the inter-war period was almost certainly diminished by both technological improvements and excess capacity in the transport sector. In the context of the world economy, the influence of transport costs was almost certainly dwarfed by the influence of tariffs and other government-sponsored barriers to trade.

Champernowne (1938, 1939a) examined the causes of regional variations in unemployment using a sample of 16 industries at three dates: 1929, 1932 and 1936. He distinguished 'Two Britains'—the prosperous Inner Britain and the depressed Outer Regions. Inner Britain comprised four of the nine regions specified by the Ministry of Labour: London, South-east, South-west and Midlands. Outer Britain comprised the remaining five regions, namely North-east, North-west, Scotland, Wales and Northern Ireland. Champernowne's statistical calculations were fairly straightforward, but the interpretation of his results proved problematic. His preliminary conclusion was that regional variations in unemployment explained industrial variations, rather than the other way round, but when challenged by Dennison (1939) and others he retreated to an agnostic position (Champernowne, 1939b).

Hatton (1982a) has re-examined the issue by applying shift-share analysis to a larger sample of 30 industries and considering each of the nine Ministry of Labour divisions separately. His results for each of the three years 1929, 1932 and 1936 are reproduced in table 10.6.

TABLE 10.6
Shift-share analysis of percentage unemployment for nine divisions of the UK labour market and 30 industries 1929–36

Division	Differential unemployment			Industrial composition component			Region-specific component		
	1929	*1932*	*1936*	*1929*	*1932*	*1936*	*1929*	*1932*	*1936*
London	−4.15	−8.40	−5.42	0.03	−0.89	−0.26	−2.09	−2.84	−3.03
South-east	−5.56	−9.01	−6.65	0.03	1.17	−0.61	−3.87	−6.02	−4.89
South-west	−2.80	−6.18	−4.57	−1.63	−2.10	−1.79	−1.96	−4.58	−3.81
Midlands	0.66	0.20	−3.10	1.09	3.13	0.49	−0.20	−1.59	−3.48
North-east	3.72	8.80	5.79	1.74	5.09	2.61	0.27	2.45	2.42
North-west	3.93	5.80	4.73	−0.14	1.55	0.17	2.34	2.64	3.36
Scotland	2.02	4.92	4.12	0.65	2.53	0.58	0.69	2.35	2.51
Wales	9.28	16.31	17.30	5.30	10.89	8.13	3.55	5.92	9.39
N. Ireland	4.83	4.91	7.90	4.20	8.21	4.13	4.84	5.01	7.72
Inner Britain	−2.90	−5.61	−4.81	−1.72	−2.17	−1.07	−1.76	−3.22	−3.56
Outer Regions	4.05	7.57	6.22	1.40	3.21	1.56	1.54	2.89	3.57

Source: Hatton (1982a), Table V, p. 13.

Three measurements are given for each year. The first is the discrepancy between the regional unemployment rate and the national unemployment rate. The statistics illustrate the concentration of unemployment in Outer Britain, and in Wales in particular. The second measurement is the discrepancy between the regional rate and what the regional rate would be if the industrial structure of the region were the same as that of the economy as a whole. This 'industry composition' component of regional unemployment is small in London, the South-east and the North-west, but fairly substantial elsewhere. The third measure is the discrepancy between the regional rate and what the regional rate would be if the national unemployment rate prevailed in each of the industries within the region. This 'region-specific' component of unemployment is fairly small to begin with in the Midlands, North-east and Scotland, but grows over time to become large in all regions by 1936.

The interpretation of the 'industry-composition' and 'region-specific' components is not without ambiguity. There is, for example, an additional interaction term generated by the statistical decomposition of the differential regional unemployment rate. This means that the two components described above do not necessarily sum to the total discrepancy between the national and regional unemployment rates. A more serious problem arises from the fact that some industries produce goods which are not tradeable between regions. Unemployment caused by unfavourable industrial composition in a given region will reduce real incomes in the region and depress demand for the non-tradeable goods produced there; it may also reduce the demand for non-tradeable intermediate products. The resulting unemployment in the non-tradeable sector will show up as region-specific, although it is causally linked to industrial composition. This suspicion is reinforced by the pattern of covariation between the industrial composition and region-specific components in table 10.6. In 1929 there is negligible association between the two components but by 1936 the association is strongly positive. This suggests that the increase in the region-specific components by 1936 may be due to the spill-over effects on industry in general of the industrial composition component present since 1929. There are grounds for believing, therefore, that shift-share analysis may overstate the importance of region-specific unemployment. Subject to this qualification, the results suggest that both industry composition and region-specific factors have an important influence on unemployment differentials although, superficially at least, the relative impact of the former declines over time and the impact of the latter increases.

The evidence above relates to unemployment rates which, as noted earlier, involve considerations of both labour demand and labour supply. In Pre-Keynesian theory it is contractions in labour demand that are regarded as the primary cause of unemployment, and it is therefore pertinent to inquire to what extent regional differences in the contraction of demand are explicable by industrial composition and by region-specific factors. Hatton (1982a) expresses the growth of employment in a given industry in a given region as a linear function of the growth of employment in the national industry, the growth of employment in the region as a whole, and a stochastic term. A statistical examination of the growth of employment in 30 industries in nine regions 1929–36 indicates that industrial composition is the major determinant of regional employment growth—especially in the depressed Outer Regions. It also shows that fluctuations in employment are much greater in the Outer Regions than in Inner Britain, and that the greater fluctuations are explained almost entirely by industrial composition. In other words, differential employment instability is due to the fact that the industries with the greatest employment instability are concentrated in the Outer Regions.

This last result ties in with the earlier result (section 10.5) that casualization of the labour force is a factor in the high unemployment of the staple industries. Casualization of the labour market (i.e. a policy of short-term hiring) is a natural response by employers to unpredictable fluctuations in demand. The majority of the staple industries are producers of durable goods, and are prone to cyclical fluctuations in demand because of the accelerator principle. Since the staple industries are most prone to fluctuation, and are concentrated in the Outer Regions, the casual unemployment problem is predominantly a problem in the Outer Regions. The main exception, noted earlier, is the building industry, where the growing demand for both industrial and residential construction attracted casual labour to the prosperous areas of Inner Britain too.

Hatton's results suggest that industrial composition is a much more important factor in the growth of employment than it is in the incidence of unemployment. Since unemployment reflects the growth of labour demand relative to the growth of labour supply, this in turn suggests that region-specific factors may be important chiefly in respect of labour supply.

It was noted earlier that region-specific factors in unemployment tend to increase in importance over time. This could reflect the changing characteristics of regional labour supply. Once unfavourable industrial composition causes a differential decline in labour demand in a region, the most adaptable labour will begin to emigrate to other regions. Myrdal's cumulative instability hypothesis (1957), for example, suggests that the migration of the most enterprising labour from regions with declining industries may transform a temporary problem of industrial composition into a long-term region-specific problem. The external benefits of the example set by enterprising people are lost, and the culture of the region becomes economically less viable as a result. This theme is explored further in section 11.7.

10.8   LABOUR MOBILITY BETWEEN INDUSTRIES
AND REGIONS

This section reviews a number of studies of labour migration in inter-war Britain. The results of these studies are broadly consistent with the Pre-Keynesian view that unemployed workers are reluctant to move to regions or industries which offered better employment prospects.

Very few studies of labour migration examine gross migration. Most studies focus upon either inward migration alone or outward migration alone; alternatively they focus upon net migration (outward *less* inward migration). Likewise there are relatively few studies which consider in detail both geographical and occupational migration. This is mainly because of data limitations regarding occupational mobility. Notwithstanding these qualifications, a fairly coherent picture of inter-war migration can be obtained by combining the results of various studies.

Makower, Marschak and Robinson (1938, 1939, 1940) are concerned chiefly with geographical migration. Their analysis of labour mobility parallels fairly closely the theory presented in chapter 6, and tested in the earlier sections of this chapter. Net migration between any two areas is related to the 'incentive to move', which is measured by differences in employment prospects between the areas. Employment prospects in an area are related variously to the unemployment rate, expected earnings (the wage bill divided by the insured population) and expected receipts (expected earnings from employment adjusted for expected dole receipts during spells of unemployment). It turns out that the last two measurements of employment prospects have no greater explanatory power than the unemployment rate alone, and as they lead to one or two anomalies, the explanation of the incentive to move in terms of unemployment is preferred (for a critique of this methodology see Creedy, 1974). This insignificance of expected earnings bears out some of the results obtained earlier with respect to the coefficients on wage rate variables.

Makower *et al.* study both net migration to Oxford from different counties and also net migration from different counties to the rest of Britain. In both studies it is found that the response of migration to the incentive to move is small. Subject to this qualification, the overall pattern of net migration—from the North and West to the

South and Midlands—is explained quite well by regional differences in employment prospects. It is also found that when employment prospects are controlled for, migration flows diminish with distance.

Makower *et al.* and Daniel (1940) found that migration was sensitive to the overall national level of unemployment. When unemployment was high, migration was low, and most of those who migrated had experienced relatively short spells of unemployment. When unemployment was lower, migration was higher and the proportion of long-term unemployed among the migrants increased. Daniel interprets these results as indicating that during a depression only the 'more mobile' workers migrate, whilst during a recovery the 'less mobile' migrate as well.

Analysts of migration frequently distinguish between the 'push' and 'pull' factors in migration. The push factors are exemplified by poor employment prospects in the area that the migrant quits, and the pull factors are exemplified by the better employment prospects in the area to which the migrant moves. Evidence on the duration of spells of unemployment before moving and after moving indicates that in inter-war Britain 'pull' factors predominated in the timing of the move. It appears that most workers were reluctant to leave an area of high unemployment unless they already knew of vacancies, or prospective vacancies, available in another area. This caution is quite natural, given that it is much easier to remain unemployed in an area with which one is familiar and where one has social ties, than to be unemployed even temporarily in an area in which one is unfamiliar.

Age was found to be a significant influence upon the propensity to migrate. Young people, especially newly married people, were relatively mobile; older men were very immobile. These results are not surprising because there are a number of reasons why this behaviour may be expected to occur. Age-dependence of migration does not, therefore, provide support for any one particular theory of migration.

Size of family is also an important influence on migration. Married workers with one or two children behaved in much the same way as married workers with no children, but married workers with three or more children were much less mobile, and endured longer average spells of unemployment before they moved than did other workers. To a certain extent this reluctance to move can be explained by the housing difficulties experienced by the larger family—particularly when seeking rented accommodation in the new area—and also by the greater disruption to the schooling of the children.

Daniel argues, however, that where the very large family is concerned, the unemployment benefit system is the major deterrent to mobility. In his sample of Welshmen who had moved to Oxford, he reports that the average wage during their first employment was 53s. per week excluding compulsory deductions.

These men were probably the more fortunate migrants, since those who did not succeed and returned home are not included in the sample. The average wage available to all migrants was almost certainly below this and probably lay between 45s. and 50s. a week. The scale allowance of a single man on unemployment assistance is 15s. a week, so that employment in his case results in a gain of some 30s. a week. A married man with children aged 2, 8, 11, and 14 would, however, be allowed 42s. 6d. To this must be added the free milk and meals available in depressed area schools, the absence of travelling or other expenses connected with employment, the few shillings which can be earned without disallowance of assistance, and also the proceeds arising from what the Commissioner for the Special Areas terms sub-economic development, e.g. Group Holdings, Cottage Homesteads, Voluntary (Local Amenities) Schemes, Allotments, and Subsistence Production Schemes (Daniel, 1940, pp. 169–70).

In considering the impact of unemployment benefit, it is also necessary to discuss the special provisions for casual workers. These allowed intermittent spells of unemployment to be consolidated into continuous spells for administrative purposes, so that the claimant could better comply with the requirements of the benefit system. Bakke (1933) notes the use of the system by London dockers, and Jewkes and Campion (1928) and Clay (1929a) refer to the exploitation of the system by employers in the cotton industry, who organized their rotas of short-time working so that their employees would qualify for benefit under the arrangement. Brinley Thomas (1931) claimed that while there was scope for the system to be exploited in the same way in the coalfields, there was no evidence of any widespread abuse—at least in the South Wales and Monmouthshire field. Nevertheless, it is clear that these provisions offered a potential subsidy to industries in which casual hiring predominated and that the subsidy became larger as short-time working was introduced. Such subsidies must to some extent have discouraged the migration of labour from these industries by raising the expected income of workers on short time.

This leads on to the question of occupational mobility in general, about which the evidence is fairly impressionistic. Statistics on mobility were provided by Hilton (1928), but these are very difficult to interpret. Daniel (1940) found that change of occupation was a significant deterrent to mobility over and above change of location. Irrespective of age and condition, unemployed men moved soonest when no change in either occupation or location was involved. They were out of work for a considerable time before they changed either their occupation or their location, and were unemployed for even longer before a movement which involved both change of occupation and change of location.

Makower *et al.* 1938 argue that differences between industries in the occupational mobility of the labour force may explain some of the differences between counties in the level of out-migration. They suggest, for example, that the relatively low level of out-migration from Lancashire may be due to the predominance of textile employment there. Employees in the metal and mining industries also appear to be reluctant to migrate, while those in agriculture are highly mobile. Makower *et al.* suggest that the main aspect of industrial composition that causes differences in out-migration between counties is the proportion of people employed in textiles as compared to agriculture.

These results apply to migration into the Oxford area, much of the movement being accounted for by migrants to the Morris and Pressed Steel works. On the face of it, it is surprising that workers in mechanized industries such as textiles and metals should be reluctant to move into motor manufacturing, when agricultural workers are very willing to do so. One explanation could be that agricultural workers are basically home-workers or itinerants, who form part of the 'disguised unemployed' (Robinson, 1936a, 1936b; Barger, 1936). Makower *et al.* argue that the discrepancy between agricultural workers and others is too great to be explained in this way. Another possibility is that because of the new methods of work organization being used in the motor industry, employers were reluctant to recruit men who were trained in more traditional working practices in the same kind of industry. There seems to be little direct evidence to support this view, though it is certainly a plausible one. There is, however, interview evidence to support an analogous explanation, namely that workers in traditional manufacturing industries were averse to the de-skilling of work in the motor industry, and the consequent diminution of the craftsman's status. Daniel (1940), for example, suggests that

. . . for a migrant from the depressed areas, a change of occupation frequently means a movement from skilled to unskilled work. A great proportion of colliery workers are engaged on comparatively skilled work and these men are naturally loth to migrate to unskilled work and to relinquish all prospects of returning to their own occupations. Rather than move away men frequently prefer to accept a less well paid job in the same industry, a job from which they can hope to recover their old employment. This explains the fact that there is hardly a mine in South Wales without qualified mining engineers working as firemen, and without firemen who can get work only as miners (Daniel, 1940, p. 152).

Similar attitudes are apparent in a study of redundant steel-workers in Yorkshire. Dawes (1934) notes that several of the better-paid skilled men had moved into retailing and insurance broking, which he ascribes to their desire to be independent. Other evidence confirms a substantial movement into small-scale retailing during the slump, and it is possible that many skilled workers preferred a move of this kind to competing for unskilled work.

In the long run, occupational redistribution of the population is supposed to occur chiefly through the re-direction of school-leavers away from declining industries and into prosperous ones. The evidence indicates, however, that this process did not work very effectively in the inter-war period. Data compiled by Makower *et al.* (1940) indicate that substantial numbers of young people continued to enter declining industries such as coal-mining, iron and steel, ship-building, textiles, and boots and shoes. In some cases the continued recruitment of young people is explained by the nature of the work—as in the cotton industry—but the damaging effect of this policy was still felt eventually, for when young people became entitled to adult wages they were made redundant and were left without suitable training for other jobs (Jewkes and Jewkes, 1938). The continuing employment of juveniles in the declining industries may be explained partly by family tradition and social ties—particularly in the cotton industry, where mother, father and children might all work at the same mill, and in isolated mining communities where sons followed their fathers down the pit. Another, more practical, reason for the pattern of juvenile unemployment, may be that when the head of the household was out of work, the 'second-best' strategy was to have juvenile members of the family employed at lower wages in the same industry: labour was supplied by the same family to the same employer, but at a cheaper rate. This 'family link' between the household and the firm may also explain why older married men with children were reluctant to migrate when their children were able to find work with a local employer—at least in the short run.

It is apparent that the links between unemployment and migration are very complex. The long-run case for labour mobility may be overwhelming, and the failure of labour to migrate may well have inhibited the development of new industries in new areas; but if the worker takes a short-run view rather than a long-run view then there are always good reasons for deferring the decision to move. It may be difficult to hear of vacancies in distant areas, and it is risky to move to such areas without a job already arranged. The larger the family the greater are the possibilities for cross-subsidization between the earners and the unemployed, and the higher is the replacement ratio if all members of the family are unemployed. When unemployment afflicts even the relatively prosperous trades then labour turnover in those trades is reduced, and the flow of vacancies dries up as a result. Only the most employable workers can afford to move under these circumstances. Finally, there is the likelihood that the vacancies are for jobs where skills have been diluted, so that the work itself may be unfamiliar, and it may prove difficult to return at a later date to the kind of job for which one has originally trained. All of these factors seem to have been present to some degree in the inter-war period, and for the time being it must remain a matter of judgement as to which of them were actually the most important.

10.9 CONCLUSION

Estimation of the labour supply function deduced in chapters 5 and 6 confirms the Pre-Keynesian view that labour supply responds only partially to labour demand. There is some evidence that the elasticity of labour supply is lowest in declining industries, and in industries with casual hiring practices and a high degree of unionization. These results are broadly consistent with results obtained from studies of labour migration, which indicate that the timing of migration is governed more by 'pull' factors—the creation of jobs in expanding industries—than by 'push' factors—the loss of jobs in declining industries. Migration studies also indicate significant differences in the level of net migration from declining industries, which may be accounted for by differences in work organization between the industries.

Shift–share analysis suggests that during the inter-war period industrial composition became less significant as a factor in regional unemployment. It is possible, though, that the increasing importance of region-specific factors is partly connected with industrial composition, and reflects progressive negative spill-over from the declining industries to other industries in the region.

At the aggregate level, the view that unemployment benefit stimulates labour supply to a significant extent is rejected. The superficial connection between aggregate unemployment and the real level of unemployment benefit may be due not to the effect of higher benefits on labour supply, but to the impact of declining labour demand on the levels of benefit set by government: the larger the number of claimants, the higher the level of benefit was set.

It should not be inferred, however, that the unemployment benefit system had no effect upon labour supply. Unemployment benefit almost certainly reinforced the incentives for unemployed workers to remain attached to existing communities and trades: in accordance with the theory, a differential impact upon workers with large families can be discerned. There is also evidence that the unemployment benefit system was exploited by employers—particularly in casual trades—to subsidize short-time working. This may have been a factor in the sluggish movement of labour out of the cotton industry, for example.

The results obtained for the aggregate impact and for the structural impact of unemployment benefit can be reconciled if it is recognized that the provisions governing eligibility for benefit may be just as important as the real level of benefit set. Certainly where the structural impact is concerned, the absence of financial penalties for workers who refused to contemplate industrial transfer or relocation may well have been important in immobilizing labour in the declining trades. This point should be kept in perspective, however: it seems that there were many skilled men who were reluctant to trade down to unskilled work quite independently of the level at which benefit was set and the way that eligibility was determined. This is reflected in the number of instances of skilled men who preferred to become self-employed rather than trade down to unskilled work or draw the dole. It is clear, therefore, that the non-pecuniary aspects of work were also an important influence on labour supply.

Underlying all this, however, the reluctance of many workers to move may reflect an erroneous judgement that the causes of their unemployment were essentially short-run. Long-run structural problems may have been mistaken for short-run disturbances. This could explain not only their reluctance to move, but—as noted in section 9.6—it could also explain their attitude to wage bargaining.

11

Pre-Keynesian Theory: Its Relevance Today

11.1 INTRODUCTION

There are a number of superficial similarities between the Pre-Keynesian diagnosis of Britain's relative decline in the 1920s and some popular diagnoses of Britain's current economic problems. Since Britain's economic problems appear to be shared increasingly by other mature industrialized economies, Pre-Keynesian theory may be relevant to other countries too. The object of this chapter is to examine to what extent the analogy between the current situation and the past can be usefully pursued.

Section 11.2 examines evidence on the relation between the demand for labour and the real wage. The evidence suggests that, just as in inter-war Britain, employment has been determined by the demand for labour rather than by the supply; recent studies suggest that the aggregate demand for labour is approximately unit-elastic with respect to the real wage. Section 11.3 discusses the determinants of the real wage itself.

Section 11.4 shows that the relation between industrial structure and regional employment growth in post-war Britain has been somewhat more complex than in the inter-war period. Labour migration is discussed in section 11.5, where it is shown that despite a reduction in obstacles to geographical mobility, the supply of unskilled labour does not readily adjust to differentials in regional employment growth. Skilled workers and professional workers, on the other hand, tend to be much more mobile. This means that when skill-intensive plants relocate in high-unemployment areas there may be substantial inward migration of skilled labour and only a small reduction in unemployment among the unskilled. Section 11.6 defends the structural unemployment thesis against the charges that the amount of structural unemployment is insignificant, or that it is chiefly a byproduct of a deficiency of aggregate demand. It is suggested that structural unemployment has been seriously underestimated by some researchers because of a misinterpretation of the evidence about unfilled vacancies.

Section 11.7 attempts to interpret all the evidence from inter-war and post-war studies in terms of a dynamic theory of structural change. The key element in the theory is a self-selection process whereby the most enterprising workers move to the innovative sectors of the economy while the unenterprising workers agglomerate in the non-innovative sectors. Once the concentration of unenterprising workers in any sector reaches a critical level, the prospect of any change is eliminated and workers and management focus their attention almost entirely on maintaining or increasing their share of the ever-diminishing product. While the theory is broadly consistent with the available evidence, much further research is needed before it can be fully endorsed. Section 11.8 considers some of the implications of this dynamic theory for other areas of economics: in particular, for theories of disequilibrium and of rational expectations.

11.2   DEMAND FOR LABOUR AND THE REAL WAGE

In chapter 9 striking confirmation was obtained for the Pre-Keynesian view that employment is determined by the demand for labour and that the demand for labour varies inversely with the real wage. The view that employment is determined by the demand for labour reflects the postulate that the real wage is too high. This postulate seems reasonable in the context of inter-war Britain, where mass unemployment prevailed for much of the time. Its relevance to post-war Britain is not so obvious, for until recently unemployment was at a much lower level than in the inter-war period. Notwithstanding this reservation, the data are consistent with the view that in post-war Britain too, employment has been determined at the short end of the labour market by the level of the real wage.

In a recent study of labour hoarding in Britain, 1965–74, Bowers, Deaton and Turk (1982) estimate the short-run employment function introduced in section 9.3. Using informal arguments rather than detailed modelling, they specify a log-linear relation between employment (the dependent variable) and current output and the own-product wage. The function is estimated independently for eight sample industries, using de-trended variables—equivalent to the inclusion of a time trend as an explanatory variable. Their results are reported in table 11.1. It can be seen that the coefficients on output are all positive and significant, and are of broadly similar magnitude to those reported in section 9.3. In seven of the eight sample industries the own-product wage has a negative impact on employment, and in five of the industries it is statistically significant. The only positive effect is recorded in the clothing industry, and is statistically insignificant.

TABLE 11.1

Log-linear regressions of employment on output and the own-product real wage using adjusted quarterly data for eight UK industries, 1965(III)–1974(II)

Industry	Constant	Current output	Own-product real wage	$\bar{R}^2$
Food	0.957*	0.274*	−0.228*	0.77
	(2.3)	(5.2)	(6.3)	
Chemicals	0.627	0.502*	−0.127	0.63
	(0.6)	(7.2)	(1.5)	
Metal manufacturing	0.748*	0.405*	−0.152*	0.80
	(2.0)	(10.6)	(3.8)	
Engineering	1.362*	0.847*	−1.206*	0.78
	(2.5)	(9.5)	(7.6)	
Textiles	0.717*	0.460*	−0.179*	0.76
	(2.7)	(5.0)	(2.2)	
Clothing	0.390	0.482*	0.131	0.56
	(0.6)	(6.5)	(0.7)	
Timber	1.284*	0.125*	−0.414*	0.32
	(3.9)	(3.7)	(2.6)	
Paper	0.778*	0.421*	−0.200	0.22
	(2.3)	(3.3)	(1.6)	

Source: Adapted from Bowers, Deaton and Turk (1982), Table 9.4.
Note: The data were de-trended using a 20-period moving average and seasonally adjusted using dummies. No measure of serial correlation is quoted. An asterisk denotes that the coefficient is statistically significant as 5 per cent in a two-tailed *t*-test

Turning to the aggregate level, Symons (1981) has studied the determinants of UK manufacturing employment over the period 1961–77. Like Bowers *et al.* he uses quarterly data. He assumes that disequilibrium in the labour market identifies a labour demand function whose arguments are the own-product wage, the price of inputs relative to outputs, normal hours of work, strike activity and a time trend. Normal hours and strike activity may proxy for some of the non-wage costs of labour (since shorter working weeks normally reduce capital utilization and increase unit labour costs, while strikes incur disruption costs). Symons finds that employment is unit-elastic with respect to the own-product wage, although the lag in employment adjustment is fairly long. It takes about seven quarters for half the effect of a permanent increase in the wage to be felt. He finds that the elasticity of employment with respect to input costs is about one-half, with a rather similar lag structure. He also finds that in the long run a decrease in normal hours has a strong tendency to reduce employment. This is consistent with the view that a decrease in normal hours increases the non-wage costs of employment per hour worked. The size of the effect, however, is so great that it is difficult to see how non-wage costs alone can explain the effect. Symons (p. 53) suggests that 'the tastes that lead to a drive for a shorter working week may also cause workers to be less productive'. This explanation is considered in more detail in section 11.7 below.

The conclusion suggested by these studies is that, notwithstanding the relatively low level of unemployment in post-war Britain, the Pre-Keynesian theory has continued to apply and employment has been governed, at least in part, by the real wage.

11.3   MONEY WAGE RIGIDITY AND REAL WAGE RIGIDITY

In the 1950s and early 1960s the fixed money wage theory of Keynes appeared to work well. Keynesian policies were credited with keeping unemployment to relatively low levels and although 'wage drift' was apparent, inflation gave little cause for concern. The government expenditure multiplier seemed to be somewhat smaller than had been anticipated, but this could be explained in terms of lags in the circular flow of income. In the late 1960s, however, there was a breakdown in a number of the behavioural regularities upon which successful Keynesian demand management depends. It seemed that the private sector had learnt to anticipate and neutralize the effects of key instruments of government policy, and additional instruments—such as incomes policies—had to be devised to counter this.

About this time there was a major revival of interest in the Pre-

Keynesian theory of real wage bargaining due to the seminal paper of Sargan (1964). In this paper Sargan argues that wages are determined by trade unions, who stipulate for a trend increase in the real wage, but with some moderation of demands in periods of high unemployment. Analysis of quarterly data for 1949–61 indicates that target, or 'equilibrium' real wages increased at about 2 per cent per annum, and that a doubling of unemployment induced a 3 per cent fall in the equilibrium wage. When equilibrium is disturbed by a change in the cost of living money wages do not adjust instantaneously: the adjustment process involves an exponentially weighted distributed lag of average length 18.5 quarters. Suppose, for example, that there is a once-for-all devaluation of sterling under a fixed exchange rate regime. If the devaluation has an immediate full impact on import prices, it will be 16 quarters before money wages have risen by half the change in import prices, and 43 quarters before they have risen by 90 per cent of the change in import prices. In other words, half the initial impact of the devaluation disappears in 4 years, and 90 per cent by the end of 11 years.

Sargan's specification of real wage bargaining can be viewed as the introduction of an additional catch-up term into the Phillips curve (Phillips, 1959; Dicks-Mireaux and Dow, 1959). A number of writers have examined the role of this real-wage catch-up term, including Johnston and Timbrell (1973); Henry, Sawyer and Smith (1976); Henry and Ormerod (1978); and Sargan himself (Sargan, 1980); the most recent study is Apps (1982). A useful summary of this work is provided by Jackman, Mulvey and Trevithick (1981, ch. 8). The main lessons of these studies seem to be that to obtain satisfactory estimates, target wages have to be adjusted for tax deductions—suggesting that trade unions bargain over real 'take-home' pay—and that the estimated impact of unemployment on the wage rate does not adequately capture the impact on wages of the pressure of demand. The shortcomings of the unemployment variable may indicate that unemployment is not the simple macro-economic aggregate that it is often supposed to be: it may be that the structure of unemployment is now far more important in explaining real wage movements than is the aggregate volume.

The results discussed above suggest that real wage bargaining has occurred throughout the post-war period, but with a catch-up of wages on prices that has been relatively slow. There is evidence to suggest, however, the lags in the catch-up process became very much shorter in the late 1960s and early 1970s. Patterson (1982) suggests that short-run money illusion in wage bargaining was much greater before 1968 than it was after 1971. Using the framework of the expectations-augmented Phillips curve (Friedman, 1968), he models the spread of inflation-awareness as a logistic process. For the UK economy, 1960–77, he finds that short-run money illusion persisted so long as inflation was low and stable (below 2½ per cent per annum). But when inflation 'took off' around 1968, within 3 years 75–80 per cent of wage bargains were made in real rather than money terms.

Further evidence on real wage rigidity comes from the stagflation that followed the oil price rise of 1973. The rate of increase of nominal labour costs per unit output rose from 9.1 per cent in 1973 to 17.4 per cent in 1974 and 28.7 per cent in 1975. At the same time unemployment increased, due partly to substantial job losses in manufacturing. The wage inflation was terminated by a deflationary budget and a new form of incomes policy. While this 'social contract' was in force the inflation of labour costs was reduced to an average of 10.1 per cent in 1977 (Graham, 1979). The experience of other Western industrialized countries was somewhat similar, though the inflationary impact was not normally quite so severe.

The stagflation experience is consistent with the view that trade unions were attempting to maintain real wages in the face of the rising oil import price induced by the OPEC cartel. Since, in the short run, energy and other oil-based products are complementary to labour in manufacturing processes, the rise in oil prices shifts downward the demand for labour and reduces the equilibrium real wage. An attempt by the trade unions to defend the real wage can be expected to lead to a sharp increase in unemployment in manufacturing industry (Maynard, 1978; Bruno, 1980). It is also interesting to note that although the terms of trade deteriorated sharply between 1972 and 1974, they improved in 1975 and this improvement was subsequently maintained, in association with a permanently higher level of unemployment. This is consistent with the model of the open economy presented in section 6.7 and tested in section 10.6. If the trade unions were attempting to maintain their members' living standards by exploiting more fully their monopoly of labour supply in certain industries, then the increase in the monopoly price of labour would be partly passed on by exporters in the form of higher relative prices. The increase that could not be passed on would induce a contraction in employment and output. While higher export prices improve the terms of trade, they also mean reduced demand and lower output, so unemployment would be higher too. The argument is independent of exchange rate adjustments since it is couched in real and not monetary terms.

The question naturally arises as to why the problem of stagflation should have been particularly acute in Britain. Stagflation has, of course, been a world-wide phenomenon, but on average the British performance has been relatively poor, as reflected in the combination of high unemployment and the depreciation of sterling against most other leading currencies. One explanation could be that real wage rigidities are more serious in Britain than they are in other countries. This would make it particularly difficult for the British economy to adjust to adverse external changes through a reduction in the real wage. This view receives support from recent work by Grubb, Jackman and Layard (1982) who compare the relative importance of real wage rigidity and money wage rigidity for 19 OECD countries over the period 1957–80. Wage rigidity is measured by the extra unemployment caused by a deflationary shock when the monetary authorities neutralize the effect of the shock on the inflation rate. More precisely, wage rigidity is defined as the number of additional 'units' of unemployment induced by a unit shock, where a unit of unemployment is a unit increase in the percentage rate of unemployment for 1 year. Money wage rigidity is greater, the greater is the response of unemployment to a monetary shock, such as an unanticipated reduction in money supply growth. Real wage rigidity is greater, the greater is the response of unemployment to a real shock such as an exogenous fall in labour productivity growth or an exogenous disturbance in the terms of trade.

It is found that in the sample countries the average level of real wage rigidity is about unity. Real wage rigidity is higher in Britain than in any other country (the coefficient is 2.39). Real wage rigidity is lowest in Switzerland and Japan (the coefficient is 0.13). On average, money wage rigidity is about half real wage rigidity; however, money wage rigidity is extremely high in the US. These results are broadly consistent with the view of Branson and Rotemberg (1980) that in the European Community countries real wage rigidity is greater than in the US, while money wage rigidity is higher in the US than in Europe.

Grubb *et al.*, find that international differences in unemployment are explained by differences in the level of real wage rigidity rather than by differences in the magnitude of the real wage shocks that are experienced. Furthermore, across countries there is a significantly positive relation between real wage rigidity and the growth of unemployment over the sample period.

Why should real wage rigidity be particularly acute in Britain? It could be argued that the importance of real wage rigidity may reflect the nature of the shocks experienced by the economy. It is more sensible for money wages to be indexed to money prices—i.e. for real wages to be rigid—in an economy where monetary shocks predominate than it is in an economy where real shocks predominate (Lucas, 1973; Gray, 1976). However, Grubb *et al.* find little evidence to support this theory. Since Britain is an international trading nation, it is reasonable to suppose that real shocks will be regularly transmitted to the manufacturing and tradeable services sectors, and that real wage rigidity should in consequence be low and not high.

An alternative explanation of real wage rigidity emphasizes the low rate of productivity growth in Britain. If productivity is high, and the trade unions' target rate of real wage increase is consequently below the rate of productivity growth, then there is some 'slack' available for real wage adjustments. But if productivity is low and the target rate of real wage increase exceeds the rate of productivity growth then no such slack exists, and the wage target becomes a binding constraint on wage settlements. Productivity is, of course, itself affected by trade union bargaining over working practices, so that both the real wage target and the level of productivity may reflect a common trade union attitude. This approach to real wage rigidity is considered further in section 11.7

11.4   THE REGIONAL PROBLEM AND INDUSTRIAL STRUCTURE IN POST-WAR BRITAIN

The pattern of regional growth and unemployment characteristic of the inter-war period has to some extent been perpetuated in the post-war period. Scotland and the North of England have continued to decline and the South has continued to grow. On the other hand, the decline of Wales has been contained and the South-west and East Anglia have grown faster than the South-east.

The regions with the slowest growth of employment have experienced the highest levels of unemployment. This result may seem too obvious to call for comment—but it emphasizes the fact that labour does not move freely between regions in response to differential rates of employment growth. If it did, there would be a tendency for unemployment rates between regions to be equalized. Failure to equalize unemployment rates is *prima facie* evidence that a substantial amount of labour is strongly attached to the declining regions, or to the industries which predominate there.

In the 1950s and early 1960s regional inequalities were not quite so pronounced, but following a spate of job losses in manufacturing in the late 1970s substantial inequalities have again emerged. During a recession, of course, unemployment tends to increase in all regions, and this means that in proportional terms the rise in the unemployment rates is greatest in the high-employment regions. In absolute terms, however, the rise in the unemployment rate during a recession tends to be greatest in the low-employment regions. Thus unemployment in the most depressed regions is more sensitive to cyclical fluctuations than is unemployment in the more prosperous regions. It appears that only part of the cyclical sensitivity of the depressed regions is explained by their industrial composition—in other words, by a concentration of cyclically sensitive industries, such as durable goods producers, there. In post-war Britain a significant part of the cyclical sensitivity has been region-specific (Brechling, 1967; Dixon and Thirlwall, 1975).

The importance of region-specific factors in regional inequalities is emphasized by a shift-share analysis of the growth of manufacturing employment in 11 British regions between 1952 and 1979. The results of this analysis, by Fothergill and Gudgin (1982), are summarized in table 11.2. Industry composition explains the relative decline of employment in Yorkshire and Humberside and the North-west, but the growth of employment in East Anglia and the South-west is explained mainly by region-specific factors. The tendency for region-specific factors to dominate suggests that the trend revealed by Hatton's study of inter-war Britain (see section 10.7) has continued in the post-war period.

Fothergill and Gudgin explain the role of region-specific factors in terms of increasing diseconomies of urbanization facing manufacturing industry. The final column of the table shows Fothergill and Gudgin's ranking of regions by urbanization (as derived from their diagrams), and it is clear that the degree of urbanization is significantly correlated with the region-specific component of employment growth. The lower is the urbanization, the more positive is the region-specific component. The urbanization factor works particularly well, for example, in explaining the relocation of industry from the urbanized South-east to rural East Anglia and the South-west.

TABLE 11.2
Shift-share analysis of percentage changes in manufacturing employment in
11 UK regions, 1952–79

Region	Differential change	Industry composition component	Region-specific component	Ranking by urbanization
East Anglia	62.5	4.1	74.0	0
South-west	17.9	3.4	30.1	2
Wales	9.7	−1.0	26.3	1
East Midlands	3.6	−1.9	21.1	3
North	0.0	−4.4	20.0	4
West Midlands	−15.6	7.3	−7.3	8
South-east	−17.7	15.1	−17.2	9
Yorkshire and Humberside	−22.5	−13.7	7.8	6
Scotland	−26.2	−6.8	−3.8	5
North-west	−32.2	−13.2	−3.5	7
Northern Ireland	−34.9	−26.7	7.1	excluded

Source: Adapted from Fothergill and Gudgin (1982), table 4.1, p. 52 and figure 5.1, p. 70.

The major exception is Northern Ireland, which has fairly low urbanization but poor employment growth, but the most obvious explanation for this anomaly is in terms of political unrest.

In the inter-war period, and in the early post-war period, it was generally believed that urbanization was associated with economies of agglomeration to industry. There are a number of reasons why this may now have changed. First, road transport has increased in importance relative to rail, and so agglomeration around rail heads is no longer so important as it was in the inter-war period. Since the road network is more comprehensive, but more prone to congestion than the rail network, economies of agglomeration around road intersections are not so great. Nevertheless, access to the motorway network is an important consideration, and the difficulties of constructing motorways in heavily built-up areas has meant that the older urban areas may now suffer a location disadvantage. Secondly, there are the housing problems of urban areas and the desire of middle-income families to move away from an industrial environment and from the high-density population areas where the low-income families live. Because many 'new' industries are relatively footloose—they are not tied to the sources of non-tradeable raw materials, for example—they can afford to move away from the older urban areas into more congenial surroundings closer to where their middle-income employees prefer to live. Finally, post-war British regional policy, and the New Town programme in particular, has encouraged industry to move to 'green-field' sites away from the older urban areas.

The urbanization thesis goes a good way towards explaining the nature of regional differentials in post-war Britain, but it may not be the complete explanation. It does not explain, for example, why region-specific factors have increased in importance relative to industry composition; it is mainly concerned with explaining why the balance of region-specific factors has changed in favour of the rural areas. To find an explanation of the diminishing importance of industrial composition and the increasing importance of region-specific factors it is necessary to analyze the situation at a higher level of disaggregation.

During the inter-war period it was fairly easy to distinguish the 'old' industries from the 'new'. By and large, the old industries relied upon the technologies of steam power and large-scale machinery, while the new industries relied upon electricity, chemistry, internal combustion and small-scale precision machinery. The products produced by the new industries were obviously dissimilar to the products produced by the old industries, and the industrial classification was accordingly adapted to identify the new industries and record their rapid growth in employment and output. Since technology changed little in the older industries, the statistics of industry growth reveal clearly the rapid growth of new industries based on new technologies relative to old industries based on old technologies.

In the post-war period, however, new technologies have increasingly invaded the 'older' industries, so that the older industries are no longer necessarily those with an old technology. With a few exceptions—such as microelectronics and jet engineering—technological progress has mainly involved the consolidation of early breakthroughs rather than the pioneering of revolutionary techniques. Few new industries have been created, but many existing industries have witnessed the obsolescence of old techniques. So far as the industrial classification is concerned, the distinction between old and new industries is no longer as clear as it was.

The crucial distinctions are now much more within industries, between firms which are tied to the old technologies and firms which have adopted the new ones. For this reason the 'industrial composition' of a region may no longer capture the 'new technology' effect in the same way as it did in the inter-war period.

The argument can be extended to provide an explanation of the importance of region-specific factors in the post-war period. When a new technology is being introduced, the innovating firm has less incentive than other firms to locate in an established industrial area. New technologies normally require new skills and working practices, and there is therefore little point in seeking to recruit labour previously employed with other firms in the same industry. The firm will need to train labour itself, rather than rely upon training imparted by others. In certain cases—for example where there are strong trade unions enforcing traditional working practices—the firm may deliberately locate away from others to avoid the risk of trade union interference.

In the nineteenth century Britain was a major exporter of technologies, but in the twentieth century it has increasingly imported technology, mostly from the US. Technology has been imported mainly through foreign direct investment by US firms (Dunning, 1958). Most of these firms have chosen to build on 'green-field' sites rather than to take over established British firms. Takeovers appear to have occurred mainly when it was marketing and management skills that were being transferred, rather than a new technology itself. The reasoning is fairly clear: there is little point in taking over a firm with obsolete capital equipment and obsolete labour skills.

The green-field investor is not tied to sites occupied by existing firms. Post-war foreign investors in Britain appear to have been susceptible to government inducements to locate in development areas and in new towns (though many of those locating in new towns have chosen sites in the south). This susceptibility to government persuasion may itself represent, to some extent, an indifference towards locating in established industrial areas. Once established, however, the foreign investor, with his new technology, may act as a magnet drawing to the area the most enterprising firms anxious to learn from the innovator. By moving close to the foreign investor, domestic firms can draw upon a labour force trained in the new technology, and possibly gain a competitive edge in tendering for any subcontracted work. The location to which the foreign investor is enticed then becomes a centre around which manufacturing employment—and service employment, too—can grow. So far as the interpretation of regional employment statistics is concerned, the presence of the innovating firm and its satellites within the region will appear as a 'region-specific' factor promoting employment growth.

To analyze this process further, it would be necessary to disaggregate not only industrially, but also spatially, and to distinguish separate areas within the regions discussed by Fothergill and Gudgin. It would be useful, for example, to distinguish new towns, low-density suburban areas and seaside residential areas as areas which—though not themselves rural—may nevertheless be attractive to innovative firms. The process of industrial relocation is almost certainly more complex than the simple urban/rural dichotomy would suggest.

11.5   EMPLOYMENT GROWTH AND LABOUR MIGRATION IN POST-WAR BRITAIN

It was argued in the previous section that some firms are more technologically progressive than others, and that progressive firms act as incubators, attracting other firms to their locality in order to learn from them. This theory may account for some aspects of regional differentials in employment growth. To transform the argument into a theory of regional differentials in unemployment it is necessary to take account of the implications of regional employment growth for regional labour supply. The growth of labour supply depends, of course, upon birth and death rates, but the most significant factor in regional differentials appears to be net migration flow.

Post-war studies of labour migration have become fairly sophisticated, and only a brief summary of the results can be provided here (for a detailed review of methodology see Mueller, 1982). It is important to distinguish between different streams of migration prompted by different motives and undertaken by different kinds of people. Short-distance migration is often prompted by residential considerations and reflects the different housing needs of individuals at different stages of the life cycle (Harris and Clausen, 1967). Long-distance migration is much more sensitive to employment prospects and—as in the inter-war studies reported in section 10.8—is governed mainly by the pull of employment growth in the destination rather than the push of unemployment at the origin.

Low-income and blue-collar workers appear to be much less mobile over long distances than high-income and white-collar workers. One explanation is that lower-paid workers face relatively higher relocation costs, particularly when the frustrations caused by controlled tenancies in the local authority and private rented sectors are taken into account. It seems, however, that housing difficulties are a relatively minor consideration. In a detailed study of housing problems and labour mobility, Johnson, Salt and Wood (1974, p. 247) conclude that 'the lack of mobility of manual workers and of lower-paid white-collar workers is probably because they do not want to move rather than because they cannot move. Not only are they more likely to obtain alternative employment locally, but they may put a higher value on social ties within a local area. . . . When they do move long distances, it tends to be to areas which are familiar to them through pre-existing ties.'

Gross migration flows tend to be largest for prime-age professional and managerial workers moving between major employment centres. There are also large commuter flows between residential areas and industrial areas. In the case of long-distance commuters, these flows may well cross the boundaries of regions or metropolitan labour areas. The post-war period has thus seen a significant integration between local labour markets where high-income workers are concerned; but where low-income workers are concerned, geographical migration has remained relatively small, and long-distance commuting insignificant. One effect of this 'dual' migration pattern is to make it easier for employers to substitute high-income skilled labour for low-income unskilled labour in areas where skilled labour was previously relatively scarce.

The impact of new technology in many industries has been to displace the unskilled worker through automation. It has also displaced the 'craftsman', who was the type of skilled worker demanded by the old technology. The new technology typically demands semi-skilled workers and professional and managerial workers to oversee them. The unskilled work available is often much lighter than before and is just as suitable for women as for men.

It seems, therefore, that the skills demanded by innovating firms are the kind that the most mobile section of the workforce is best equipped to supply. An innovating firm locating on a green-field site need have little fear of local labour shortages, since the kinds of workers it requires are relatively mobile. It will need to pay wages and salaries above the norm for the industry as a whole in order to attract the workers it requires. But there will be sufficient workers responsive to economic incentives to move to the expanding area. It is likely, therefore, that the growth of employment in expanding areas will attract significant inward migration, and this is, in fact, the pattern that is observed (Gordon, 1979; Burridge and Gordon, 1981).

If the innovating firm happens to be located in an older urban area with high unemployment (for example, a supplier of office services in an inner city), then although employment will expand, unemployment may not decrease. The discrepancy between the attitudes of the unemployed and the requirements of the firm may lead to the employment needs being accommodated entirely by inward migration (or, of course, by commuting instead). In cases of this kind, where an innovating firm is located as an 'enclave' in an area of high unemployment, the 'duality' of the labour market is almost complete (Doeringer and Piore, 1971; Bosanquet and Doeringer, 1973).

The tendency for innovating firms to rely upon mobile skilled labour is reinforced by the concentration of innovative activity in large entrepreneurial firms (typically multinational firms) who produce using a network of branch plants. Such firms provide an internal labour market for their employees, which further enhances the geographical mobility of the career-minded worker. A firm of this kind could staff a new branch plant entirely from its own internal labour resources and recruit only replacement staff for the plants already operating. In this way the local direct employment effect of the new branch plant would be negligible—and for other reasons, the indirect effects might be fairly small too.

11.6   THE EXTENT OF STRUCTURAL UNEMPLOYMENT IN BRITAIN: A CRITIQUE OF PREVIOUS STUDIES

The preceding discussion suggests that Britain has suffered from a continuing structural problem involving workers who are wedded to obsolete production technologies. Two groups of workers in particular are affected: the 'craftsmen', who were the aristocracy of the workforce under the old technology, and the unskilled workers who did the kind of heavy work that the new technology has dispensed with. To this might be added a third group: young people who, because of family or educational background, lack the industrial discipline necessary for working with new technologies involving expensive and delicate equipment.

Some writers, such as Cheshire (1973) and Nickell (1982), have denied that structural unemployment has been significant in post-war Britain. They argue instead that the principal causes of unemployment have been aggregative factors, and in particular a Keynesian deficiency of aggregate demand. Their arguments can be criticized on two main grounds.

First, these writers take a very narrow view of structural unemployment. Cheshire, for example, identifies structural unemployment with a situation in which unemployment in one occupation or region is matched by a corresponding number of unfilled vacancies in another occupation or region. It is further required that these vacancies cannot be filled from the unemployed already attached to that occupation or region: this requirement is met, according to Cheshire, only if the number of unfilled vacancies exceeds the numbers unemployed in the occupation or region concerned. It follows from this that structural unemployment can exist only when, in some occupation or region, there is an excess of unfilled vacancies over the numbers unemployed. The existence of unemployment in other occupations or regions (in excess of the unfilled vacancies in those occupations or regions) is then *prima facie* evidence of a structural mismatch caused by geographical or occupational immobility.

The main difficulty with this concept of structural unemployment is that it involves some very strong implicit assumptions about the role of unfilled vacancies (for other problems see Armstrong and Taylor, 1981). It was pointed out in section 3.5 that new vacancies constitute a flow, while unfilled vacancies are a stock: the stock of unfilled vacancies is determined both by the flow of new vacancies and also by speed with which vacancies are filled. If vacancies are filled very quickly then the stock of unfilled vacancies will tend to be small compared to the stock of unemployed. Competition between employers anxious to fill vacancies quickly will bid up wages until either workers appear to fill them or the wage is so high that jobs are no longer economic and the vacancies are withdrawn. The failure of the unemployed workers in one sector to move to jobs in another sector may therefore be reflected, not in a stock of unfilled vacancies, but simply in a higher wage. The absence of a stock of unfilled vacancies with which to match the unemployed cannot, therefore, be used as an argument against structural unemployment.

Studies of post-war Britain show that the stock of unfilled vacancies is typically smaller than the stock of unemployment. This has been interpreted as evidence of a persistent deficiency of aggregate demand. This interpretation may well be false. If the costs to an employer of the disruption caused by a vacancy remaining unfilled exceed the costs to an unemployed worker of prolonging his search for a job, then workers may take longer to find jobs than employers take to fill vacancies. For any level of job turnover in the labour market, therefore, the stock of unfilled vacancies may well be less than the stock of unemployed, irrespective of the level of aggregate demand. Once again, the failure to distinguish properly between stocks and flows can lead to a misinterpretation of the data.

Advocates of the demand–deficiency view argue that if demand were stimulated then labour mobility would increase and structural unemployment would be substantially reduced. There is an element of truth in this argument, though the policy implication as a whole appears to be false. If real wages in general are too high, then non-wage rationing of jobs occurs along the lines described in chapter 5. Those who have jobs are reluctant to quit them to search for better jobs because of the low probability of becoming re-employed within a reasonable time. Unemployment becomes concentrated upon those unfortunate enough to have recently been made redundant or—like young people just entering the labour force—to have had no previous opportunity of a job. If a reflationary policy can reduce the real wage (through money illusion, for example) then the immediate effect will be the creation of new vacancies. These vacancies may not all be directly suitable for the unemployed. There will, however, be knock-on effects, for workers who have been reluctant to quit their jobs during a recession may now be encouraged by the flow of new vacancies to quit in order to seek more suitable work. This provides still more vacancies for the unemployed to choose from, and so makes it more likely that a suitable placement can be found, particularly if employers relax their hiring standards at the same time. The expansion of employment makes the labour market more fluid, and improves the chances of matching the unemployed to suitable jobs.

For the policy to have lasting benefits, however, the real wage must be kept permanently depressed, otherwise job losses will ensue and the problem will recur. For reasons already discussed, it is doubtful if Keynesian reflation alone can succeed in depressing the real wage for long (a modern Keynesian might therefore press for an incomes policy too). There is the added problem that a reflation engineered through fiscal policy may lead to a distortion of resource allocation. The direct effect of Keynesian policy is to create employment in the public sector, or in private industries servicing public sector demand. Because of inertia, public sector demand remains at a high level when the real wage rises, and the burden of taxation causes a contraction of private demand, and consequent loss of jobs in private sector firms sourcing private demand. A further reflation is then called for to offer the newly unemployed replacement jobs by a further expansion of the public sector. This kind of Keynesian policy—a variant of which was pursued in Britain in the 1950s and 1960s—has the long-run effect of creating structural problems by allocating an excessive amount of labour to the public sector (Bacon and Eltis, 1976). The reflation may promote the mobility of labour, but it moves the labour into the wrong sectors of the economy.

To conclude, it appears that empirical work on structural unemployment in post-war Britain has been marred by a confusion over the significance of the stock of unfilled vacancies. It has been assumed, wrongly, that there is some underlying stable relationship between unemployment and unfilled vacancies, and that there is some sort of equilibrium when the two are equal. This view has led to structural unemployment being wrongly diagnosed as the result of a deficiency of aggregate demand.

Post-war Keynesian policies, by largely ignoring the structural aspects of unemployment, have probably made structural problems worse. It is rather ironic that one of the main objectives of post-war economic policy was to avoid the mistakes that it was believed had been made in the inter-war period, yet in the event the same mistake of inhibiting structural adjustment has been repeated. Keynesian policies have been applied to avoid the slump conditions of 1929–33, which were seen—quite out of proportion—as the main problem of the inter-war period. 'Fine-tuning' was developed to avoid repetition of the 'boom and bust' conditions which prevailed immediately after World War I. Yet part of the problem of this post-war boom was that demobilized labour was directed back to the wrong industries (notably the munitions industry), encouraged by government promises that workers could have their old jobs back (Pigou, 1947). After World War II workers have again been encouraged by government policy to move into jobs which have no long-term future—this time, to service temporary public sector demand. In the short run this policy helped to disguise structural problems, and it is only in the late 1970s and early 1980s that the full implications of the policy have become obvious.

11.7   ENTERPRISE AND THE PROCESS
OF STRUCTURAL CHANGE

The analysis of employment growth and labour mobility in section 11.5 suggests that the most mobile workers will tend to agglomerate around innovating firms in areas of expanding employment, leaving the less mobile workers attached to firms using obsolete technologies in areas of declining employment. Underpinning this analysis is the view that there are important differences in the labour force with respect to attitudes to work. Perhaps the most crucial difference is between the enterprising worker and the unenterprising worker. The enterprising worker may be defined as someone who is strongly committed to work as a means of generating income and improving his status, and who takes a broad view of his economic environment and a long view of his own employment prospects. The enterprising worker is therefore responsive to economic incentives such as higher wages, relatively unconcerned by the social disruption caused by migration, recognizes the need for education and training, is hard-working in pursuit of promotion, and regularly scans vacancies in case there is a better job with another firm. The enterprising worker is therefore skilled, adaptable and mobile. The opinion may be ventured that the typical enterprising worker is younger rather than older, and is likely to have been reared by enterprising parents.

By contrast, the unenterprising worker may be defined as someone who is either committed to work only because he likes the kind of work involved, or he is not committed to work at all, but to leisure or social activities instead. He attaches little importance to economic advancement: income is demanded chiefly to support his leisure or social activities. His lack of interest in economic advancement means that he attaches little importance to education and training, he has a narrow view of his economic environment, and little awareness of what other opportunities are open to him. Because he does not perceive work as an avenue of promotion he has little interest in working hard unless he is on a piece-work system. Even then, because of his short-run perspective he has little concern with earning an income above his current consumption needs, and under piece-work he may therefore prefer shorter hours to a large income out of which he can save. The unenterprising worker who is interested in his work may well be skilled, but will be unadaptable and therefore occupationally immobile; the unenterprising worker who is uninterested in his work will be unskilled, unadaptable to semi-skilled work, and geographically immobile.

The continuing process of structural change carries the enterprising workers along the path of career development, and leaves the unenterprising workers behind. Social processes of this kind are now receiving increasing analytical attention (Nelson and Winter, 1982; Olson, 1982). The connection between structural change and regional decay was in fact pointed out some years ago in a seminal work by Wilbur R. Thompson, which described the process as 'hardening of the arteries'.

A powerful 'long wave' may be at work in the process of urban growth. An established centre of an industry has a strong comparative advantage in the early period of the industry's development due to all the external economies which are so familiar. . . . But a radical change in industrial technology not only undercuts some of the older centre's comparative advantage but may even reverse it if the veteran labour force resists work standard changes dictated by the new technology. And if, as frequently happens at the blue-collar level, the new production techniques are less demanding of skill than the old, the 'labour-harassed' firm is likely to relocate. . . . The steady migration of textiles from New England to the South Atlantic region probably had more than a little of this force underlying it: labour's collective resistance to increasing the number of spindles tended in the textile mills is very much in line with this kind of development. The influence of work standards on industrial location is, moreover, not likely to lessen in the near future, with even more changes in industrial technology in the offing (e.g., computers) (Thompson (1964), p. 43, quoted in Sternlieb and Hughes (1975), p. 165).

It does not follow that, as a result of this process, the unenterprising workers must become unemployed. Provided the unenterprising workers are content with low real wages then they can remain employed. Since the unenterprising workers have fairly limited aspirations, they may not demand a very high real wage. The wage they demand, however, may be high in relation to their productivity, which will be low because of their attitude to work.

The craftsman may work hard, but his satisfactions come from the quality of the product rather than the quantity. Greater quantity of the same quality means greater speed of work and more stress, while greater quantity with lower quality removes the satisfactions of work altogether. The unskilled worker has no reasons to work any harder than his supervisor requires, since he is not interested in promotion, while the viability of the firm as a whole depends upon how hard other people in general work, rather than how hard he in particular works. Having a narrow economic perspective, the unenterprising worker cannot see the need for changes in working practices to improve productivity: all he can see is the difficulty of adaptation and the likelihood of more strenuous work in store.

It can be argued that in twentieth-century Britain these unenterprising attitudes to work have become increasingly common. The attitudes are articulated particularly well by leaders and militants in the trade union movement. They are usually couched in terms of the worker's right to self-government in industry, and the need to push back the 'frontier of control' (Goodrich, 1920). The object of self-government is to give the worker control of his own work process, usually with a view to resisting harmful change. This reactionary aspect is quite explicit in the guild socialism of G. D. H. Cole (1918, 1920) which harks back to the control of quality and limitation of output by the medieval guilds. The ideology of guild socialism was much favoured by members of craft unions in the early twentieth century, and appears to have influenced the demands made by employers during the industrial unrest of 1919 (Hinton, 1973).

Guild socialism is essentially a democratic movement of the kind favoured by Fabian socialists. Syndicalism, on the other hand, pursues the same objective by revolutionary means. It is a 'progressive' rather than reactionary movement and is closely allied to Marxism. Unlike guild socialism, which emphasizes the value of the craftsman's work, syndicalism emphasizes the tedium of unskilled work under capitalism, and the benefits to be derived from disruption. It was favoured mainly by the industrial unions, and provided ideological support for the General Strike (Hannington, 1936; Skelley, 1976).

These ideological movements were not confined to Britain, of course. Nevertheless guild socialism, with its democratic emphasis and romantic view of the past, seems a typical product of the British imagination. Its preoccupation with the value of small-scale production, and the tradition of 'learning by doing' institutionalized in the system of masters and apprentices, accords with the view that British labour has a comparative advantage in skilled work carried out in small plants (Prais, 1981). The appeal of guild socialism to the worker is obvious. From the economic point of view its main disadvantage is that by over-emphasizing the craftsman's status it encourages him to oppose the dilution of skill and discourages him from trading down to unskilled work when his opposition to dilution results in unemployment. Given the large body of craftsmen created by the extreme specialization of the nineteenth-century British economy, the existence of guild socialist attitudes among the unenterprising ones may have been an important factor inhibiting structural adjustment after the turn of the century.

Syndicalism has a less immediate effect on structural adjustment, for it emphasizes the unity of interest between unskilled workers in different industries, and encourages workers to view themselves as members of a single proletariat (Harley, 1912), As emphasized in section 9.6, the syndicalist motive for raising real wages is not primarily to improve the standard of living under capitalism, but rather to undermine the viability of capitalist organization. At the same time, therefore, anything that reduces productivity—such as claims for shorter hours, working to rule, or unofficial strike action—is to be encouraged.

There is thus a dual approach—on the wages front and on the productivity front—encouraging a trend increase in the real wage and a trend decline in productivity. On the productivity front, a number of productivity-inhibiting objectives are simultaneously pursued. Just as guild socialism appeals to the unenterprising craftsman, so syndicalism appeals to the unenterprising unskilled worker. It encourages him to believe that, under capitalism, work is an evil, and that by doing less of it he is performing a service—perhaps even discharging a duty—to other members of the working class.

It was shown earlier that structural change involves a self-selection process in which the most enterprising workers move to innovating firms or industries, leaving behind the least enterprising workers in the firms or industries which continue with obsolete technology. The increasing concentration of unenterprising workers in the non-innovative sectors leads to a significant proportion of the workforce in those sectors becoming opposed to change. Having a naturally parochial view, the preponderance of similar views among them stiffens their resistance to innovation, and it is easy for trade unions to persuade the workers to combine against change. Once the critical point is reached at which the majority 'dig in their heels' there is little the employers can do except either seek government subsidies or go into liquidation. If a sufficient number of workers are involved and they are concentrated in key constituencies then vote-seeking politicians may be lobbied to provide subsidies in the form of tariff protection, price support schemes or nationalization. If the workers have little political influence then the firms will close down and the workers go on the dole. Even then, though, if there are sufficient workers on the dole, government may be persuaded to raise the real level of benefits.

This self-selection process explains how bad industrial relations may develop in the non-innovative sector, and thereby hasten the decline of the sector by reducing productivity. It must be recognized, however, that the deterioration of industrial relations may also be prompted by bad management practice. Just as the most enterprising workers are attracted to the innovative sector, so the most enterprising managers will be attracted there too. The less able managers who remain behind may be tempted to maintain their authority by tyranny rather than by the winning of respect. Cannan (1919b) suggested to the Coal Industry Commission that syndicalist sentiments were stimulated by the attitudes of bad employers. Many British employers seem to have had dual standards, by which they supported the transfer of the British concept of democracy to colonial peoples but regarded any desire for democracy by their own workers as an impertinence. They failed, for example, to recognize the resentment caused by the primitive hiring practices in the casual labour markets. It is not unreasonable to suggest that syndicalist sentiments thrived where personnel policies were most ruthless—in the docks, the mines and the textile industry, for example. The legacy of bitterness is likely to be greatest where these practices were most common—such as Merseyside, the North-east and South Wales. It could be argued that the impact of this legacy on labour attitudes is one of the region-specific factors in employment decline—together with the lack of enterprise in the labour force caused by the self-selection process involved in migration.

The preceding remarks are, of course, highly speculative, and it is difficult to test them using official statistics. For example, so long as the real wage remains high in declining areas, marginal productivity will remain high and therefore average productivity will be fairly high too. Thus low productivity will not show up in the output and employment statistics, but merely in the low level of employment. To test the theory it would be necessary to have data on job losses and job gains, and it would also be useful to know the reasons given by employers for moving away from declining regions, or for not moving to them. Limited evidence of this kind is available (cf. Dennis, 1980) and suggests that shortages of suitable labour may be one of the factors in firms moving away from urban areas. The fact that a firm may have to move away from a large urban area to find suitable labour suggests that there may be something seriously wrong with the quality of the labour in the urban area. Other evidence comes from the comparison of the performance of different branch plants within a multi-regional firm. Some case studies of individual firms reveal substantial differences in worker attitudes between plants in different regions (see e.g. Roeber, 1975). Much further research is needed, however, before any definite conclusions can be drawn from this sort of evidence.

11.8 IMPLICATIONS FOR ECONOMIC THEORY

When Pre-Keynesian theory is discussed in a dynamic context, it is apparent that it has a number of important implications for current economic research.

To begin with, the assumption of labour market disequilibrium which underpins the theory of unemployment is not primarily concerned with doubts about the market-clearing mechanism, such as the absence of the Walrasian auctioneer emphasized by Clower (1965) and Leijonhufvud (1968). It is, in a sense, even more radical than this. It reflects a scepticism about the model of human motivation underlying conventional 'economic man'. It questions the way that workers' preferences are defined only over the consumption of private goods. It also questions the view that people are basically well-informed about their environment, and that they interpret their environment in much the same way that the orthodox economist does. Enterprising workers may broadly conform with conventional economic man, but unenterprising workers do not.

The unenterprising worker's preferences are concerned very much with the non-income attributes of work and with the consumption of unpriced goods such as social standing; it follows that additional income may do little to enhance his welfare. He is ill-informed about the economic environment in which he operates and often interprets his position with respect to an ideological model alien to the orthodox economist—for example, in terms of the working-class struggle against capitalism. To explain this worker's attitude to wage bargaining it is necessary first to understand the kind of model with which he operates—an ill-defined model which often relies more upon mystical and symbolic expression than analytical structure (de Man, 1928).

Conventional economic theory can, in principle, accommodate these objections by allowing that individuals are rational only in the context of their own subjective perceptions of their situation. The requisite modifications to the theory are difficult to effect, however, and in the meantime the assumptions introduced in this book—that workers resist both real and money wage reductions and have strong attachments to particular working practices—may serve to capture some of the key aspects of unenterprising behaviour.

The dynamic structural view also has an important lesson for the 'rational expectations' approach to macroeconomics (Lucas, 1973; Lucas and Sargent, 1981; Begg, 1982). The point is often made, of course, that people are not fully rational and do not agree upon the economist's model. A more substantive point is that when analyzing shocks to the economic system, structural changes may be peculiarly difficult for people to detect. It may be much easier to determine whether a shock has affected everyone, or just oneself, than to assess whether a shock has affected some general subset of the population (I am indebted for this point to Paul Roth). It has, in fact, been suggested in section 11.6 that several economists have mistaken structural problems for a problem of aggregate demand deficiency. If economists cannot easily distinguish between aggregate shocks and structural shocks, then it is not surprising that other people may fail to distinguish between them too. If economic shocks are diagnosed wrongly, then expectations that are conditional upon the diagnosis will be erroneous too, and adjustment to a full rational expectations equilibrium will be delayed until people learn from their mistake. Given that unenterprising people are slow to learn, disequilibrium may prevail for some considerable time. This argument suggests that not only do structural problems give rise to disequilibrium, but that the most persistent disequilibria are the ones most likely to have a structural cause. This is consistent with the Pre-Keynesian view that the persistent unemployment in inter-war Britain had a structural cause.

Following on from this, the dynamic structural approach suggests that the theories of 'long waves' in economic life, mentioned in section 1.1, may not be as fanciful as they sometimes seem (for a review see van Duijn, 1983). The long wave may be explained either by the bunching of key technological innovations, or in terms of social psychological processes: it may be, for example, that the frequency of the 50-year Kondratieff cycle is explained by the time it takes one generation to forget the lessons that the previous generation has learnt. Although this is a highly speculative branch of economics, it is one that will repay more serious study.

Finally, it should be mentioned that some of the structural problems discussed with respect to the British economy are most commonly analyzed in the context of international trade and investment. The analogy between international trade and interregional trade is well known. On a more practical level, the open-ness to trade of the British economy makes it useful, for some purposes, to regard Britain simply as a region of Europe. In this context, insight into regional problems within the British economy can sometimes be obtained by regarding Britain itself as a declining region of Europe. Certainly the explanation of regional decline presented in this book has its analogy in explanations of the economic decline of Britain in the international economy. Interesting theoretical work is being done on structural disequilibrium in the international economy, which makes it possible to carry forward the Pre-Keynesian analysis into the international sphere (see for example, Lorie and Sheen, 1982).

11.9 SUMMARY

This chapter has sought to place the Pre-Keynesian theory of unemployment within the broader context of a theory of structural change. It has been shown that the Pre-Keynesian theory is consistent with the post-war experience of the British economy, and it has been suggested that if the lessons of the inter-war period had been better understood, some of the problems created by post-war economic management could have been avoided.

The theory of structural change combines two aspects of Pre-Keynesian thought: the importance of adapting labour supply to the changing employment demands created by new technologies and tastes, and the difficulties of maintaining full employment when workers attached to declining industries resist both relative and absolute reductions in their real wage. It is not claimed that the Pre-Keynesians actually formalized the theory presented in this chapter, and it is not particularly helpful to say that 'this is what the Pre-Keynesians would have said today'. What can be claimed, however, is that a modern analysis of structural problems leads directly back to the Pre-Keynesian ideas. The issues debated by the Pre-Keynesians in the 1920s continue to be major policy issues to this day.

12

Summary and Conclusions

The Pre-Keynesian theory of unemployment was developed in the late 1920s in order to explain the slow growth and high unemployment of Britain relative to other countries. The most important Pre-Keynesian theorist, A. C. Pigou, was a disciple of Alfred Marshall. He extended Marshall's analysis of the labour market by introducing short-run money illusion and long-run real-wage rigidity. These innovations enabled him to develop a theory of short-run industrial fluctuations and also a theory of long-run unemployment. In both theories unemployment arises because the demand for labour is reduced when the real wage is too high.

Despite the depletion of the capital stock during World War I, the average real wage rate in Britain in the 1920s was substantially above its pre-war level. The Pre-Keynesians attributed this primarily to the increasing strength of trade unions, whose membership had risen substantially between 1900 and 1920. General unions representing the unskilled and lower paid were a rising force in the 1920s, and it may be partly for this reason that the wages of the unskilled rose relative to those of skilled workers.

The Pre-Keynesians argued that trade union aggressiveness was underpinned by the relatively high level of unemployment benefit, and by leniency in its administration. The unemployment insurance system may have stimulated unemployment for other reasons too: the employer's contribution represented a tax upon the employment of labour, and some employers also exploited the benefit system to subsidize casual methods of labour recruitment. The precise strength of these effects is, however, difficult to quantify; the simplistic argument that unemployment benefit encourages people to be work-shy receives little support from the evidence.

Henry Clay emphasized that it was not just the *average* wage that was too high, but that wage relativities had failed to adjust to maintain employment in the declining staple industries. Coal, iron, textiles, shipbuilding and heavy engineering were facing severe competition in export markets from the newly industrializing countries. Many traditional export markets were lost for good when supplies of British products were interrupted during World War I. Wages in the declining industries had fallen, but they had not fallen far enough to maintain full employment.

If labour were very mobile, then a small change in relative wages would be sufficient to transfer labour from declining industries to expanding ones. This would not only avoid unemployment in the declining industries but would also provide an abundant supply of cheap labour for the expanding industries, encouraging them to innovate and grow. A mechanism of this kind seems to have promoted the early industrialization of Britain, with workers switching in large numbers out of agriculture into factory work. This process was stimulated by Poor Law reform which made it difficult for unemployed workers to remain attached to agriculture.

During the 1920s, however, labour was relatively immobile. One explanation is that industrial workers had become strongly attached to traditional working practices, and that many of them were unwilling to forego their 'craftsman' status by trading down to semi-skilled employment. Just as in the early stages of industrialization, it seems to have been the agricultural workers who were most mobile, and who took up many of the unskilled and semi-skilled jobs in the new industries. There is evidence that the more enterprising workers did move, but there was a substantial unenterprising core of long-term unemployed who were left behind. It is possible that the unenterprising workers mistook a permanent structural change in the economy for a temporary aggregate fluctuation in trade; indeed, those who remained unemployed long enough would have had their beliefs apparently confirmed, for from 1933 onwards rearmament revived employment in many of the declining industries.

The hypothesis that real wages are too high in the declining sectors of the economy can easily be formalized using disequilibrium theory. This theory provides a consistent analysis of the spill-over effects of unemployment on other sectors of the economy. An important feature of real-wage bargaining is that these spill-overs do not feed back upon the level of employment because the feedbacks are neutralized by the wage-bargaining mechanism. A corollary is that only by intervention in the labour market can government influence the level of employment; fiscal and monetary policies will not work. Once the real wage has been fixed, expansionist fiscal and monetary policies will be purely inflationary: 'crowding out' in the product market will be complete, and the employment multiplier will be zero.

It is only in the short run, when the money wage and not the real wage is fixed that fiscal and monetary policy can be used to promote employment. This point was recognized by Pigou long before the publication of Keynes' *General Theory*. Pigou regarded the argument as an elaboration of the Marshallian theory of labour, and therefore dissented from Keynes' view that the discovery of the multiplier effect in a fixed money-wage economy constituted a revolution in economy theory. Pigou suggested that the exploitation of money-wage rigidities through a reflationary policy could only be temporary, because trade unions would seek to increase the money wage to compensate for the induced rise in the cost of living. The evidence suggests that in the 1930s Pigou's anxieties may have been excessive, but that during the mild but persistent inflation of the 1960s they were confirmed. Trade unions learnt to neutralize the effect of Keynesian policies: macroeconomic policy became ineffective, and employment was determined principally by trade union policy on the real wage.

Pigou's historical perspective on the evolution of unemployment theory is supported by recent analytical developments in labour economics which have moved away from the elaboration of Keynesian concepts towards the classic issues studied by Marshall. This book has attempted to forge a further link in this chain by synthesizing disequilibrium and job-search theories of the labour market. It is argued that workers search for rationed job vacancies offered at the trade union wage, and distribute themselves between the various sectors of the economy in response to differentials in *expected* wages. This theory formalizes insights into labour-market adjustment which were presented by Pigou as early as 1914. The theory exposes a number of weaknesses in earlier studies of structural unemployment, and suggests that the magnitude of structural problems may have been seriously underestimated as a result. It is apparent that current research stands firmly in the tradition of Marshall and Pigou; this should encourage researchers to reformulate more of their classic work in modern terms.

The problems of real-wage rigidity and of structural imbalance are just as relevant today as they were in the 1920s. Moreover the problems are not confined to Britain. Many of the mature industrializing countries face severe problems of structural adjustment as they respond to import competition arising from the 'new international division of labour', which has exported many unskilled and semi-skilled jobs to low-cost locations in South East Asia and elsewhere. Some developing countries, too, have faced new adjustment problems. In common with the mature industrial countries, the newly industrializing countries have had to adjust to the higher real cost of energy, which has reduced the value productivity of labour in energy-intensive industries, and in the extractive industries which produce their raw materials. Unemployment in the developed countries (generated by structural rigidities) has led to a decline in their demand for exports from the developing countries. Developing countries have therefore faced additional problems of substituting resources out of their traditional export trades.

In the short run, the symptom of structural maladjustment to international conditions is usually an increasing deficit in the balance of trade. The short-run solution is to finance this deficit by short-term borrowing, but unless structural adjustment is vigorously pursued, the resources may not be generated to repay this debt. If no structural adjustments are made then international financial equilibrium will be achieved through exchange-rate depreciation and domestic inflation, which will reduce the real value of international debt. In the early 1930s the international payments system was unable to cope with the drastic revaluation of debt, and it remains an open question whether the international payments system of today will be any more robust than it was 50 years ago.

The Pre-Keynesians did not believe that there were any quick and simple measures for promoting structural adjustment. They considered that employment subsidies (including the reduction of employers' national insurance contributions) would be more effective than tariffs and other protective measures in maintaining employment in the short run. But unless workers and employers clearly perceived these measures as temporary, they would inhibit adjustment in the long run. For reasons already explained, reflationary fiscal and monetary policies would have no lasting effect, though they could be used to compensate temporarily for over-pessimistic expectations about profitability and prices.

The main long-term remedy for structural maladjustment is labour mobility. Industrial transference policy in inter-war Britain had little success because it focused upon moving the long-term unemployed rather than on moving the most employable sections of the labour force. Institutional reforms such as removing controls on the housing market, standardizing the provision of education and social services across the country, subsidizing retraining, providing personal loans to migrants and reducing unemployment benefit for non-migrants may all contribute marginally to worker mobility. But the main obstacles to mobility appear to be worker's inflexible social attitudes and their myopic perception of their situation. In this respect the social conditions generated by industrialization – for example, the agglomeration of workers in large plants which dominate local labour markets – may give workers a very distorted view of their competitive environment. The lack of diversity in local employment opportunities and the consequent development of family traditions of work with the same employer may encourage workers to view their employer's competitive position as unassailable, and to prompt them to make exaggerated claims both for real-wage increases and for changes in working practices which reduce productivity. Workers' ambitions may centre on making their employer respect the cultural values of the local community rather than upon strengthening the economic position of their employer in international markets.

The promotion of structural adjustment is not, of course, without its social costs. Young people, for example, are more mobile than the old, and the promotion of mobility may disrupt family links between generations, and the young may no longer be able to pro-vide adequate support for the old. It must remain a political issue as to how far governments should trade off the economic benefits of structural adjustment against the social costs involved.

Appendix A

The Cross-section Study of Employment

A.1 DATA

The following data were obtained for the three years 1924, 1930 and 1935 for 63 industries: total employment (N), net output (Y), and average weekly earnings of all employees (E). In addition data on basic wage rates (W) were obtained for 38 of these industries.

The data on N, Y, and E were obtained from Schwartz and Rhodes (1939), Tables I–XI and IA–XIA. They in turn draw upon two main sources: the Censuses of Production for 1924, 1930 and 1935, and the wage inquiries of the Ministry of Labour reported in various issues of the *Ministry of Labour Gazette*, 1926–7, 1933 and 1937. The employment statistics are rounded to the nearest hundred. Net output is a measure of value added at current prices, obtained by deducting the cost of materials from gross output; adjustments for excise duty are made where applicable. Earnings are measured by weekly income in shillings and are rounded to the nearest sixpence. The earnings figures relate only to a sample week, so that the error caused by temporary fluctuations in the state of trade may be quite severe. The indices of W are available for 38 industries from Ramsbottom (1935, 1938, 1939). The indices are available for the ends of the three years, and are calculated on the basis that in each industry the average for the whole of the year 1924 is 100.

The 63 industries were selected entirely on the basis of the quality of data available. Very small industries were excluded on the grounds that percentage errors of measurement were likely to be high—particularly when first differences were calculated. Industries where the Census and Ministry of Labour data were difficult to match were excluded, as were industries for which crucial observations were missing. The manner in which the classifications of the remaining industries were matched up is indicated in table A.1. Column 1 gives an abbreviated name for the industry, column 2 gives the heading under which production and employment data are

TABLE A.1
Matching of industrial classifications 1924, 1930, 1935

Industry (1)	Class used for output and employment statistics (2)	Class used for earnings statistics (3)	Class used for wage index (4)
Cement	Cement*	Cement	Cement manufacture
Brick	Brick and fireclay*	Brick, tile, etc.	Brick manufacture
China	China and earthenware*	Pottery (1924, 1930), Earthenware, china and porcelain (1935)	Pottery
Glass	Glass	Glass (1924, 1930), including bottles (1935)	n.a.
Chemicals	Chemicals, dyestuffs and drugs	Chemicals (1924, 1930), Heavy chemicals, including dyes, and Drugs and fine chemicals (1935)	Heavy chemicals and Drugs and fine chemicals
Explosives	Explosives and fireworks*	Explosives	n.a.
Paint	Paint, colour and varnish	Paint, colour and varnish	Paint, colour, varnish, etc
Soap	Soap, candle and perfumery; and Oil and tallow	Soap, candle, oil and tallow (1924, 1930); Soap, candles, glycerine; Oil cake manufacture; Animal fat extracting; Mineral oil refining; Other oil refining, and combinations (1935)	Soap and candles
Iron	Blast Furnaces	Pig iron	Iron and steel
Steel	Smelting and rolling	Iron and steel smelting and rolling	Iron and steel

Foundries	Foundries	Light castings (1924, 1930); Stove, grate and light castings (1935)	Light castings
Tinplate	Tinplate	Tinplate	Tinplate
Hardware	Hardware, hollow-ware, metallic furniture and sheet metal	Hollow-ware	n.a.
Chain	Chain, nail, screw and miscellaneous forgings	Chain and anchor	n.a.
Tubes	Wrought iron and steel tubes	Iron and steel tubes	Tube manufacture
Wire	Wire drawing, weaving	Wire netting, ropes	n.a.
Tool	Tool and implement, cutlery	Cutlery, tools (1924, 1930); Cutlery (1935)	n.a.
Needle	Needle, pin, fish-hook and metal smallwares	Needles, pins, fish-hooks, etc. (1924, 1930); Pins (1935)	n.a.
Copper	Copper and brass*; and Lead, tin, aluminium and other non-ferrous metals	Smelting, rolling and casting non-ferrous metals (1924, 1930); Non-ferrous metals (1935)	n.a.
Brass	Finished brass	Brass founding and finishing (1924, 1930); Brass and yellow metal goods (1935)	Brass wares
Jewellery	Gold and silver refining, and plate and jewellery	Gold, silver, jewellery	Gold, silver, electroplate, etc.
Aircraft	Aircraft	Aircraft	n.a.
Electrical engineering	Electrical engineering	Electrical machinery and scientific instruments (1924, 1930); Electrical engineering (1935)	Engineering

Industry (1)	Class used for output and employment statistics (2)	Class used for earnings statistics (3)	Class used for wage index (4)
Ship-building	Ship-building	Ship-building	Ship-building and repairing
Motor vehicle	Motor and cycle (manufacturing and repairing)	Motor vehicle and cycle, larger firms	Vehicle-building
Railway vehicle	Railway carriage, wagon	Railway carriage, wagon	Engineering
Cotton	Cotton spinning and cotton weaving*	Cotton	Cotton
Woollen	Woollen and worsted	Woollen and worsted	Woollen and worsted
Silk	Silk and artificial silk*	Silk (1924, 1930); Silk spinning and weaving (1935)	Silk
Hosiery	Hosiery	Hosiery	Hosiery
Lace	Lace	Lace	Lace
Jute	Jute	Jute spinning and weaving	Jute
Bleaching	Bleaching, printing and dyeing	Bleaching, printing, dyeing and finishing	Textile bleaching, dyeing, etc.
Linen	Linen and hemp*	Linen (1924, 1930); Flax and hemp (1935)	Flax etc.
Glove	Gloves	Gloves	n.a.
Hat	Hat, bonnet and cap	Felt and silk hat (1924, 1930); Felt hat (1935)	Hat, cap and millinery trades
Boot	Boot and shoe	Boot and shoe (ready-made) (1924, 1930); Boot, shoe, slipper (1935)	Boot and shoe manufacture

Fur	Fur	Fur	n.a.
Saddlery	Saddlery, harness and leather goods	Saddlery and leather goods (1924, 1930); Saddlery and harness, bags, trunks, etc.; and Other (1935)	Leather goods
Milling	Grain milling	Grain milling (larger firms only 1935)	Flour milling
Bread	Bread and biscuits	Bread baking (1924, 1930); Bread and flour—larger firms (1935)	Baking
Sugar	Sugar and glucose*	Sugar refining (1924, 1930); Sugar making and refining (1935)	Sugar confectionery and food-processing
Cocoa	Cocoa and sugar confectionery	Cocoa, chocolate and sugar confectionery (1924, 1930); Chocolate and sugar confectionery (1935)	n.a.
Bacon	Bacon curing and sausage	Bacon and sausage (1924, 1930); Bacon, ham, lard, sausage (1935)	n.a.
Fish-curing	Fish-curing	Fish-curing	n.a.
Brewing	Brewing and malting	Brewing, malting, bottling (1924, 1930); Brewing (1935)	Brewing
Spirits	Spirit distilling; and Spirit rectifying, compounding and methylating	Spirit distilling and compounding	n.a.
Cordials	Aerated waters, cider, vinegar and British wines	Aerated waters, cider, etc., (1924, 1930); Mineral and aerated waters, larger firms (1935)	Aerated waters
Tobacco	Tobacco	Tobacco	Tobacco

Industry (1)	Class used for output and employment statistics (2)	Class used for earnings statistics (3)	Class used for wage index (4)
Timber	Timber (sawmilling, etc.)	Mill sawing, machine joinery (1924, 1930); Mill sawing and joinery, larger firms (1935)	n.a.
Box	Wooden crates, boxes	Packing case, box, etc. (1924, 1930); Wooden box, packing case (1935)	n.a.
Furniture	Furniture and upholstery	Furniture (1924, 1930); Cabinet and furniture, larger firms (1935)	Furniture
Paper	Paper	Paper (1924, 1930); Paper and board (1935)	Paper manufacture
Wallpaper	Wallpaper	Wallpaper	n.a.
Cardboard	Cardboard box	Cardboard box	n.a.
Stationery	Manufactured stationery	Manufactured stationery (1924, 1930); Paper bags, envelopes, stationery (1935)	n.a.
Newspapers	Printing and publication of newspapers, etc.	Newspaper and general printing (1924, 1930); Newspaper and periodicals (1935)	n.a.
Rubber	Rubber	India rubber (1924, 1930); Rubber goods (1935)	n.a.
Musical instruments	Musical instruments*	Musical instruments (1924, 1930); Pianos and organs and other musical instruments (1935)	n.a.

Brush	Brush-making	Brooms and brushes	n.a.
Electricity	Electricity*	Electricity, excluding local authorities	Electricity supply
Gas	Gas	Gas, excluding local authorities	Gas supply
Water	Water	Water, excluding local authorities	n.a.

Notes: n.a.: Not available.
* Significant change in scope of industrial classification between 1930 and 1935.

recorded, and column 3 the heading under which earnings data are recorded.

In eleven of the industries the Census industrial classification changes significantly between 1930 and 1935; these industries are indicated by an asterisk in column 2. Estimates of the impact of the reclassification on the measurement of net output are presented in the 1935 Census, and are recorded by Schwartz and Rhodes. In many industries the classification of the earnings statistics also differs between these dates, as the entries in column 3 indicate. In some cases the 1935 average earnings has been calculated by combining several of the earnings figures given by Schwartz and Rhodes; this is indicated by the appearance of multiple-industry classes in column 3. In these cases the 1935 average-earnings figure is a weighted average of the constituent average-earnings figures, where the weights are the numbers employed in the consituent industries, as recorded in the *Ministry of Labour Gazette*, 1937. The industrial classifications used to match the wage index to the other data are indicated in column 4 of the table.

A.2   METHODOLOGY

The data were transformed to provide measures of percentage changes in each of the variables over the two sub-periods 1924–30, 1930–5 and over the whole period 1924–35. Each percentage change was interpreted, where appropriate, as an approximation to a logarithmic first-difference. Changes in earnings, and changes in the wage index, were interpreted as alternative measures of the change in the wage rate. The data were analysed using the Minitab program developed by the Statistics Department, Pennsylvania State University.

Arithmetic means, medians, standard deviations and histograms were obtained for the full sample of 63 industries and the reduced sample of 38 industries. Selected results are reported in table A.2. Comparison of the results reveals that the reduced sample contains a disproportionate number of low-growth industries and relatively few high-growth industries. The arithmetic mean of the percentage growth of output over the full period is only 9.74 for the reduced sample, as against 16.94 for the full sample, and the percentage growth of employment is only 7.41 as compared with 14.42. The results of dropping the eight of the 38 industries for which there were significant Census reclassifications increases further the preponderance of low-growth industries. The mean growth of output is reduced from 9.74 to 8.62 per cent. At the same time, the standard deviation of the growth of output falls from 34.40 to 27.84, probably on account of the reduction in measurement error through the elimination of reclassifications.

TABLE A.2.

Comparison of univariate distributions for full and reduced samples

	1924–30		1930–35		1924–35	
Percentage increase in	*Mean and median*	*Standard deviation*	*Mean and median*	*Standard deviation*	*Mean and median*	*Standard deviation*
Full sample (63 observations)						
Output	5.06	27.10	11.46	20.67	16.94	37.98
	3.50		11.76		18.30	
Employment	6.42	21.57	5.48	18.25	14.42	41.03
	2.69		5.17		9.01	
Earnings	−1.60	9.91	4.18	7.02	2.35	11.39
	−0.20		3.57		1.61	
Wage rates	—	—	—	—	—	—
	—		—		—	
Reduced sample (38 observations)						
Output	0.84	26.44	8.96	17.61	9.74	32.74
	0.90		9.30		13.47	
Employment	2.67	20.33	2.75	14.66	7.41	34.40
	0.44		3.43		6.31	
Earnings	−3.44	6.60	5.24	6.71	1.48	8.02
	−2.79		5.26		1.72	
Wage rates	−1.26	4.46	−2.25	3.59	−3.42	6.56
	0.00		−1.41		−2.47	

Regressions based on the full sample failed to provide any evidence of a significant relation between growth of earnings and growth of employment. Table A.3 shows that in the full sample the coefficient on growth of output is significantly positive over each period, but the coefficient on growth of earnings is insignificant, and in two out of the three cases has the 'wrong' sign. However, as explained in the text, regressions based on the reduced sample detect a significant

negative relation between growth of employment and growth of the
wage index over the full period. The question then arises as to
whether this result is due to the true significance of the wage index or
to biases in the selection of the reduced sample. This issue cannot be
fully resolved, but some indirect evidence is available from a
comparison of the regressions on earnings in the full and reduced
samples. The results in table A.3 show that the regressions of growth
of employment on growth of output and growth of earnings are
broadly similar in the two samples. The coefficients on growth of
output remain positive and significant, and the coefficients on
growth of earnings remain insignificant. This suggests that the
problem of sample bias is a fairly small one. There is, however, a
tendency for the coefficient on the growth of output to be lower in
the reduced sample, and for the coefficient on growth of earnings to
be lower as well; indeed the coefficient on growth of earnings is
consistently negative (though insignificant) in the reduced sample. A
possible explanation is that in the faster-growing industries which
have been excluded from the reduced sample, the growth of output

TABLE A.3.

Comparison of the full and reduced sample estimates of the effect of
the growth of earnings on the growth of employment in the
cross-section study of UK industries 1924–30–35

Period	Sample	Constant	Growth of output	Growth of earnings	R^2	DW
1924–30	Full	0.034*	0.639*	0.118	66.8	1.96
		(0.017)	(0.061)	(0.166)		
	Reduced	0.015	0.610*	−0.202	59.5	2.08
		(0.025)	(0.091)	(0.366)		
1930–35	Full	−0.016	0.697*	−0.206	63.2	1.76
		(0.018)	(0.069)	(0.204)		
	Reduced	−0.012	0.607*	−0.290	53.8	2.01
		(0.023)	(0.096)	(0.251)		
1924–35	Full	−0.022	0.971*	0.082	81.7	1.35
		(0.025)	(0.061)	(0.203)		
	Reduced	−0.011	0.906*	−0.259	72.3	1.62
		(0.032)	(0.096)	(0.392)		

Note: An asterisk denotes that the coefficient is significant at 5 per cent in a two-tailed *t*-test.

exerts a relatively strong influence on the growth of employment, while in the slower-growing industries which predominate in the reduced sample the growth of earnings is a relatively strong factor in the contraction of employment. Further study of this hypothesis lies, unfortunately, outside the scope of the present book.

Because of the statistical insignificance of earnings, the results reported in the text are based on the reduced sample alone. The following features of the reduced sample data were found particularly useful when comparing the regression results for the two sub-periods with each other, and with the results for the period as a whole.

(1) There is a large variation between industries in their growth of output, especially between 1924 and 1930, but also between 1930 and 1935. In four of the 38 industries output contracted by more than 30 per cent during the period 1924–30, while in three industries it increased by more than 30 per cent, and in one case by more than 70 per cent.

(2) There is no significant correlation across industries between the growth of output over the period 1924–30 and the subsequent growth of output 1930–5. This is compatible with the view that underlying trends in the growth or decline of individual industries were heavily masked by temporary disturbances associated with the slump conditions of 1930. Thus trend growth rates were positively correlated, deviations from trend were negatively correlated, and the deviations were about as great as the trend, and so the two correlations just about cancelled one another out.

(3) Employment growth varied less than output growth over the sub-periods 1924–30, but by more than output growth over the whole period. During the period 1924–30, employment growth was very high in a few industries, but slightly negative in many. This situation was reversed during 1930–5, with a few industries experiencing large contractions in employment, and most either contracting only slightly or enjoying a modest growth. The pattern of employment growth is consistent with the view that labour was being hoarded during the slump of 1930, but that hoarding had been eliminated by 1935, by which time the utilization of labour had been restored to its 1924 level.

(4) Earnings fell by more than wage rates between 1924 and 1930, but rose between 1930 and 1935 while wage rates continued to fall. Over the whole period, 1924–35, earnings rose by more than wages: in the sample industries nominal earnings rose on average by 1.5 per cent while wage rates fell by 3.4 per cent. The dispersion of wage rate changes across industries was much lower than the dispersion of changes in earnings.

Appendix B

The Time-series Study of Employment

B.1   DATA

The following annual data were collected for five manufacturing industries for the period 1920–38:

employment of wage earners (N);
average annual earnings of wage earners (E);
an index of basic wage rates (W);
an index of production (Y);
an index of the price of output (P).

The five industries are iron and steel, mechanical engineering, electrical engineering, ship-building and vehicles.

The statistics of employment are from Chapman and Knight (1953), table 44, and are rounded to the nearest 100. The statistics of earnings for iron and steel, electrical engineering and vehicles are from Chapman and Knight, table 47, and for mechanical engineering and ship-building they have been calculated from tables 44 and 45 (so as to exclude respectively the ordnance factories and the naval dockyards). The earnings figures are rounded to one decimal place.

The indices of basic wage rates are from Ramsbottom (1935, 1938, 1939). The Ramsbottom engineering wage index has been applied to both mechanical and electrical engineering. The Ramsbottom indices exclude the years 1921, 1923, 1925, 1927, 1931 and 1933; these have been estimated by linear interpolation. The alternative to interpolation is to omit the years altogether, but that would result in the loss of too many degrees of freedom. The use of interpolation means, however, that the lag structure of the estimated employment functions must be interpreted with great care.

The indices of production are taken from Feinstein (1972), table 52, using 1913 as a base year, and are measured to one decimal place. The price index for iron and steel is taken from Mitchell and Deane (1962), table 'Prices 5, Parts A and B'; the statistics for 1930–8 have been converted to the same base (1913) as the statistics for 1920–9 using the ratio of the 1934 price indices on the 1913 and 1930 bases (a factor of 1.11). This means that part of the change in the index between 1929 and 1930 may be attributable to a change in weights rather than to a change in prices. The price indices for mechanical and electrical engineering are based upon the price index for plant and machinery, originally constructed for the adjustment of investment statistics, reported in Feinstein (1972), table 63. The price indices for ship-building and vehicles come from the same source.

The five industries chosen for analysis were selected on three main criteria:

(1) the availability of data;
(2) the quality of the data; and
(3) their relevance to the hypotheses under examination.

There are only a limited number of industries for which suitable time series on all five variables are available, and even fewer for which the employment and earnings statistics are reliable. For the five industries chosen the employment and earnings data are judged by Chapman and Knight to be reliable (grade B or above). The five industries use broadly similar types of labour, and include two growing industries (electrical engineering and vehicles) and two declining industries (iron and steel, and ship-building). It is reasonable to suppose that structural adjustments will involve the transfer of labour between the declining industries and the growing industries, and so the relation between wages and employment in these industries is of particular interest.

B.2 METHODOLOGY

The data were analysed using the Minitab program referred to in Appendix A. At the outset all the variables were transformed to logarithms. Following this, N was regressed on various combinations of E, W, Y, P and a linear time trend T, without parameter restrictions. The estimates showed that Y and P had normally positive effects on employment, that W had on balance a negative effect, and that E had little effect at all. However, the coefficients were unstable across equations.

Restrictions were then introduced by replacing the three variables E, W and P with just two variables: own-product earnings, E/P, and the own-product wage, *W/P*. The resulting equations had much more stable coefficients. The re-estimation confirmed that earnings were insignificant, and so the variable *E/P* was dropped altogether. It is the remaining results that are discussed in the text.

The Minitab program provides facilities for analysing residuals, detecting outliers and varying the sample period. A limited amount of experimentation suggested that there were few problems with extreme observations, and that the results are fairly robust to marginal changes in the set of observations used.

Appendix C

The Time-series Study of Labour Supply

C.1 DATA

Annual data on the following variables were obtained for five industries for the period 1923–38:

employment of wage earners(N);
average annual earnings of wage earners (E);
annual wage payments (Z);
an index of basic wage rates (W);
an index of the insured workforce (L_1);
an index of the percentage of insured workers unemployed (U).

The five industries are electrical engineering, motor vehicles (manufacture and repair), printing, publishing and bookbinding (including His Majesty's Stationery Office), cotton textiles, and ship-building.

Statistics of N, E and Z were obtained from Chapman and Knight (1953), tables 44, 45 and 47, and statistics of W from Ramsbottom (1935, 1938, 1939). Two measures of labour supply were used: an index, L_1, taken from various issues of the *Ministry of Labour Gazette*, and a measure

$$L_2 = N/(100 - U)$$

based on a related index of unemployment, U, given in Mitchell and Deane (1962), table 'Labour Force 4'. It should be noted that there were a number of changes in the measurement of labour supply over the period concerned, and also important changes in eligibility for unemployment benefits, which may have affected the supply of insured workers (see e.g. Cohen, 1938). It is well known that during this period insured workers account for only about 60 per cent of total workers.

The data described above were supplemented by:

a consumer price index, P (1913 = 100; Feinstein, 1972, p. T113);

average annual earnings per man year in all industries, E^*
(Chapman and Knight, 1953, p. 27);

an index of weekly wage rates in manufacturing industry, W^*
(Ramsbottom, 1935, 1938, 1939);

total unemployment as a percentage of the insured workforce,
U_1^* (Feinstein, 1972, p. T128, column 10);

insured unemployment as a percentage of the insured workforce,
U_2^* (Feinstein, 1972, p. T128, column 9);

weekly benefit entitlement (shillings) for an adult male with one
adult dependent and two dependent children, B (Burns, 1941,
p. 368, reproduced in Ormerod and Worswick, 1982, p. 401);

population aged 15–64 inclusive (millions), V (Feinstein, 1972,
p. T123).

The wage, earnings and unemployment data W^*, E^*. U_1^*, U_2^*
were interpreted as measures of wages, earnings and unemployment
in the rest of the economy—i.e. the economy excluding the industry
being studied. No attempt was made to adjust the figures by
deducting from the aggregate figures the component due to the
industry concerned. Failure to adjust may introduce some bias, but
the industries are sufficiently small that the bias is likely to be
negligible.

C.2 METHODOLOGY

Basic wages and earnings were used as alternative measures of wage
rates, both for the individual industry (E and W) and for the rest of
the economy (E^* and W^*). Wages and earnings were normalized by
the consumer price index, P. The two measures of industry labour
supply, L_1, L_2 were also used as alternatives, as were the measures of
unemployment in the rest of the economy, U_1^*, U_2^*.

Experimentation with different permutations indicated that the
most sensible results (as regards the signs of the estimated coefficients) were obtained with earnings rather than basic wages (E and
E^* rather than W and W^*), the measure of labour supply based upon
the unemployment index (L_2 rather than L_1) and the unemployment
measure based upon total unemployment rather than insured
unemployment (U_2^* rather than U_1^*). This overt data-mining is
justified only on the grounds that the data are highly imperfect and it
would be a pity to reject a theory simply because the most

appropriate measurement of a variable had not been used. Apart from this, the only other data searches carried out were those described in the text.

Appendix D

The Cross-section Study of Labour Supply

D.1 DATA

Data were obtained for a cross-section of 27 industries for 1920, 1924, 1930 and 1935. The selection of industries was governed by the quality of the available data. The industries chosen are listed in the left hand column of table D.1.

The theory was tested on data relating to wage-earners: salary-earners were excluded. Employment and earnings data were taken from various tables in Chapman and Knight (1953). Labour supply for 1920 was estimated by the method described in the text. It was assumed that cross-section variation in unemployment rates was very low in 1920, because of the high level of employment that prevailed. This implies that in a cross-section of industries, employment will proxy for labour supply up to a constant of proportionality which depends upon the 1920 unemployment rate. Because of the log-linear specification that is assumed, this constant of proportionality is captured by the size of the intercept term. Labour supply for the other dates was estimated by applying the unemployment rates reported by Mitchell and Deane (1962), table 'Labour Force 5' to the employment figures described above. The unemployment data are based upon statistics reported in the *Ministry of Labour Gazette*, and provide a convenient summary of the published evidence on labour supply. It should be noted that in the figures for 1930 and 1935, people aged over 65 years are not counted.

The growth rate of employment in each industry was estimated from the ratio of employment in 1935 to employment in 1924. The base year was chosen as 1924 rather than 1920 because in 1920 some industries were still experiencing temporary after-effects of the war.

Indexes of the four other industry characteristics were compiled from a variety of sources: a considerable amount of judgement was used in some cases, and for this reason the data are reported in full in table D.1. The index of the standardization of technology was

TABLE D.1
Industry characteristics data used in cross-section study of labour supply

Industry	Standardization of technology	Trade union membership density	Casualization	Geographical concentration
Fishing	1	−1	1	1
Coal mining	0	1	1	1
Brick and tile	1	0	0	1
Pottery	1	0	0	0
Mechanical engineering	0	0	−1	−1
Electrical engineering	−1	0	−1	−1
Vehicles	−1	0	−1	−1
Ship-building	1	1	1	1
Cotton textiles	1	1	1	−1
Wool	1	1	1	−1
Linen	1	1	1	−1
Hosiery	1	1	1	−1
Boots and shoes	1	0	1	−1
Bread, cakes, etc.	1	0	0	−1
Drink	1	0	0	−1
Sawmilling	1	0	0	−1
Furniture	1	0	−1	−1
Printing	1	1	−1	−1
Building	1	0	1	−1
Gas, water, electricity	0	1	−1	−1
Railways	1	1	−1	−1
Trams and buses	0	1	−1	−1
Other road transport	−1	1	0	−1
Docks and harbours	1	1	1	1
Distributive trades	0	−1	1	−1
Hotels	1	−1	1	−1
Laundries	1	−1	1	−1

Note: High value +1; medium value 0; low value −1.

compiled from business and industrial histories and from a general knowledge of the history of technology. The index of trade union membership density was compiled partly from Bain and Price (1980) and partly by matching the statistics of trade union membership by industrial group reported in the *Ministry of Labour Gazette* to the statistics of employment given in Chapman and Knight. Trade union histories were a useful source of supplementary data. The index of casualization of labour markets was compiled from various works in industrial and labour history.

The index of geographical concentration was based not upon the actual concentration of the industries concerned, but upon the extent to which the industries were actually tied to particular locations because of their function or because of the need to be close to raw materials. Thus although the textile industry was heavily concentrated in Lancashire and Yorkshire, it is not classified as geographically concentrated because by the 1920s it could probably have operated just as well elsewhere. Similar reasoning applies, for example, to the pottery industry. Only fishing, coal mining, brick-making, ship-building and docks are regarded as inevitably confined to particular geographical areas.

D.2 METHODOLOGY

The logarithm of the change in labour supply was first regressed upon the logarithm of the change in earnings, the logarithm of the change in employment and five other variables involving industry characteristics, as indicated in the text. Regressions were estimated for each of the six periods 1920–4, 1920–30, 1920–35, 1924–30, 1924–35 and 1930–5. The change in earnings variable was then dropped. The results of the re-estimation are reported in table 10.2. Dropping some of the industry characteristics variables did not in general alter the sign or significance of any of the remaining variables.

Bibliography

Alchian, A. A. (1971). Information costs, pricing and resource unemployment. In E. S. Phelps *et al*. *Microeconomic Foundations of Employment and Inflation Theory*. London: Macmillan.

Aldcroft, D. H. (1970). *The Inter-War Economy: Britain, 1919–1939*. London: Batsford.

Alford, B. W. E. (1981). New industries for old? British industry between the wars. In R. Floud and D. McCloskey (eds), *The Economic History of Britain since 1700*. Vol. 2: *1860s to the 1970s*. Cambridge: Cambridge University Press.

Allen, G. C. (1930). Labour transference and the unemployment problem. *Economic Journal*, **40**, 242–8.

Allen, R. G. D. and B. Thomas (1937). The London building industry and its labour recruitment through employment exchanges. *Economic Journal*, **47**, 465–82.

Allen R. G. D. and B. Thomas (1939). The supply of engineering labour under boom conditions. *Economic Journal*, **49**, 259–75.

Apps, R. J. (1982) The real wage hypothesis: some results for the U.K. In M. J. Artis, C. J. Green, D. Leslie and G. W. Smith (eds), *Demand Management, Supply Constraints and Inflation*. Manchester: Manchester University Press.

Armstrong, H. and J. Taylor (1981). The measurement of different types of unemployment. In J. Creedy (ed.), *The Economics of Unemployment in Britain*. London: Butterworth.

Bacon, R. W. and W. A. Eltis (1976). *Britain's Economic Problem: Too Few Producers*. London: Macmillan.

Bain, G. S. and R. Price (1980). *Profiles of Union Growth: A Comparative Statistical Portrait of Eight Countries*. Oxford: Basil Blackwell.

Bakke, E. W. (1933). *The Unemployed Man: A Social Study*. London: Nisbet.

Ball, R. J. and E. B. A. St Cyr (1966). Short-term employment functions in British manufacturing industry. *Review of Economic Studies*, **33**, 179–207

Barger, H. (1936). Disguised unemployment: a comment. *Economic Journal*. **46**, 756–9.

Barlow Commission (1940). *Report of the Royal Commission on the Distribution of the Industrial Population*. London: His Majesty's Stationery Office, Cmd 6153.

Barro, R. J. and H. I. Grossman (1971). A general disequilibrium model of income and employment. *American Economic Review*, **61**, 82–93.

Barro, R. J. and H. I. Grossman (1976). *Money, Employment and Inflation*. Cambridge: Cambridge University Press.

Begg, D. K. H. (1982). *The Rational Expectations Revolution in Macroeconomics*. Deddington, Oxon: Philip Allan.

Benjamin, D. K. and L. A. Kochin (1979). Searching for an explanation of unemployment in interwar Britain. *Journal of Political Economy*, **87**, 441–78.

Benjamin, D. K. and L. A. Kochin (1982). Unemployment and unemployment benefits in twentieth century Britain: a reply to our critics. *Journal of Political Economy*, **90**, 410–36.

Beveridge, W. H. (1909). *Unemployment: A Problem of Industry*. London: Longmans, Green & Co.

Beveridge, W.H. (1930). *Unemployment: A Problem of Industry (1909 and 1930)*. London: Longmans, Green & Co.

Beveridge, W. H. (1931). *Causes and Cures of Unemployment*. London: Longmans Green

Bienefeld, M. (1972). *Working Hours in British Industry: An Economic History*. London: Weidenfeld & Nicolson for London School of Economics.

Bleaney, M. (1976). *Underconsumption Theories: A History and Critical Analysis*. London: Lawrence & Wishart.

Bodkin, R. G. (1969). Real wages and cyclical variations in employment: an examination of the evidence. *Canadian Journal of Economics*, **2**, 353–74.

Booth, A. E. and S. Glynn (1975). Unemployment in interwar Britain: a multiple problem. *Journal of Contemporary History*, **10**, 611–37.

Bosanquet, N. and P. B. Doeringer (1973). Is there a dual labour market in Great Britain? *Economic Journal*, **83**, 421–35.

Bowers, J., D. Deaton and J. Turk (1982). *Labour Hoarding in British Industry*. Oxford: Basil Blackwell.

Bowley, A. L. (1930). *Some Economic Consequences of the Great War*. London: Thornton Butterworth (Home University Library of Modern Knowledge).

Bowley, A. L. (1934). F. Y. Edgeworth. *Econometrica*, **2**, 113–24.

Bowley, A. L. and M. H. Hogg (1925). *Has Poverty Diminished?* London: P. S. King & Son.

Boyle, A. (1979). *Climate of Treason*. London: Hutchinson.

Branson, W. H. and J. J. Rotemberg (1980). International adjustment with wage rigidity. *European Economic Review*, **13**, 309–32.

Brechling, F. P. R. (1967). Trends and cycles in British regional unemployment. *Oxford Economic Papers*, **19**, 1–21.

Bruno, M. (1980). Import prices and stagflation in the industrial countries: a cross-section analysis. *Economic Journal*, **90**, 479–92.

Burns, E. M. (1941). *British Unemployment Programs, 1920–1938*. Washington: Social Science Research Council.

Burridge, P. and I. R. Gordon (1981). Unemployment in the British metropolitan labour areas. *Oxford Economic Papers*, **33**, 274–97.

Buxton, N. K. and D. H. Aldcroft (eds) (1978). *British Industry between the Wars: Instability and Industrial Development, 1919–39*. London: Scolar Press.

Cannan, E. (1893). *A History of the Theories of Production and Distribution in English Political Economy from 1776 to 1848*. London: Percival.

[Cannan, E. (ed.) (1896)]. *Lectures on Justice, Police, Revenue and Arms*, by Adam Smith. Oxford: Clarendon Press.

[Cannan, E. (ed.) (1904)]. *An Inquiry into the Nature and Causes of the Wealth of Nations*, by Adam Smith. London: Methuen.

Cannan, E. (1912). *The Economic Outlook*, London: T. Fisher Unwin.

Cannan, E. (1918). *Money: Its Connexion with Rising and Falling Prices*. London: P. S. King & Son.

Cannan, E. (ed.) (1919a). *The Paper Pound of 1797 to 1821*. London: P. S. King & Son.

Cannan, E. (1919b). *Coal Nationalisation: Precis and Evidence offered to the Coal Industry Commission*. London: P. S. King & Son.

Cannan, E. (1927a). *An Economist's Protest*. London: P. S. King & Son.

Cannan, E. (1927b). *A Review of Economic Theory*, London: P. S. King & Son.

Cannan, E. (1928). Review of 'Report of the Industrial Transference Board' *Economic Journal*. **38**, 673–7.

Cannan, E. (1930). The problem of unemployment; a review of the 'Post-war Unemployment Problem', by Henry Clay. *Economic Journal*, **40**, 45–55.

Cannan, E. (1931). *Modern Currency and the Regulation of its Value*. London: P. S. King & Son.

Cannan, E. (1933). *Economic Scares*. London: P. S. King & Son.

Casson, M. C. (1979). *Youth Unemployment*. London: Macmillan.

Casson, M. C. (1981). *Unemployment: A Disequilibrium Approach*. Oxford: Martin Robertson.

Champernowne, D. G. (1938). The uneven distribution of unemployment in the United Kingdom, 1926–36: Part I. *Review of Economic Studies*, **5**, 93–106.

Champernowne, D. G. (1939a). The uneven distribution of unemployment in the United Kingdom, 1926–36: Part II. *Review of Economic Studies*, **6**, 111–24.

Champernowne, D. G. (1939b). The main cause of variation of the unemployment percentage between industries — a correction. *Review of Economic Studies*, **6**, 125–6.

Chang, D. (1936). *British Methods of Industrial Peace: A Study of Democracy in Relation to Labour Disputes*. New York: Columbia University Press.

Chapman, A. L. and R. Knight (1953). *Wages and Salaries in the United Kingdom, 1920–1938*. Cambridge: Cambridge University Press.

Cheshire, P. C. (1973). *Regional Unemployment Differences in Great Britain*. Cambridge: Cambridge University Press.

Clay, H. (1918). Industrial reconstruction and the government. *The Round Table*, **33**, 135–62.

Clay, H. (1926). Letter to Edwin Cannan, 13 January 1926. London: British Library of Political and Economic Science, Cannan Papers, No. 1029, Folio 1.

Clay, H. (1928). Unemployment and wage rates. *Economic Journal*, **38**, 1–15.

Clay, H. (1929a). *The Post-war Unemployment Problem*. London: Macmillan.

Clay, H. (1929b). The public regulation of wages in Great Britain. *Economic Journal*, **39**, 323–43.

Clay, H. (1929c). *The Problem of Industrial Relations and Other Lectures*. London: Macmillan.

Clay, H. (1930). Dr Cannan's views on unemployment. *Economic Journal*, **40**, 331–5.

Clower, R. W. (1965). The Keynesian counterrevolution: a theoretical appraisal. In F. H. Hahn and F. Brechling (eds), *The Theory of Interest Rates*. London: Macmillan.

Coates, B. E., R. J. Johnston and P. L. Knox (1977). *Geography and Inequality*. Oxford: Oxford University Press.

Cohen, P. (1938). *Unemployment Insurance and Assistance in Great Britain*. London: Harrap.

Cole, G. D. H. (1918). *Self-Government in Industry*. London: G. Bell & Sons.

Cole, G. D. H. (1920). *Guild Socialism Re-stated*. London: Leonard Parsons.

Collard, D. (1981). A. C. Pigou, 1877–1959. In D. P. O'Brien and J. R. Presley (eds), *Pioneers of Modern Economics in Britain*. London: Macmillan.

Collier, P. and J. Pemberton (1981). Alternative approaches to unemployment. *University of Reading Discussion Papers in Economics*, No. 124.

Collins, M. (1982). Unemployment in interwar Britain: still searching for an explanation. *Journal of Political Economy*, **90**, 369–79.

Corry, B. and D. Laidler (1967). The Phillips relation: a theoretical explanation. *Economica* (N.S.), **34**, 189–97.

Creedy, J. (1974). Inter-regional mobility: a cross-section analysis, *Scottish Journal of Political Economy*, **21**, 41–53.

Crick, B. (ed.) (1981). *Unemployment*. London: Methuen.

Cross, R. (1982). How much voluntary unemployment in interwar Britain? *Journal of Political Economy*, **90**, 380–5.

Dalton, H. (1927). Professor Cannan's general contribution. In T. E. Gregory and H. Dalton (eds), *London Essays in Economics: In Honour of Edwin Cannan*. London: George Routledge & Sons.

Dalton, H. (1953). *Call Back Yesterday: Memoirs 1887–1931*. London: Frederick Muller.

Daniel, G. H. (1940). Some factors affecting the movement of labour. *Oxford Economic Papers*, **3**, 144–79.

Davis, E. G. (1981). R. G. Hawtrey, 1879–1975. In D. P. O'Brien and J. R. Presley (eds), *Pioneers of Modern Economics in Britain*. London: Macmillan.

Davis, J. R. (1971). *The New Economics and the Old Economists*. Ames, Iowa: Iowa State University Press.

Davis, J. R. and F. J. Casey, Jr (1977). Keynes's misquotation of Mill. *Economic Journal,* **87**, 329–30.

Dawes, H. (1934). Labour mobility in the steel industry. *Economic Journal*, **44**, 84–94.

'Deacon, R.' [McCormick, D.] (1979). *The British Connection: Russia's Manipulation of British Individuals and Institutions*. London: Hamish Hamilton.

de Man, H. (1928). *The Psychology of Socialism*. Translated from the second German edition by E. and C. Paul. London: George Allen & Unwin.

Dennis, R. (1980). The decline of manufacturing employment in Greater London, 1966–74. In A. Evans and D. Eversley (eds), *The Inner City: Employment and Industry*. London: Heinemann for the Centre for Environmental Studies.

Dennison, S. R. (1939). *The Location of Industry and the Depressed Areas*. London: Oxford University Press.

Dicks-Mireaux, L. A. and J. C. R. Dow (1959). The determinants of wage inflation: United Kingdom, 1946–1956. *Journal of the Royal Statistical Society* (Series A), **122**, 145–74.

Dixit, A. K. (1978). The balance of trade in a model of temporary equilibrium with rationing. *Review of Economic Studies*, **45**, 393–404.

Dixon, R. J. and A. P. Thirlwall (1975). *Regional Growth and Unemployment in the United Kingdom*. London: Macmillan.

Doeringer, P. B. and M. J. Piore (1971). *Internal Labour Markets and Manpower Analysis*. Lexington, Mass: D. C. Heath.

Dow, S. C. and P. E. Earl (1982). *Money Matters: A Keynesian Approach to Monetary Economics*. Oxford: Martin Robertson.

Dunlop, J. T. (1938). The movement of real and money wage rates. *Economic Journal*, **48**, 413–34.

Dunlop, J. T. (1939). Trends in the 'rigidity' of English wage rates. *Review of Economic Studies*, **46**, 189–99.

Dunning, J. H. (1958). *American Investment in British Manufacturing Industry*. London: George Allen & Unwin.

Durbin, E. F. M. (1933). *Purchasing Power and Trade Depression: A Critique of Under-consumption Theories*. London: Jonathan Cape.

Eshag, E. (1963). *From Marshall to Keynes: An Essay on the Monetary Theory of the Cambridge School*. Oxford: Basil Blackwell.

Fay, C. R. (1935). *Edwin Cannan: The Tribute of a Friend*. Private manuscript in Cannan Collection, British Library of Political and Economic Science. Abridged version in *Economic Record*, **13** (1937), 1–21.

Feinstein, C. H. (1972). *National Income, Expenditure and Output of the United Kingdom, 1855–1965*. Cambridge: Cambridge University Press.

Feldstein, M. (1967). Specification of the labour input in the aggregate production function. *Review of Economic Studies*, **34**, 375–86.

Fisher, A. G. B. (1926). *Some Problems of Wages and Their Regulation in Great Britain since 1918*. London: P. S. King & Son.

Fisher, A. G. B. (1945). *Economic Progress and Social Security*, London: Macmillan.

Ford, P. (1934). *Work and Wealth in a Modern Port: an Economic Survey of Southampton*. London: George Allen & Unwin.

Fothergill, S. and G. Gudgin (1982). *Unequal Growth: Urban and Regional Employment Change in the U.K.* London: Heinemann Educational Books.

Foxwell, H. S. (1886). Irregularity of employment and fluctuations of employment. In J. Oliphant (ed.), *The Claims of Labour*, Edinburgh: Cooperative Printing Co.

Freeman, C., J. Clark and L. Soete (1982). *Unemployment and Technical Innovation: A Study of Long Waves and Economic Development*. London: Frances Pinter.

Friedman, M. (1957). *A Theory of the Consumption Function*. Princeton: Princeton University Press.

Friedman, M. (1968). The role of monetary policy. *American Economic Review*, **58**, 1–17.

Garraty, J. A. (1978). *Unemployment in History*. New York: Harper & Row.

Glynn, S. and P. G. A. Howells (1980). Unemployment in the 1930s: the Keynesian solution reconsidered. *Australian Economic History Review*, **20**, 28–45.

Goodrich, C. L. (1920). *The Frontier of Control*, new edition (ed. R. Hyman). London: Pluto Press.

Gordon, I. R. (1979). Regional unemployment elasticity: the neglected role of migration. *Scottish Journal of Political Economy*, **16**, 97–106.

Gordon, R. J. and J. A. Wilcox (1981). Monetarist interpretations of the Great Depression: an evaluation and critique. In K. Brunner (ed.), *The Great Depression Revisited*. Boston: Kluwer Nijhoff.

Graham, A. W. M. (1979). Inflation. In D. Morris (ed.), *The Economic System in the U.K.*, 2nd edn. Oxford: Oxford University Press.

Gray, J. A. (1976). Wage indexation: a macroeconomic approach. *Journal of Monetary Economics*, **2**, 221–35.

Gregory, T. E. (1927). Professor Cannan and contemporary monetary theory. In T. E. Gregory and H. Dalton (eds), *London Essays in Economics: In Honour of Edwin Cannan*. London: George Routledge & Sons.

Grubb, D., R. Jackman and R. Layard (1982). Wage rigidity and unemployment in OECD countries. London: Centre for Labour Economics, London School of Economics, *Discussion Paper* 135.

Hancock, K. J. (1960). Unemployment and the economists in the 1920s. *Economica*, **37**, 305–21.

Hancock, K. J. (1962). The reduction of unemployment as a problem of public policy, 1920–29. *Economic History Review*, 2nd series, **15**, 328–43.

Hannington, W. (1936). *Unemployed Struggles 1919–1936*. New edition, London: Lawrence & Wishart, 1977.

Harley, J. H. (1912). *Syndicalism*, London: T. C. and E. C. Jack: The People's Books.

Harris, A. I. and R. Clausen (1967). *Labour Mobility in Great Britain, 1953–63*. London: Her Majesty's Stationery Office.

Harris, J. (1977). *William Beveridge: A Biography*. Oxford: Clarendon Press.

Harris, J. R. and M. P. Todaro (1970). Migration, unemployment and development: a two-sector analysis. *American Economic Review*, **60**, 126–42.

Harrod, R. F. (1951). *The Life of John Maynard Keynes*. London: Macmillan.

Hatton, T. J. (1980). Unemployment in Britain between the world wars: a role for the dole? Colchester: University of Essex. *Essex Economic Papers*, No. 139.

Hatton, T. J. (1981). Employment functions for U.K. industries between the wars. Colchester: University of Essex. *Essex Economic Papers*, No. 181.

Hatton, T. J. (1982a). Structural aspects of unemployment between the wars. Colchester: University of Essex. *Essex Economic Papers* No. 196.

Hatton, T. J. (1982b). Unemployment in the 1930s and the 'Keynesian solution': some notes of dissent. Colchester: University of Essex. *Essex Economic Papers*, No. 197.

Hawtrey, R. G. (1919). *Currency and Credit*. London: Longmans Green.

Hayek, F. A. von (1931). *Prices and Production*. London: George Routledge & Sons.

Hayek, F. A. von (1933). *Monetary Theory and the Trade Cycle* (trans. N. Kaldor and H. M. Croome). London: Jonathan Cape.

Hazeldine, T. (1981). Employment functions and the demand for labour in the short run. In Z. Hornstein, J. Grice and A. Webb (eds), *The Economics of the Labour Market*. London: Her Majesty's Stationery Office.

Hendry, D. F. (1980). Predictive failure and econometric modelling in macroeconomics: the transactions demand for money. In P. Ormerod (ed.), *Economic Modelling*. London: Heinemann Educational Books.

Henry, S. G. B. and P. Ormerod (1978). Incomes policy and wage inflation: empirical evidence for the U.K., 1961–77. *National Institute Economic Review*, **85**, 31–9.

Henry, S. G. B., M. C. Sawyer and P. Smith (1976). Models of inflation in the United Kingdom: an evaluation. *National Institute Economic Review*, **77**, 60–71.

Hicks, J. R. (1932). *The Theory of Wages,* London: Macmillan.

Hilton, J. (1924). Enquiry by sample: an experiment and its results. *Journal of the Royal Statistical Society*, **87**, 545–70.

Hilton, J. (1928). Some further enquiries by sample. *Journal of the Royal Statistical Society*, **91**, 519–40.

Hinton, J. (1973). *The First Shop Stewards' Movement*. London: George Allen & Unwin.

Howson, S. (1981). Slump and unemployment. In R. Floud and D. McCloskey (eds), *The Economic History of Britain since 1700, Vol. 2: 1860 to the 1970s*. Cambridge: Cambridge University Press.

Howson, S. and D. Winch (1977). *The Economic Advisory Council 1930–1939: A Study in Economic Advice during Depression and Recovery*, Cambridge: Cambridge University Press.

Hutchison, T. W. (1978). *On Revolutions and Progress in Economic Knowledge*. Cambridge: Cambridge University Press.

Hutt, W. H. (1939). *The Theory of Idle Resources*. London: Jonathan Cape.

Jackman, R., C. Mulvey and J. Trevithick (1981). *The Economics of Inflation*, 2nd ed. Oxford: Martin Robertson.

Jevons, H. S. (1931). The second industrial revolution. *Economic Journal*, **41**, 1–18.

Jewkes, J. and H. Campion (1928). The mobility of labour in the cotton industry. *Economic Journal*, **38**, 135–7.

Jewkes, J. and S. Jewkes (1938). *The Juvenile Labour Market*. London: Victor Gollancz.

Jewkes, J. and S. Jewkes (1971). Sir Henry Clay (1883–1954). In E. T. Williams and H. M. Palmer (eds), *Dictionary of National Biography, 1951–1960*. London: Oxford University Press.

Johansson, P.-O. and K. G. Lofgren (1981). The effects of tariffs and real wages in a Barro-Grossman model of an open economy. In L. Matthiessen and S. Strom (eds.), *Unemployment: Macro and Microeconomic Explanations*. London: Macmillan.

Johnson, H. G. (1975). Keynes and British economics. In M. Keynes (ed.), *Essays on John Maynard Keynes*. Cambridge: Cambridge University Press.

Johnson, H. G. (1978). Arthur Cecil Pigou, 1877–1959: an obituary. In E. S. Johnson and H. G. Johnson, *The Shadow of Keynes: Understanding Keynes, Cambridge and Keynesian Economics*. Oxford: Basil Blackwell.

Johnson, J. H., J. Salt and P. A. Wood (1974). *Housing and the Migration of labour in England and Wales*. Farnborough, Hants: Saxon House.

Johnston, J. and M. Timbrell (1973). Empirical tests of a bargaining theory of wage rate determination. *Manchester School*, **41**, 141–67.

Jones, D. C. (ed.) (1934). *The Social Survey of Merseyside*, 3 vols. Liverpool: University Press of Liverpool, and London: Hodder & Stoughton.

Kadish, A. (1982). *The Oxford Economists in the Late Nineteenth Century*, Oxford: Clarendon Press.

Kahn, R. F. (1931). The relation of home investment to unemployment. *Economic Journal*, **41**, 173–98.

284 *Bibliography*

Kent, R. A. (1981). *A History of British Empirical Sociology*. Aldershot: Gower Press.

Keynes, J. M. (1919). *The Economic Consequences of the Peace*. London: Macmillan.

Keynes, J. M. (1922). *A Revision of the Treaty*. London: Macmillan.

Keynes, J. M. (1924). A comment on Professor Cannan's article. *Economic Journal*, **34**, 65–68.

Keynes, J. M. (1931). An economic analysis of unemployment. In P. Q. Wright (ed.), *Unemployment as a World-Problem: Lectures on the Harris Foundation 1931*. Chicago: University of Chicago Press.

Keynes, J. M. (1932). Halley Stewart Lecture. In Sir A. Salter *et al.*, *The World's Economic Crisis and the Way of Escape*. London: George Allen & Unwin.

Keynes, J. M. (1936). *The General Theory of Employment, Interest and Money*. London: Macmillan.

Lachman, L. M. (1940). A reconsideration of the Austrian theory of industrial fluctuations. *Economica*, N.S., **7**, 179–96.

Lavington, F. (1922). *The Trade Cycle*, London: P. S. King & Son.

Law, C. M. (1980). *British Regional Development since World War 1*. Newton Abbot: David & Charles.

Layard, P. R. G. (1981). Unemployment in Britain: causes and cures. London: Centre for Labour Economics, London School of Economics.

Layard, P. R. G. and S. J. Nickell (1980). The case for subsidising extra jobs. *Economic Journal*, **90**, 51–73.

Leijonhufvud, A. (1968), *On Keynesian Economics and the Economics of Keynes*. New York: Oxford University Press.

Lindley, R. M. (ed.) (1980). *Economic Change and Employment Policy*, London: Macmillan.

Lorie, H. R. and J. R. Sheen (1982). Supply shocks in a two country world with wage and price rigidities. *Economic Journal*, **92**, 849–67.

Lucas, R. E. Jr (1973). Some international evidence on output–inflation tradeoffs. *American Economic Review*, **63**, 326–34.

Lucas, R. E. Jr and L. A. Rapping (1969). Real wages, employment and inflation. *Journal of Political Economy*, **77**, 721–54.

Lucas, R. E. Jr and L. A. Rapping (1972). Unemployment in the Great Depression: is there a full explanation? *Journal of Political Economy*, **80**, 59–65.

Lucas, R. E., Jr and T. J. Sargent (eds.) (1981). *Rational Expectations and Econometric Practice*. London: George Allen & Unwin.

Macfie, A. L. (1934). *Theories of the Trade Cycle*. London: Macmillan.

Makower, H., J. Marschak and H. W. Robinson (1938). Studies in the mobility of labour: a tentative statistical measure. *Oxford Economic Papers*, **1**, 82–123.

Makower, H., J. Marschak and H. W. Robinson (1939). Studies in the mobility of labour: analysis for Great Britain: Part I. *Oxford Economics Papers*, **2**, 70–97.

Makower, H., J. Marschak and H. W. Robinson (1940). Studies in the mobility of labour: analysis for Great Britain: Part II. *Oxford Economic Papers*, **4**, 39–62.

Malinvaud, E. (1977). *The Theory of Unemployment Reconsidered*. Oxford: Basil Blackwell.

Massey, D. and R. Meegan (1982). *The Anatomy of Job Loss: The How, Why and Where of Employment Decline*. London: Methuen.

Maynard, G. W. (1978). Keynes and unemployment today. *Three Banks Review*, No. 120.

McCrone, G. (1969). *Regional Policy in Britain*. London: Allen & Unwin.

Metcalf, D., S. J. Nickell and N. Floros (1982). Still searching for an explanation of unemployment in interwar Britain. *Journal of Political Economy*, **90**, 386–99.

Middleton, R. (1981). Constant employment budget balance and British budgetary policy 1929–39. *Economic History Review*, **34**, 266–86.

Middleton, R. (1982). The Treasury in the 1930s: political and administrative constraints to acceptance of the 'New Economics'. *Oxford Economic Papers*, **34**, 48–77.

Minford, P. (1981). Labour market equilibrium in an open economy. Liverpool University, *mimeo*.

Mitchell, B. R. and P. Deane (1962). *Abstract of British Historical Statistics*. Cambridge: Cambridge University Press.

Moggridge, D. E. (1972). *British Monetary Policy 1924–1931: The Norman Conquest of $4.86*. Cambridge: Cambridge University Press.

Moggridge, D. E. (1975). The influence of Keynes on the economics of his time. In M. Keynes (ed.) *Essays on John Maynard Keynes*. Cambridge: Cambridge University Press.

Mueller, C. F. (1982). *The Economics of Labour Migration: A Behavioural Analysis.* New York: Academic Press.

Myrdal, G. (1957). *Economic Theory and Underdeveloped Regions.* London: Duckworth.

Nash, E. F. (1935). *Machines and Purchasing Power.* London: George Routledge & Sons.

Neary, J. P. (1980). Non-traded goods and the balance of trade in a neo-Keynesian Temporary Equilibrium. *Quarterly Journal of Economics,* **94**.

Neftci, S. B. (1978). A time series analysis of the real wages–employment relationship. *Journal of Political Economy,* **86**, 281–91.

Nelson, R. R. and S. G. Winter (1982). *An Evolutionary Theory of Economic Change.* Cambridge, Mass: The Belknap Press of Harvard University Press.

Nickell, S. J. (1982). The determinants of equilibrium unemployment in Britain. *Economic Journal,* **92**, 555–75.

Okun, A. M. (1981). *Prices and Quantities,* Oxford: Basil Blackwell.

Olson, M. (1982). *The Rise and Decline of Nations: Economic Growth, Stagflation and Social Rigidities.* New Haven: Yale University Press.

Ormerod, P. A. and G. D. N. Worswick (1982). Unemployment in interwar Britain. *Journal of Political Economy,* **90**, 400–9.

Patinkin, D. (1965). *Money, Interest and Prices,* 2nd edn. New York: Harper & Row.

Patinkin, D. (1978). Keynes's misquotation of Mill: comment. *Economic Journal,* **88**, 341–2.

Patinkin, D. (1982). *Anticipation of the General Theory.* Oxford, Basil Blackwell.

Patterson, K. D. (1982). A simple non-stationary Markov model of the transition between mutually exclusive groups: modelling the end of money illusion. *Bulletin of the Oxford Institute of Statistics.* 305–20.

Pemberton, J. (1981). A two-sector model of inflation, unemployment and aggregate demand. *University of Reading Discussion Papers in Economics,* No. 123.

Phelps Brown, E. H. (1959). *The Growth of British Industrial Relations: a Study from the Standpoint of 1906–14.* London: Macmillan.

Phillips, A. W. (1959). The relation between unemployment and the rate of change of money wage rates in the United Kingdom, 1861–1957. *Economica* (N.S.), **25**, 283–99.

Pigou, A. C. (1901). *Robert Browning as a Religious Teacher*. London: C. J. Clay & Sons.

Pigou, A. C. (1903). *The Riddle of the Tariff*. London: R. Brimley Johnson.

Pigou, A. C. (1905). *The Principles and Methods of Industrial Peace*. London: Macmillan.

Pigou, A. C. (1906). *Protective and Preferential Import Duties*. London: Macmillan.

Pigou, A. C. (1912). *Wealth and Welfare*. London: Macmillan.

Pigou, A. C. (1914). *Unemployment*. London: Williams & Norgate (Home University Library of Modern Knowledge).

Pigou, A. C. (1927a). Wage policy and unemployment. *Economic Journal*, **37**, 355–68.

Pigou, A. C. (1927b). *Industrial Fluctuations*. London: Macmillan.

Pigou, A. C. (1931). Evidence. In *Minutes of Evidence taken before the Committee on Finance and Industry*, Vol. II. London: His Majesty's Stationery Office.

Pigou, A. C. (1932). *The Economics of Welfare*, 4th edn. London: Macmillan.

Pigou, A. C. (1933). *Theory of Unemployment*. London: Macmillan.

Pigou, A. C. (1935a). *Socialism and Capitalism*. London: Macmillan.

Pigou, A. C. (1935b). *The Economics of Stationary States*. London: Macmillan.

Pigou, A. C. (1936). Mr J. M. Keynes' General Theory of Employment, Interest and Money, *Economica* (N.S.), **3**, 115–32.

Pigou, A. C. (1941). *Employment and Equilibrium*. London: Macmillan.

Pigou, A. C. (1945). *Lapses from Full Employment*. London: Macmillan.

Pigou, A. C. (1947). *Aspects of British Economic History, 1918–1925*. London: Macmillan.

Pigou, A. C. (1949). *The Veil of Money*. London: Macmillan.

Pigou, A. C. (1950). *Keynes's 'General Theory': a Retrospective View*. London: Macmillan.

Pilgrim Trust (1938). *Men Without Work: a Report Made to the Pilgrim Trust*. Cambridge: Cambridge University Press.

Political and Economic Planning (1939). *Report on the Location of Industry in Great Britain*. London: PEP.

Pool, A. G. (1938). *Wage Policy in Relation to Industrial Fluctuations*. London: Macmillan.

Prais, S. J. (1981). *Productivity and Industrial Structure*. Cambridge: Cambridge University Press.

Presley, J. R. (1979). *Robertsonian Economics*. London: Macmillan.

Ramsbottom, E. C. (1935). The course of wage rates in the United Kingdom, 1921–1934. *Journal of the Royal Statistical Society*, **98**, 639–73.

Ramsbottom, E. C. (1938). Wage rates in the United Kingdom, 1934–1937. *Journal of the Royal Statistical Society*, **101**, 202–4.

Ramsbottom, E. C. (1939). Wage rates in the United Kingdom in 1938. *Journal of the Royal Statistical Society*, **102**, 289–91.

Rees, A. (1970). On equilibrium in labour markets. *Journal of Political Economy*, **78** 306–10.

Richardson, H. W. (1962). The basis of economic recovery in the nineteen-thirties: a review and a new interpretation. *Economic History Review*, 2nd series, **15**, 344–63.

Richardson, H. W. and D. H. Aldcroft (1968). *Building in the British Economy between the Wars*. London: George Allen & Unwin.

Robbins, L. (1927). The optimum theory of population. In T. E. Gregory and H. Dalton (eds), *London Essays in Economics: In Honour of Edwin Cannan*. London: George Routledge & Sons.

Robbins, L. (1934). *The Great Depression*. London: Macmillan.

Robbins, L. (1949). Edwin Cannan (1861–1935). In L. G. Wickham Legg, (ed.) *Dictionary of National Biography, 1931–40*. London: Oxford University Press.

Robbins, L. (1971). *Autobiography of an Economist*. London: Macmillan.

Robertson, D. H. (1915). *A Study of Industrial Fluctuation*. London: P. S. King & Son.

Robertson, D. H. (1926). *Banking Policy and the Price Level: an Essay in the Theory of the Trade Cycle*. London: P. S. King and Son.

Robinson, E. A. G. (1935). Review of 'Reports of Investigations into the Industrial Conditions in Certain Depressed Areas'. *Economic Journal*, **45**, 183–92.

Robinson, E. A. G. (1971). Arthur Cecil Pigou (1877–1959). In E. T. Williams and H. M. Palmer (eds), *Dictionary of National Biography, 1951–1960*. London: Oxford University Press.

Robinson, E. A. G. (1977). Keynes and his Cambridge colleagues. In D. Patinkin and J. C. Leith, *Keynes, Cambridge and the General Theory*. London Macmillan.

Robinson, J. V. (1936a). Disguised unemployment. *Economic Journal*, **46**, 225–37.

Robinson, J. V. (1936b). Disguised unemployment: a rejoinder. *Economic Journal*, **46**, 759–60.

Roeber, J. (1975). *Social Change at Work: The ICI Weekly Staff Agreement*. London: Duckworth.

Rosen, H. S. and R. E. Quandt (1978). Estimation of a disequilibrium aggregate labour market. *Review of Economics and Statistics*, **60**, 371–9.

Routh, G. (1980). *Occupation and Pay in Great Britain, 1906–79*. London: Macmillan.

Rowe, J. W. F. (1928). *Wages in Practice and Theory*. London: George Routledge & Sons.

Saltmarsh, J. and P. Wilkinson (1960). *Arthur Cecil Pigou, 1877–1959, Fellow and Professor of Political Economy: a Memoir prepared by Direction of the Council of King's College, Cambridge*. Cambridge: King's College.

Samuelson, P. A. (1947). *Foundations of Economic Analysis*, Cambridge, Mass: Harvard University Press.

Sargan, J. D. (1964). Wages and prices in the United Kingdom: a study in econometric methodology. In P. E. Hart, G. Mills and J. K. Whittaker (eds), *Econometric Analysis for National Economic Planning*. London: Butterworth.

Sargan, J. D. (1980). A model of wage–price inflation. *Review of Economic Studies*, **47**, 97–112.

Sargent, T. J. (1978). Estimation of dynamic labour demand schedules under rational expectations. *Journal of Political Economy*, **86**, 1009–44.

Schwartz, G. L. and E. C. Rhodes (1939). *Output, Employment and Wages in The United Kingdom, 1924, 1930, 1935*. London: London and Cambridge Economic Service, Special Memorandum 47.

Sells, D. (1923). *The British Trade Boards System*. London: P. S. King & Son.

Sims, D. J. (1978). *Youth Unemployment in the 1930s and 1970s: a Comparative Study of Social Policy Responses*. M.Soc.Sci. thesis, University of Birmingham.

Singer, H. W. (1939a). The process of unemployment in the depressed areas (1935–1938). *Review of Economic Studies*, **6**, 177–88.

Singer, H. W. (1939b). Regional labour markets and the process of unemployment. *Review of Economic Studies*, **7**42–58.

Singer, H. W. (1940). *Unemployment and the Unemployed*. London: P. S. King & Son.

Skelley, J. (ed.) (1976). *The General Strike, 1926*. London: Lawrence & Wishart.

Smith, H. L. (1930–5). *The New Survey of London Life and Labour*, 9 vols. London: P. S. King & Son.

Steigum, E. Jr (1981). Keynesian and classical unemployment in an open economy. In L. Matthiessen and S. Strom (eds), *Unemployment: Macro and Microeconomic Explanations*. London: Macmillan.

Stein, H. S. (1969). *The Fiscal Revolution in America*. Chicago: University of Chicago Press.

Sternlieb, G. and J. W. Hughes (eds) (1975). *Post-Industrial America: Metropolitan Decline and Inter-Regional Job Shifts*. New Brunswick, N.J.: Centre for Urban Policy Research, Rutgers University.

Symons, J. S. V. (1981). The demand for labour in British manufacturing. London: Centre for Labour Economics, London School of Economics, *Discussion Paper* No. 91.

Tarshis, L. (1939). Changes in real and money wages. *Economic Journal*, **49**, 150–4.

Thirlwall, A. P. (1981). Keynesian employment theory is not defunct. *Three Banks Review*, **131**, 14–29.

Thomas, B. (1931). Labour mobility in the South Wales coal industry, 1920–30. *Economic Journal*, **41**, 216–26.

Thompson, W. (1964). *A Preface to Urban Economics*. Baltimore: Johns Hopkins University Press.

Todaro, M. P. (1969). A model of labour migration and urban unemployment in less developed countries. *American Economic Review*, **59**, 138–48.

Todaro, M. P. (1976). Urban job expansion, induced migration and rising unemployment: a formulation and simplified empirical test for LDCs. *Journal of Development Economics*, **3**, 211–25.

Trade Union Congress General Council (1931). Statement of Evidence (Part II). In *Minutes of Evidence taken before the Committee on Finance and Industry*, Vol. II. London: His Majesty's Stationery Office.

Vanderkamp, J. (1968). The Phillips relation: a theoretical explanation — a comment. *Economica* (N.S.), **35**, 179–83.

van Duijn, J. J. (1983). *The Long Wave of Economic Life*. London: George Allen & Unwin.

Wensley, A. J. and P. Sargent Florence (1940). Recent industrial concentration, especially in the West Midlands. *Review of Economic Studies*, **7**, 139–58.

Wigham, E. (1976). *Strikes and the Government 1893–1974*. London: Macmillan.

Williams, G. (1936). *The State and the Standard of Living*. London: P. S. King & Son.

Winch, D. (1969). *Economics and Policy: A Historical Study*. London: Hodder & Stoughton.

Author Index

Alchian, A.A. 85
Aldcroft, D.H. 3, 29
Alford, B.W.E. xiii
Allen, G.C. 144
Allen, R.G.D. 155
Apps, R.J. 226
Armstrong, H. 237
Ashley, W.J. 21
Auspitz, R. 116
Austin, H. 30

Bacon, R.W. 239
Bain, G.S. 180
Bakke, E.W. 25, 216
Ball, R.J. 167
Barger, H. 217
Barro, R.J. 66, 80, 111, 167
Begg, D.K.H. 246
Benjamin, D.K. 2, 208–9
Beveridge, W.H. 25, 37, 39, 130, 154–5
Bleaney, M. 23
Bienefeld, M. 27
Bodkin, R.G. 177
Booth, A.E. 3
Booth, C. 25
Bosanquet, N. 236
Bowers, J. xiv, 223–4
Bowley, A.L. 22, 25, 180
Boyle, A. 33
Branson, W.H. 228
Brechling, F.P.R. 230
Bruno, M. 227
Burridge, P. 236

Campion, H. 216
Cannan, E. 9, 18–24, 32, 37, 42–3, 57, 128, 150, 156, 160, 244
Casey, F.J., Jr. 158
Casson, M.C. 25, 66, 80, 168

Catchings, W. 67
Champernowne, D.G. 210
Chang, D. 27
Cheshire, P.C. 4, 237
Clark, J. 4
Clausen, R. 234
Clay, H. 9, 18–9, 26, 32, 41–60, 141, 148, 150, 156, 180, 199, 216
Clower, R.W. 72, 80–2, 245
Coates, B.E. 4
Cole, G.D.H. 240–5
Collard, D. 17
Collier, P. 115
Collins, M. 3
Corry, B.A. 112
Creedy, J. 214
Crick, B. 4
Cross, R. 208–9

Dalton, H. 21–2, 149
Daniel, G.H. 215–8
Davis, E.G. 23
Davis, J.R. 158, 160
Dawes, H. 218
Deacon, R. 17
Deaton, D. xiv, 223–4
de Man, H. 245
Dennis, R. 244
Dennison, S.R. 54, 210
Dicks-Mireaux, L. 226
Dillard, D. 159
Dixit, A.K. 122
Dixon, R.J. 230
Doeringer, P.B. 4, 236
Douglas, C.H. 24, 67
Dow, J.C.R. 226
Dunlop, J.T. 177–8, 185–7
Dunning, J.H. 233
Durbin, E.F.M. 23

Earl, P.E. 1
Edgeworth, F.Y. 22, 116
Einstein, A. 158
Eltis, W.A. 239
Eshag, E. 23, 38

Fay, C.R. 22
Feldstein, M.S. 168
Fisher, A.G.B. 155, 185
Fisher, I. 71, 159
Floros, N. 3
Ford, H. 28, 30
Ford, P. 25
Foster, W.T. 67
Fothergill, S. xiv, 4, 230–2
Foxwell, H.S. 15, 38
Freeman, C. 4
Friedman, M. 72, 227

Garraty, J.A. 25
Glynn, S. 3
Goodrich, C. 242
Gordon, I.R. 236
Gordon, R.J. 3
Graham, A.W.M. 227
Gray, J.A. 229
Grossman, H.I. 66, 80, 111, 167
Grubb, D. 228–9
Gudgin, G. xiv, 4, 230–2

Hancock, K.J. xiii, 153
Hannington, W. 242
Hansen, A.H. 67, 159
Harley, J.H. 243
Harris, A.I. 234
Harris, J. 25
Harris, J.R. 86, 115
Harrod, R.F. 158
Hatton, T.J. xiv, 2–3, 210–3
Hawtrey, R.G. 7, 23
Hayek, F.A. von 24, 26, 156
Hazeldine, T. 167
Hendry, D.F. 169
Henry, S.G.B. 226
Hicks, J.R. 24
Hilton, J. 25, 216
Hinton, J. 242
Hobson, J.A. 67
Hogg, M.H. 25
Howells, P.G.A. 3
Howson, S. xiii, 14

Hughes, J.W. 241
Hutchison, T.W. 160
Hutt, W.H. 24

Jackman, R. 112, 226, 228
Jevons, H.S. 138
Jevons, W.S. 38
Jewkes, J. 18, 25, 216, 218
Jewkes, S. 18, 25, 218
Johansson, P-O. 122
Johnson, H.G. 15, 152
Johnson, J.H. 235
Johnston, J. 226
Johnston, R.J. 4
Jones, D.C. 25
Jones, J.H. 163

Kadish, A. 21
Kahn, R.F. 23
Kent, R.A. 25
Keynes, J.M. 2, 51, 67, 72, 79–83, 142,
   148ff, 185–6, 225
Klein, L.R. 159
Knox, P.L. 4
Kochin, L.A. 3, 208–9
Kondratieff, N.D. 1, 246

Lachmann, L.M. 24
Laidler, D.E.W. 112
Lavington, F. 23
Law, C.M. 4
Layard, P.R.G. 130, 228
Leijonhufvud, A. 80, 245
Lieben, R. 116
Lindley, R.M. 4
Lofgren, K.G. 122
Lorie, H.R. 122, 247
Loyd, S.J. (Lord Overstone) 38
Lucas, R.E., Jr. 2, 3, 229, 246

Macfie, A.L. 23
Makower, H.J. 214–19
Malinvaud, E. 66
Marschak, J. 214–19
Marshall, A. 15, 37–8, 132
Martin, P.W. 67
Massey, D. 4
Maynard, G.W. 227
McCormick, D. 17
McCrone, G. 153
Meegan, R. 4

Metcalf, D. 3
Metzler, L.A. 159
Middleton, R. 2
Mill, J.S. 37, 150
Minford, A.P.L. 115
Mises, L. von 24
Moggridge, D.E. 16, 158
Morris, W. 30
Mueller, C.F. 234
Mulvey, C. 112, 226
Myrdal, G. 213

Nash, E.F. 23
Neary, P. 122
Neftci, S.B. 178
Nelson, R.R. 241
Nickell, S.J. 3–4, 130, 237
Noel-Baker, P. 15
Norman, M. 19

Okun, A.M. 168
Olson, M . 241
Ormerod, P. 209, 226
Overstone, Lord; *see* Loyd, S.J.

Pareto, V. 116
Patinkin, D. 23, 158, 167
Patterson, K.D. 226–7
Pemberton, J. 115
Phelps Brown, E.H. 26
Phillips, A.W. 226
Pigou, A.C. xiii, 8–9, 14–18, 21, 24,
    37–41, 44–6, 48–52, 55–61, 96, 116,
    129–38, 150ff, 180, 183, 185, 239
Pilgrim Trust 25
Piore, M.J. 4, 236
Poole, A.G. 57–9
Prais, S.J. 242
Presley, J.R. 23
Price, L.L. 21
Price, R. 180

Quandt, R.E. 166

Ramsey, F.P. 139
Rapping, L.A. 3
Rees, A. 3
Richardson, H.W. 3
Robbins, L. 9, 20, 23–4, 26, 37, 156–7
Robertson, D.H. 7–8, 23, 159
Robinson, E.A.G. 15, 17, 128, 142–4

Robinson, H.W. 214–19
Robinson, J.V. 217
Roeber, J. 245
Rosen, H.S. 166
Rotemberg, J.J. 228
Roth, P. 246
Routh, G. 180
Rowe, J.W.F. 180
Rowntree, B.S. 25

Salt, J. 235
Saltmarsh, J. 15, 17
Samuelson, P.A. 159, 167
Sargan, J.D. 179, 226
Sargent, T.J. 178, 246
Sargent Florence, P. 54
Say, J.B. 81
Sells, D. 27
Sheen, J.R. 122, 247
Sidgwick, H. 37, 150
Sims, D. 25
Singer, H. 25
Skelley, J. 242
Smith, A. 20, 37, 150
Smith, A.L. 19
Smith, H.L. 25
Smith, P. 226
Soete, L. 4
St Cyr, E.B.A.167
Stamp, J. 180
Steigum, E., Jr. 122
Stein, H.S. 160
Sternlieb, G. 241
Symons, J.S.V. 224–5

Tarshis, L. 177–8
Taylor, F.W. 28
Taylor, J. 237
Thirlwall, A.P. 167, 230
Thomas, B. 155, 216
Thompson, W.R. 241
Timbrell, M. 226
Todaro, M.P. 86, 115
Toynbee, A.J. 21
Trevithick, J. 112, 226
Turk, J. xiv, 223–4

Vanderkamp, J. 112
van Duijn, J.J. 246

Webb, B. 25, 33, 37

Webb, S. 21, 25, 33, 37
Wensley, A.J. 54
Wilcox, J.A. 3
Wilkinson, P. 15, 17
Williams, G. 25
Winch, D. xiii, 2, 14

Winter, S.G. 241
Wood, P.A. 235
Worswick, G.D.N. 209

Young, A. 156

Subject Index

Accelerator principle, 213
Adjustment costs, 168–73
Aggregation in macroeconomics, 6
Arbitration, 27
Austrian economics, 24, 156

Bankruptcy, 52–3, 156–7
Barlow Commission on the
    Distribution of the Industrial
    Population, 32
Basic industries, 6, 29–30
Belgium, 5
Benefit, unemployment benefit, 2,
    32–3, 42–3, 46–7, 93–5, 98–100,
    179ff, 190ff, 208–9, 216
Boot and shoe industry, 224
Building industry, 34, 181, 203

Casual labour markets, 38, 42, 45, 86,
    197–204, 213
Centre of economy, 31, 101, 210ff
Chamberlain-Bradbury Committee on
    the Currency and Bank of England
    Note Issues, 16
Chemical industry, 31, 224
Clothing industry, 224
Coal industry, 40, 56, 153, 161, 181,
    203, 216, 218
Coal Industry Commission, 21, 27, 244
Construction industry; see Building
    industry
Consumer goods, 31, 35
Consumption function, 72, 80–2
Craftsmanship, 28, 31, 197–202, 235–6,
    240–2
Crowding out, 2, 79, 83
Cunliffe Committee on Currency and
    Foreign Exchanges after the War, 16
Cyclical unemployment, 38, 39, 49

Debt burden, 49, 52–3
Declining industries, 5, 101ff
Demand management; see Keynesian
    theory and policy
Discouraged workers, 84ff, 217
Disequilibrium, 62ff, 245–6
Disguised unemployment, 34, 217
Distributive trades, 25
Dock industry, 41, 181, 216
Dual decision hypothesis, 81
Dual labour market, 4, 236

Employers' contribution under National
    Insurance, 46–7
Employment function, 167–79
Employment subsidies, 130–3, 137–8
Engineering industry, 30–1, 55–6, 132,
    161, 164, 176, 181, 193–6, 224, 232
Entrepreneurship, 5, 12, 30, 240–5
Export industries, 28, 122–8, 148,
    204–9, 227–8

Fabians, 21, 242
Family commitments, 54, 216–19
Female labour, 35, 59, 180–2
Filtering information, 50, 246
Food industry, 224
Foreign direct investment, 31, 233
Frictional unemployment, 39, 41–3

General Strike, 22, 242
Germany, 31, 34
Gold Standard, 16, 52, 157, 160
Growth, 29, 35
Guild socialism, 27, 240–5

Heavy industry, 5; see also Basic
    industries
Hoarding of labour, 167–73, 223–4

Hours of work, 27, 225
Housing, 54, 235

Identification problem, 199
Import duties, 5, 31, 33, 133–8, 243
Import substituting industries, 8, 28, 31, 122–8
Incomes policy, 2, 225, 227
Industrial democracy, 26
Industrial transference, 128–30, 153–5
Inflation, 1–2, 79, 83, 185–7, 225–9
Investment, 142–6
Involuntary unemployment, 38
Iron and steel industry, 5, 28, 56, 176, 218

Japan, 5, 28, 34, 228
Juveniles: *see* Youth labour

Keynesian revolution, 11, 62; *see also* Keynes, J.M.
Keynesian theory and policy, 1, 6, 238–9

Labour supply, 48–50, 68–70, 86–9, 190ff; *see also* Mobility of labour
Life-cycle of an economy, 5
Lobbying, 132, 243
Long-term unemployment, 6, 39–40, 42

Macmillan Committee on Finance and Industry, 14, 50, 151–2, 161
Marxism, 187–9, 242–5
Metal industry, 55
Microelectronics, 232
Midlands, 144
Ministry of Labour, 25, 154, 180, 193, 210ff
Mobility of industry, 53–4, 142–6
Mobility of labour, 5, 12, 53–61, 190ff, 234–45
Money illusion, 48–53, 96, 184, 227
Money supply, 49–52, 70–6
Money wage, 3, 49–53, 70ff, 107–112, 162, 166ff
Motor industry, 5, 30–1, 176, 193–6, 217–8
Multicollinearity, 193, 208
Multiplier, 34

National insurance, 27–8, 39, 42–3, 46–7; *see also* Benefit

Neoclassical macroeconomics, 2–3, 7
New classical macroeconomics; *see* Neoclassical macroeconomics, Rational expectations
New industries, 6, 30, 101ff
New towns, 232–3

Oil price, 227

Paper industry, 224
Preference lists, 42, 45–6
Periphery of economy, 31, 101, 210ff
Phillips curve, 112, 179, 226–7
Printing industry, 193–6
Prisoner's dilemma, 50
Productivity, 10–11, 28–9, 34–5, 210
Profits, 63–8
Protection; *see* Import duties
Public works, 142–6, 159–61

Quality control, 30
Quantity theory of money, 71, 76, 105
Queue unemployment, 44–5, 86ff

Railways, 132, 181
Rational expectations, 246–7
Rationalization, 138–42
Real wage, 10, 48–9, 68ff, 113–20, 162–3, 166ff, 222ff
Rearmament, 34, 147, 155, 164
Regional aspects of unemployment, 4, 209–21, 229–34
Registered unemployment, 65, 89–91
Royal Commission on the Income Tax, 16, 27
Royal Commission on the Poor Laws, 25
Royal Commission on Unemployment Insurance, 19
Rubber industry, 30
Russia, 26

Samuelson – Le Chatelier principle, 167
Saving, 70ff
Scientific management, 28, 30
Search for jobs, 84ff
Seasonal unemployment, 42
Service industries, 34
Shift-share analysis, 210–13
Shipbuilding industry, 5, 28, 55, 132, 164, 176, 193–6, 203, 218

Shop stewards, 27
Short-side rule, 62–5
Short-time working, 38, 40
Skill differentials, 31, 59–60, 101ff, 180, 235ff
Special Areas Commissioners, 154
Spill over effects, 65ff
Steel industry; *see* Iron and steel industry
Strikes, 27; *see also* General Strike
Structural aspects of unemployment, 3, 7–8, 53–61, 101ff, 236ff
Structural change, 30
Subsidies; *see* Employment subsidies
Switzerland, 228
Syndicalism, 21, 27, 187–9, 242–5

Tariffs; *see* Import duties
Terms of trade, 122–8, 148, 204–9, 227–8
Textile industry, 5, 25, 27–8, 35, 40, 53–4, 141, 161, 181, 193–6, 203, 216, 224
Timber industry, 224
Trade unions, 27, 31, 44–6, 162–3, 180–1, 185–9, 197–204, 226–9, 240–5
Trade Union Congress, 163
Transfer of labour, 57, 113; *see also* Industrial transference, Mobility of labour
Treasury view, 2; *see also* Crowding out

Unemployment; *see* Benefit, Cyclical unemployment, Frictional unemployment, Involuntary unemployment, Long-term unemployment, Registered unemployment, Seasonal unemployment, Structural unemployment
United States, 5, 31, 148, 159, 178, 228, 233
Utilitarianism, 37, 40. 150

Vacancies – unfilled, 4, 113ff, 197
Vehicles; *see* Motor industry
Velocity of circulation of money, 71, 76

Wage cut, 89–92
Wage drift, 112
Wage rate; *see* Money wage, Real wage
Wage rigidity, 3, 10, 48–53, 63–8, 107ff, 183–9, 199–200, 225–9
Wage setting, 43
Women in the labour force; *see* Female labour
Working practices, 27–8, 197–202

Youth labour, 25, 153, 161, 197, 218, 236, 238